T0367974

A D V A N C E S   I N

DEVELOPMENT ECONOMICS

A D V A N C E S   I N

DEVELOPMENT ECONOMICS

Editor

Dipak Basu

Nagasaki University, Japan

World Scientific

NEW JERSEY · LONDON · SINGAPORE · BEIJING · SHANGHAI · HONG KONG · TAIPEI · CHENNAI

Published by

World Scientific Publishing Co. Pte. Ltd.

5 Toh Tuck Link, Singapore 596224

USA office: 27 Warren Street, Suite 401-402, Hackensack, NJ 07601

UK office: 57 Shelton Street, Covent Garden, London WC2H 9HE

Library of Congress Cataloging-in-Publication Data
Advances in development economics / edited by Dipak Basu.
    p. cm.
    ISBN-13 978-981-283-487-4
    ISBN-10 981-283-487-7
    1. Development economics--Developing countries. 2. Developing countries--Economic policy.
    I. Basu, Dipak R.

    HC59.7 .A736 2009
    330.9172'4--dc22

                                                            2008045610

British Library Cataloguing-in-Publication Data
A catalogue record for this book is available from the British Library.

Typeset by Stallion Press
Email: enquiries@stallionpress.com

Printed in Singapore.

DEDICATION

This volume is dedicated to the Memory of Professor Thomas Kronsjo.

Professor Thomas Kronsjo

CONTENTS

INTRODUCTION

In this volume, selected authors have tried to push forward the frontier of the economics of the developing countries using all available methods without distinctions: mathematical, computational, and analytical. This was the philosophy of Prof. Tom Kronsjo, who made significant contributions on analytical methods of development planning and applications over some decades and in whose memory this volume is dedicated.

Takashima has proposed a new model for the East Asian economies to analyze how initial conditions for growth and the policy undertaken have sustained the growth process continuously. The model negates the alternative analysis proposed by both Krugman and Lucas. It is a novel approach to theorize effectively the historical process of the East Asian countries.

Mats Lundahl has developed a theory of population growth and it is on economic growth following the original ideas of Wicksell. The author has developed a general equilibrium model to analyze the impacts of emigration from an old country to a new country and their corresponding effects on income, investments, and trade.

The question of immigration on economic growth was also analyzed by Partha Sen in a new model of growth with immigrations. Exogenous growth models predict a fall in steady-state welfare (or, equivalently in descriptive models, consumption per capita) following an increase in the growth rate of population — accompanied by an increase in the growth rate of the economy. This prediction certainly does not match the facts of those economies that received large number of immigrants over long periods, e.g., the US, Australia, and Canada. Under certain conditions, it can be shown that in a two-sector overlapping generations model, an increase in the rate of growth of population (or immigration) of (raw) labor can raise the welfare of all steady-state generations.

The question of migration was analyzed further in the section for Labor Economics. Shimada, assuming a two-country economy with labor migration, investigates which of the two regimes — inter-government monetary cooperation between two independent monetary authorities or centralization of monetary policies by a single monetary authority under a monetary union — is advantageous under certainty and under supply or demand shocks. He showed that the utility of the monetary authority does not differ across regimes under certainty, whereas centralization of the monetary policies under a monetary union tends to be advantageous to the monetary authority if a two-country economy is subject to supply or demand shocks. Most important of all, he showed that the utility of the workers does not differ across regimes under certainty and under supply or demand shocks. This suggests that in reality, centralization of the monetary policies under a monetary union appears to be preferable to inter-government monetary cooperation between the two independent monetary authorities. The results are very useful for situations when a country is sending its excess labor forces to another superior economy, which may demand coordination of economic policies of the two countries.

Microeconomics of labor market, the relationship between employment relations, and financial behavior of the firms are analyzed by Garvey and Gaston. Previous research indicates that firms increase their leverage in order to moderate wage demands by organized labor. While firms will use more debt when bargaining power is the primary cause of high wages, Garvey and Gaston show that they will use less debt if wages are driven by incentive considerations. For a sample of large firms, the authors confirm previous findings that firms in more unionized industries use more debt. However, holding constant unionization and other well-known determinants of the capital structure, there would be a negative relationship between debt and employee compensation as predicted by the specific human capital approach. Along with the economic reform program, as more and more developing countries are adopting capitalistic employment relations, it is crucially important for the developing countries to consider the financial implications for the firms in relation to the structure of the employment relations.

The conflict between the objectives of equity and decentralization in models of resource allocation is very important for the development policy. Lahiri considers a new model of allocation, where at most one object is allocated to each individual, with no two individuals sharing one or more objects, and possibly some allocations being defined infeasible. In the existing literature, such problems are known as house allocation problems. In the traditional Arrow-Debreu economy, where the concepts of decentralization are independent of concepts of egalitarianism, the preference structure of the agents exhibits the property that "more is preferred to less". It is this characteristic of the preference structure of the agents, which is supposed to be egalitarian. With having no such hypothesis built into the preference structure, this analysis would provide an important insight about the issues concerning equity in an economy comprising indivisible objects. In the context of organization where resources are indivisible but got to be allocated fairly and efficiently, this analysis can open new horizons.

In the light of his own experience as the regulator of the British electricity sector, Littlechild considers the role of negotiated settlements as an alternative to regulation in the resolution of conflicts between customers and companies within the utility sector. As well as suggesting a way ahead for more-developed countries, this can provide lessons for the newly emerging countries as they increasingly consider the relative roles of public and private enterprises and representatives of customer groups.

Uchida and Ahmed have examined whether the Japanese financial system can provide any lesson for the developing countries. In the Japanese system instead of the stock market firms depend on a main bank for their financial needs, which give them the stability and long-range view regarding investment decisions. The authors have examined the behavior of this financial system on small- and medium-sized firms in Japan and whether this model can be imitated for a developing country like Bangladesh with undeveloped stock market.

Structural adjustment program for India was analyzed using an adaptive optimal control model of the fiscal policy structure of India by Dipak Basu. Fiscal policy structure of an emerging capitalistic economy as implemented during 1990–1995 was compared with an alternative fiscal policy structure based on a mixed economic system of a planned economy. The method of adaptive control system was used where the model will undergo changes along with the optimization process. The results show that a mixed economic plan would be able to provide similar economic growth as a reformed economy. The implications are important. A mixed economic system can possibly maintain a more balanced society whereas a reformed economy by creating an unequal society would create social imbalances.

Guncavdi and Selim made an attempt to investigate the gender-biased distributional consequences of trade reform and openness in Turkey. Women are the most vulnerable group in developing countries, and are negatively affected by economic reforms in general, and liberalization in trade regimes in particular. Therefore, they are considered as the main source of poverty in these countries. Despite this nature of women, the gender issue has largely been ignored in the literature. This paper aims to fill this gap in the literature. Their research shows that female-headed households (FHHs) are poorer than the male-headed households (MHHs) in Turkey and that an involvement in an economic activity in internationally open and highly export-oriented sectors increases the possibility of being poor for FHHs.

Tisdell has analyzed the process of economic growth of China, its relationship with other major trading blocks and examined the hypothesis of Kuznets in view of the growing environmental problems in the Chinese economy. The author has concluded that the conclusion of Kuznets regarding income inequality is not valid for China where rising economic growth has resulted in rising income inequality.

Issues of globalization was discussed by Victoria Miroshnik, who has compared the corporate management systems of Toyota Motor Company in both Japan and India. Globalization can, according to some, create a global corporate culture, but the results show that a multinational company normally strive to transplant its own culture to its foreign subsidiary rather than to accept the global culture. Japanese management system is unique and very different from the standard Western management system. Thus, it is possible for a developing country to have diverse management systems rather than to have any specific management system even in the days of globalization.

The book covers most of the important areas of development economics with the basic analytical framework to formulate a logical structure and then suggest and implement methods to quantify the structure to derive applicable policies. We hope the book would be a source of joy for anyone interested to make development economics a useful discipline to enhance human welfare.

TOM OSKAR MARTIN KRONSJO: A PROFILE

Dr. Lydia Kronsjo

Professor in Computer Science
University of Birmingham, England

Tom Kronsjo was born in Stockholm, Sweden, on 16 August 1932, the only child of Elvira and Erik Kronsjo. Both his parents were gymnasium teachers.

In his school days, Tom Kronsjo was a bright popular student, often a leader among his school contemporaries and friends. During his school teaching years, he organized and chaired a National Science Society that became very popular with his school colleagues.

From an early age, Tom Kronsjo's mother encouraged him to learn foreign languages. He put those studies to a good test during a 1948 summer vacation when he hitchhiked through Denmark, Germany, the Netherlands, England, Scotland, Ireland, France, and Switzerland. That same year he founded and chaired a Technical Society in his school. In the summer vacation of 1949, he organized an expedition to North Africa by seven members of the Technical Society, their ages being 14 to 24. The young people traveled by coach through the austere post-Second World War Europe. All the equipment for travel, including the coach, were donated by sympathetic individuals and companies, who were impressed by an intelligent, enthusiastic group of youngsters, eager to learn about the world. This event caught a wide interest in the Swedish press at the time and was vividly reported.

Tom Kronsjo used to mention that as a particularly personally exciting experience of his school years he remembered volunteering to give a series of morning school sermons on the need for the world governmental organizations, which would encourage and support mutual understanding of the needs of the people to live in peace.

Tom Kronsjo's university years were spent at both sides of the great divide. Preparing himself for a career in international economics, he wanted to experience and see for himself the different nations' ways of life and points of view. He studied in London, Belgrade, Warsaw, Oslo, and Moscow, before returning to his home country, Sweden, to take examinations and submit required work at the Universities of Uppsala, Stockholm, and Lund for his Fil.kand. Degree in Economics, Statistics, Mathematics, and Slavonic Languages, and Fil.lic. Degree in Economics. By then, Tom Kronsjo, besides his mother tongue Swedish, was fluent in six languages — German, English, French, Polish, Serbo-Croatian, and Russian. During this period, Tom was awarded a number of scholarships for study in Sweden and abroad.

Tom Kronsjo met his wife while studying in Moscow. He was a visiting graduate student at the Moscow State University and she was a graduate student with the Academy of Sciences of the USSR. They married in Moscow in February 1962. A few years later, a very happy event in their family life was the arrival of their adoptive son from Korea in October 1973.

As a post-graduate student in economics, Tom Kronsjo was one of a new breed of Western social scientists that applied rigorous mathematical and computer-based modeling to economics. In 1963, Tom Kronsjo was invited by Professor Ragnar Frish, later Nobel Prize Winner in Econometrics, to work under him and Dr. Salah Hamid in Egypt as a visiting Assistant Professor in Operations Research at the UAR Institute of National Planning. His pioneering papers on optimization of foreign trade were soon considered classic and brought invitations to work as a guest researcher by the GDR Ministry of Foreign Trade and Inner German Trade and by the Polish Ministry of Foreign Trade.

In 1964, Tom Kronsjo was appointed an Associate Professor in Econometrics and Social Statistics at the Faculty of Commerce and Social Sciences, the University of Birmingham, UK. He and his wife then moved to the UK.

In Birmingham, together with Professor R.W. Davies, Tom Kronsjo developed Diploma and Master of Social Sciences courses in National Economic Planning. The courses, offered from 1967, attracted many talented students from all over the world. Many of these students then stayed with Tom Kronsjo as research students and many of these people are today university professors, industrialists, and economic advisors. In 1969, at the age of 36, Tom Kronsjo was appointed Professor of Economic Planning. By then Tom Kronsjo had published over 100 research papers.

Tom Kronsjo has always had a strong interest in educational innovations. He was among the first professors at the University to introduce a television-based teaching, making it possible to widen the scope of the materials taught.

Tom Kronsjo was generous towards his students with his research ideas, stimulating his students intellectually, unlocking wide opportunities for his students through this generosity. He had the ability to see the possibilities in any situation and taught his students to use them.

Tom Kronsjo's research interests were wide and multifaceted. One area of his interest was planning and management at various levels of the national economy. He developed important methods of decomposition of large economic systems, which were considered by his contemporaries a major contribution to the theory of mathematical planning and programming. These results were published in 1972 in a book *Economics of Foreign Trade* written jointly by Tom Kronsjo, Dr. Z. Zawada, and Professor J. Krynicki, both of the Warsaw University, and published in Poland.

In 1972, Tom Kronsjo was invited as a Visiting Professor of Economics and Industrial Administration at Purdue University, Purdue, USA.

In 1974, Tom Kronsjo was a Distinguished Visiting Professor of Economics, at San Diego State University, San Diego, USA.

In the year 1975, Tom Kronsjo found himself as a Senior Fellow in the Foreign Policy Studies Program of the Brookings Institution, Washington, D.C., USA. In collaboration with three other scientists, he was engaged in the project entitled "Trade and Employment Effects of the Multilateral Trade Negotiations". In the words of his colleagues, Tom Kronsjo made an indispensable contribution to this project. Tom Kronsjo's ingenious, tireless, conceptual, and implementing efforts made it possible to carry out calculations involving millions of pieces of information on trade and tariffs, permitting the Brookings model to become the most sophisticated and comprehensive model available at the time for investigation into the effects of the current multilateral trade negotiations. In addition, Tom Kronsjo conceived and designed the means for implementing, perhaps the most imaginative portion of the project, the calculation of "optimal" tariff cutting formulas using linear programming and taking account of balance of payments and other constraints on trade liberalization. A monograph on *Trade, Welfare, and Employment Effects of Trade Negotiations in the Tokyo Round* by Dr. W.R. Cline, Dr. Noboru Kawanabe, Tom Kronsjo, and T. Williams was published in 1978.

Tom Kronsjo's general interests have been in the field of conflicts and cooperation, war and peace, ways out of the arms race, East-West joint enterprises, and world development. He published papers on unemployment, work incentives, and nuclear disarmament.

Tom Kronsjo served as one of the five examiners for one of the Nobel Prizes in Economic Sciences. From time to time, he was invited to nominate a candidate or candidates for the Nobel Prize in Economics.

Tom Kronsjo took an early retirement from the University of Birmingham in 1988 and devoted subsequent years working with young researchers from China, Russia, Poland, Estonia, and other countries.

Tom Kronsjo was a great enthusiast of vegetarianism and veganism, of Buddhist philosophy, yoga, and inter-space communication, of aviation and flying. He learned to fly in the USA and held a pilot license since 1972.

Tom Kronsjo was a man who lived his life to the full, who constantly looked for ways to bring peace to the world. He was an exceptional individual who had the incredible vision and an ability to foresee new trends. He was a man of great charisma, one of those people of whom we say "a man larger than life".

Tom Oskar Martin Kronsjo died in June 2005 at the age of 72.

BIOGRAPHY OF CONTRIBUTORS

Sarwar Uddin Ahmed, Assistant Professor, Independent University of Bangladesh, has obtained his PhD from Nagasaki University, Japan. He was previously a Lecturer in Nagasaki University.

Olav Bjerkholt, Professor in Economics, University of Oslo, was previously the Head of Research at the Norwegian Statistical Office and an Assistant Professor of Energy Economics at the University of Oslo. He has obtained his PhD from the University of Oslo. He was a Visiting Professor in the Massachusetts Institute of Technology and was a consultant to the United Nations and the International Monetary Fund (IMF).

Gerald Garvey, previously Professor of Financial Management, Drucker School of Management, Claremont Graduate School, USA, is currently the Managing Director at Barclays Global Investors. He has obtained his PhD from the University of California, Los Angeles and has held faculty positions at the Australian National University, Sydney University, and the University of British Columbia, Canada.

Noel Gaston is Professor of Economics and the Director of the Globalisation and Development Centre at Bond University. He obtained his PhD from the Cornell University and was an Associate Professor in Tulane University, USA. He was a Visiting Professor at Hitotsubashi University, Osaka University, the University of Konstanz, and the University of Tokyo. He has also been a Shimomura Fellow at the Development Bank of Japan and Visiting Economist at the Cabinet Office of the Japanese Government.

Oner Guncavdi is currently a Professor of International Trade and Economic Development at Istanbul Technical University, Turkey. He received his PhD from the University of Nottingham, England; MSc, from Warwick University, England; and MA in Economics from Istanbul Technical University.

Somdeb Lahiri is a Professor in the Institute for Petroleum Management, Gandhinagar, India. He obtained his PhD from the University of Minnesota, USA. He was previously Professor in the Institute of Financial Management and Research, Madras, India; University of Witwatersrand, Johannesburg, South Africa; Indian Institute of Management, Ahmedabad, India; and in the Indian Institute of Technology, Kanpur, India.

Stephen Littlechild, Professor Emeritus, University of Birmingham, England, was educated at the University of Birmingham and obtained his PhD from the University of Texas, Austin, USA. He was previously the Director General of Electricity Supply, UK and Professor in the Aston University, England and Head of the Department of Industrial Economics, University of Birmingham. He was a Visiting Professor in the University of Chicago. He is now a Senior Research Fellow, Judge Business School, University of Cambridge.

Mats Lundahl, Professor of Development Economics, Stockholm School of Economics, has obtained his PhD from the University of Lund, Sweden. He was previously an Assistant Professor in the University of Lund, and the Chairman of the Department of International Economics and Geography, Stockholm School of Economics from 1987 to 1994. He was a Visiting Professor in Boston University, Corporación de Investigaciones Económicas para Latinoamérica (CIEPLAN), Santiago de Chile, Swedish School of Economics and Business Administration, Helsinki, Swedish Collegium for Advanced Study in the Social Sciences (SCASSS), Uppsala, Universidad de Sevilla and Stanford University, USA.

Victoria Miroshnik, is currently an Adam Smith Research Scholar, Faculty of Law and Social Sciences, University of Glasgow, Scotland. She was educated at the Moscow State University and was an Assistant Professor in Tbilisi State University, Georgia. She has published two books and a large number of scientific papers in leading management journals.

Akira Shimada is an Associate Professor of Economics at Nagasaki University, Japan. He was educated at the Tohoku University and was a

Lecturer at Morioka College, Japan. He has published a number of scientific papers in leading academic journals.

Raziye Selim is currently an Associate Professor of International Trade and Economic Development at the Istanbul Technical University. She has obtained her PhD and MSc from Istanbul Technical University.

Partha Sen, Professor in Economics, Delhi School of Economics, University of Delhi, India, obtained his PhD from the London School of Economics. He has received his MA from the University of Delhi and MSocSci from the University of Birmingham. He was previously a Professor of Economics, Indian Statistical Institute, and Assistant Professor, University of Illinois. He was also the Head, Department of Economics, Delhi School of Economics from 2004 to 2006 and Managing Director, Centre for Development Economics, Delhi School of Economics since 2007. He was a Visiting Professor at the National University of Singapore, City University Hong Kong, Kobe University, University of New South Wales, University of St. Andrews, University of Illinois, University of Washington, and University of Michigan.

Makoto Takashima, Dean and Professor (Retired), Faculty of Economics, Nagasaki University, Japan was educated at the University of Tokyo, Japan. He was previously an Associate Professor in the University of Tokyo Institute of Education in Tsukuba and was a Visiting Professor in the University of East Anglia, England.

Clem Tisdell, Professor Emeritus in Economics, University of Queensland, Australia, obtained his PhD in Economics from the Australian National University and subsequently was a Visiting Fellow at the Princeton University and at Stanford University. He has held professional and administrative positions at the Australian National University, The University of Newcastle and The University of Queensland as well as visiting positions in Nankei University, China, and the Chinese Academy of Social Sciences.

Shigeru Uchida, Professor in Monetary Economics, Nagasaki University, Japan, was educated in Osaka and Tsukuba University in Tokyo before obtaining his PhD from Kyoto University, Japan. He has published a number of books and scientific papers.

ABOUT THE EDITOR

Prof. Dipak Basu is currently a Professor in International Economics in Nagasaki University in Japan. He obtained his PhD from the University of Birmingham, England and did his post-doctoral research in Cambridge University. He was previously a Lecturer in Oxford University — Institute of Agricultural Economics: Senior Economist in the Ministry of Foreign affairs, Saudi Arabia; and Senior Economist in charge of Middle East & Africa Division of Standard & Poor (Data Resources Inc). He has published six books and more than 60 research papers in leading academic journals.

PART 1

GROWTH AND DEVELOPMENT

CHAPTER 1

THE SUSTAINED GROWTH AND ITS RELATION
TO THE INITIAL CONDITIONS

Makoto Takashima

Nagasaki University, Japan

1.1. Introduction

In recent years, deep interest has been shown not only by economic historians
and policy makers but also by scholars of economic theory in rapid economic
developments that have been accomplished by Asian economies with Japan as a
leading country of the industrialization during the latter half of the 20th century in
the long-term process of world economic development.

The accelerated rapidity of growth of these economies is presented statistically
in Table 1.1, where changes in GDP per capita are compared among four typical
countries (UK, USA, Japan, and South Korea) which have achieved their industrialization one after another for these 300 years. In order to compare the rapidity
of economic growth among them, it is considered to the point to see the changes
after they accomplished take-off for their industrialization. As regards South Korea,
the last runner of the take-off among four, Rostow (1983) has indicated that the
economy entered the take-off stage in and has completed it for subsequent sustained
growth until 1968. With his suggestion being applied to the historical changes in
GDP per capita of that country in Table 1.1, the advent of industrialization in South
Korea is to have occurred when the economy reached around $200 of GDP per
capita.

Assuming that this is the case for the other three economies, we compare the
number of years needed for each of them to reach $500 of GDP per capita after they
are in the take-off stage of $200. Considering the year of start of its industrialization
to be 1600, the UK took about 230 years. As for Japan, regarding the beginning
of development policy taken by the Meiji Government in 1868 as the start of its

3

Table 1.1. Historical change in GDP per capita of four countries.

	1700	1800	1840	1871	1916	1940	1958	1967	1976	1989
UK	288	385	603	1015	1633	2004	2458	3092	3671	4933
USA		417	526	785	1869	2383	3565	4614	5412	7041
Japan				251	552	852	975	2203	3752	5075
S. Korea							144	185	543	1706

Sources: Maddison (1979) and UN-National Account Statistics.
Notes: Figures are represented in terms of PPP conversion US$ in 1970 price.
Those for South Korea are in terms of market exchange rate conversion.
US$ in the same fixed price (author's estimates).

industrialization, it took 48 years. In South Korea, it needed only eight years, taking 1968 as the end of its take-off stage according to Rostow. For the more advanced stage beyond $1000 of GPD per capita, Japan took no more than eight years until the economy reached $2000 from $1000 and South Korea would be found to have needed at most four years for it if the data for recent years become available, whilst the UK took 70 years and the USA, 38 years, to double their GDP per capita from $1000. The years when the economies have reached their advanced stage of the level of $2000 of GDP per capita are 1940, 1923, 1967, and presumably 1991 for UK, US, Japan, and South Korea, respectively, showing that the two Western representatives of advanced industrialized countries, the UK and the USA, have already accomplished the level of $2000 before the Second World War, whilst the other two North-East Asian countries, Japan and South Korea, have reached it in the process of industrialization after the War.

Such a rapid and sustained growth as accomplished by Japan and South Korea has been followed by other Asian economies like Hong Kong, and Taiwan, China and more recently it has extended to other Asian economies called Newly Industrializing Economies (NIEs) — Thailand, Malaysia, and Indonesia. It has been accompanied by great social transformation of each country such as urbanization, growing enrollment in general and higher education, and rise in living standards, among other things.

The problems of this sustained and high growth of these Asian economies have been tackled by a number of researchers and scholars theoretically for example, Krugman (1987), Lucas (1988, 1993), Matsuyama (1991), Murakami (1982), Romer (1986) and empirically for example, The World Bank (1991, 1993), Park and Kwon (1995), Muscatelli, Stevenson and Montagna (1995), Kim and Lau (1994), Young (1992, 1994), Edwards (1992), Chen (1979), Tsao (1985, 1986), Wong (1986), Lau and Wan, Jr. (1993), Amsden and Singh (1994) to explain the reasons, identify the sources, and recognize whether the growth will be able to be sustained.

As a matter of course, it is a common feature of the literature by these authors that special emphasis is placed on change in productivity of production processes and a technological factor in international trade. Traditional theories in international trade, however, pay little attention to a role which technology plays in changes in trade patterns, and, therefore, works have been done at first to accommodate a technological factor in trade theories in order to shed light on the "Asian miracle." The introduction of the technological effects in the traditional Ricardian comparative advantage theory was argued by Dornbusch, Fischer, and Samuelson (1977) and the role of technology was discussed by Jones (1970) in the conventional Heckscher–Ohlin's factor-proportions theory. In contrast to these standard static trade theories, Posner (1961) and Vernon (1966) presented a dynamic conception explaining changes in trade patterns through a life cycle of goods, stating that a commodity is initially invented and produced only in developed rich countries and part of the product is exported to developing countries, being followed by the mature stage when it can be produced by them with transferred technology and their advantage of lower labor costs, whilst the country which initially produced and exported it turns importer.

Each of these trade theories was separately contrived with special emphasis on an important but particular economic aspect in production and trade by each of the celebrated economists and has been extended so as to accommodate the effects of technological changes generally in a neoclassical framework by the followers to explain the patterns of trade flows. It seems, however, that the factor-proportions theory, to say the least of it, in the static models and the dynamic product-cycle theory could be incorporated into a single trade theory by explicitly introducing a technological factor in a theoretical framework: technical changes in production process of a commodity in the transition of maturity stages will alter the optimal factor-proportions for production, and the patterns of trade flows will undergo changes accordingly through a life cycle of a good. In this connection, special attention should be paid to policy efforts by the developing economies to introduce new goods and technology when we consider the sources of "Asian miracle" and analyze real features of that sustained high growth.

Although the Richard's and Heckacher–Ohlin's theories have been sophisticated in mathematical frameworks by many economists, Vernon's product-cycle theory remained a descriptive conceptual model. It has to be expressed in a model of some mathematical expression in order to be directed to rigid examination and analysis of economic growth of developing countries. The first achievement, to the best of my knowledge, of formulating the product-cycle model in a mathematical framework was made by Krugman (1979), who developed a simple general-equilibrium model to analyze North-South trade, attempting to explicitly introduce innovation in North and eventual transfer of that technology to South so as to determine the pattern of world trade and its changes over time. According to Krugman's model of the product cycle, it is neatly explained that the trade balance of a developed country which initially introduced a new good changes from a surplus to a deficit in terms of that commodity after a certain lapse of time and that the balance gradually tends to zero as the technology gap reduces between the developed and developing countries.

Some empirical findings, however, indicate that the real behavior of trade patterns may differ from the results of the theoretical investigations. Gognon and Rose (1995), for instance, empirically examined with the use of disaggregated four-digit SITC level data of trade commodities whether most international trade flows change dynamically as the product-cycle theory states. Their investigation shows mainly "an extremely high degree of persistence" in patterns of international trade flows in terms of individual goods. As a matter of fact, there are some robust evidences that patterns of trade has changed significantly in these years in Asian countries like South Korea, and this will be explained compatibly by changes in factor endowments exerted by rapid industrialization as they state. In this discussion, too, emphasis should be received on the need that the traditional static Heckscher–Ohlin's trade theory of factor-proportions is incorporated with the dynamic technological theory of product-cycle.

Another direction of researches on "Asian miracle" and North-South trade is the development or suggestion of new growth theories by Lucas (1988, 1993), Murakami (1982), Matsuyama (1991), Romer (1986), Stokey (1988, 1991a, 1991b), Grossman and Helpman (1991) and others, besides Krugman (1979) as mentioned above in relation with the product-cycle model, which explicitly take into consideration increasing returns to scale, accumulation of technological knowledge, or innovative and R&D activities in their theories. A characteristic common to this line of researches lies in constructing a model by paying an attention of great significance to the human capital or accumulation of technological knowledge by learning-by-doing, which may cause increasing returns to scale, of developing economies as an important source of high growth rate of per capita income in Asian countries.

This paper attempts to contribute to an understanding of the way in which the sustained high growth could be accomplished in not a few Asian economies during these two or three decades and to know the reasons why some can make such a "miracle" and some cannot in the same Asian region. Although it explicitly takes not only a technological factor but also a governmental policy aspect in consideration in order to analyze the problems of Asian economic growth in line with the actual environment of the economies, the model represents only the fundamental aspects of growth structure in a simple mathematical framework. Thus, it does not design to develop a full theory to integrate the standard static trade theories and the dynamic technological ones, which would require further considerable amount of work, but to be of some help to theoretically understand the "Asian miracle" and to have some insight into the future development of this region.

Following this introductory section, this paper refers in Section 1.2 to Krugman's analysis and opinion about the "Asian miracle." As mentioned above, Krugman is one of the scholars who have made most influential researches into North-South problems including the recent developments of Asian economies. With his deep academic studies and deliberate considerations as a backing, Krugman has recently documented his views about the "Asian miracle" and the future possibilities of the Asian economies in journals like *Harvard Business Review* (Krugman, 1994a) and *Foreign Affairs* (Krugman, 1994b). I briefly discuss his opinion in reference to Lucas's paper "Making a Miracle" (Lucas, 1993) and propose my own idea, which leads to a model for growth of the Asian economies.

Section 1.3 presents a simple growth model placing emphasis on accumulation of technological knowledge and governmental policy efforts associated with it. This is designed for explanation of the Asian developing economies and for consideration of the conditions for the sustained growth. According to this mathematical model, the possible growth paths are investigated, subsequently. In Section 1.4, the conditions for sustained growth are discussed in connection to structural and industrial policies of the developing economies. Differences in the policies of economic development among Asian economies (especially, between North-East and South-East Asian economies) and their changes during these two or three decades are taken into consideration in this discussion. The considerations and discussions of this paper conclude with Section 1.5 stating the implications of the whole analyses for the "Asian miracle."

1.2. Recent Discussions about "Asian Miracle"

There has appeared a great amount of literature, academic as well as general, on the Asian economies on account of their sustained high growth achieved in the last few decades of this century. Almost all the books and professional papers on them describe the remarkability of high and sustained growth of Japan, South Korea, and some other rapidly growing Asian economies as "Asia's miracle" and attempt to find out the sources or analyze its reasons. Some of these theoretical attempts are those which are mentioned in the previous section, proposing new growth theory by explicitly assuming production functions with increasing returns to scale, innovative activities, or technology transfer mechanisms.

It is the general tone of the argument in the literature about the Asian economies (for instance, the World Bank, 1993) that their growth can be positively appraised because it resulted in the rapid rise in per capita GDP with comparatively high equalization of income distribution and that the success was accomplished by social, industrial, and financial policies of making the fundamental conditions well-suited to domestic and international environments of each country and, at the same time, by the strong, sometimes almost coercive (Song (1990), p. 58), interventions to the market and the industry. Amidst this general argument, Paul Krugman expresses a different view to the Asian economic growth in his recent article titled "The Myth of Asia's Miracle," which appeared in *Foreign Affairs*, saying that "Popular enthusiasm about Asia's boom deserves to have some cold water thrown on it. Rapid Asian growth is less of a model for the West than many writers claim, and the future prospects for that growth are more limited than almost anyone now imagines" (Krugman (1994b), p. 64). He first mentions the growth and slowdown of the Soviet economy in the following way. The growth of that economy was driven almost by increases in such inputs for production as employment (moving laborers from farms to cities, pushing women into the labor force, and people into longer working hours) and the stock of physical capital (machines and equipment, factories, roads, and other infrastructure) and the contribution of increased efficiency or technical progress in the broad sense of production and management processes, the other important element of growth, was "virtually nonexistent"; the increase in efficiency in using labor and capital in production is essential for continuity of economic growth because mere increases in inputs must eventually lead to diminishing returns, and thus it was inevitable that the growth of the Soviet economy had to come to an end.

Then, Krugman sees "surprising similarities" between the Asian economies of recent years and that of the Soviet Union of three decades ago. Referring to empirical researches about the newly industrialized East Asian economies conducted by Kim and Lau (1994) and Young (1992, 1994 a,b) finding that there is little evidence of improvements in efficiency, he says that rapid growth of Asian economies seems to be driven in large part by an astonishing mobilization of resources of labor and capital and not to be achieved by gains in efficiency, and thus remarks that "Asian economic growth, incredibly, ceases to be a mystery." Accordingly, he calls into question many writers' opinion that the technology gaps between the advanced industrialized countries and the rapidly growing ones will vanish owing to the diffusion of technology, which will undermine the technological advantages and industrial base of the former. Even Japan, he mentions from the recent observation of its rapid economic slow-down, may never overtake America in terms of the level of per capita income even if its technology is gaining on that of the United States because Japan shows a lack of continuous productivity growth comparable to the United States.

Krugman develops a consideration on this issue more deliberately by using models of South-North trade in his article "Does Third World Growth Hurt First World Prosperity?" published in *Harvard Business Review* (Krugman, 1994a). What he virtually wanted to say about the developing economies is not the manifestation of the everlasting supremacy of the Western society over the Third World in terms of economic efficiency, but the warning against disguised protectionism taken by the First World on the basis of the popular but questionable view that competition from the Third World is the biggest threat to the prosperity of the developed countries and of the misguided belief that the First World will be allowed to take measures to protect their living standard. What he really meant is the hopes for realization of a decent living standard for a vast number of people of the Third World through widespread economic development accomplished by free economic activities. This is typically expressed in the last sentence of his article in *Harvard Business Review* above cited, saying that "Economic growth in the Third World is an opportunity, not a threat; it is our fear of Third World success, not that success itself, that is the real danger to the world economy." This is rated as a highly convincing opinion for the development of world economy.

Krugman also extends his argument to the common assertion that the sophisticated industrial policies and selective interventions in economic activities by Asian governments have proved effective to the rapid growth. He says that if these strategic policies had really contributed to the growth, the benefits should have been measured as increases in efficiency in the researches of growth accounting for the Asian economies which have been conducted so far.

This recognition slightly differs from the results of the analysis made by the World Bank in *The East Asian Miracle Economic Growth and Public-Policy* (The World Bank, 1993). This analysis admits that efficiency growth is not the dominant factor to the East Asian success, but it positively appraises higher rise in productivity in this region than in other developing economies, explaining that it was accomplished "by the combination of unusual success at allocating capital to high-yielding investments and at catching up technologically to the industrial economies" (p. 8), which was driven by the policy efforts, that is, implementation of "industrial policy deliberate, government-sponsored interventions to alter industrial structure" (p. 259).

The study also mentions rapid accumulation of human capital as one of the fundamental ingredients of the high, sustained growth in the East Asian economies (pp. 192–203). The accumulation of human capital is effectuated in both quantity and quality aspects. Whilst its accumulation in terms of quantity means mobilization of a greater number of workers into production, human capital in terms of quality is augmented by higher and more expanded schooling in educational facilities among people and by greater acquisition of vocational skills and knowledge through various channels, for instance, firm-level training, on-the-job training, introduction of foreign techniques, and so on. The latter aspect of accumulation of human capital can be considered to be related to technical advance embodied in labor input. Krugman does refer to the remarkable upgrading of educational standards of work force in Asian countries, especially in Singapore. But, he regards it as a mere increase in labor input because he probably takes the rise in labor quality relying on a formal educational system not to last long.

This argument puts aside a question that advance in labor quality due to accumulation of knowledge other than school education will substantially contribute to technical advance in production and that the general upgrading of educational standards of labor force through expanded schooling in the nation will provide the economy with a sound basis for the acquisition of best-practiced technology and management know-how causing the efficiency growth. In relation to this, Lucas constructs a theoretical model explicitly incorporating the role of the growth of human capital into an aggregate production function in order to explain, or to narrow the theoretical possibilities of the problem of, the growth miracles of East Asia (Lucas, 1993). After the discussions on this model with special attention to the on-the-job accumulation of human capital (learning by doing), he concludes that the main engine of growth is the accumulation of human capital (knowledge) and physical capital accumulation plays no more than a subsidiary role. In particular, learning on the job on a sustained basis seems to be by far the most central for the rapid and sustained rise in living standard of a nation.

This paper constructs a simple theoretical model to understand the rapid growth and its possible conditions of Asian economies, placing emphasis on two important ingredients: accumulation of knowledge and policy efforts of the government. Krugman has not fully investigated the role of the accumulation of knowledge and Lucas has not explicitly considered a process of the accumulation, either. The latter ingredient, governmental policy, has been ignored in the discussions of both the scholars, at least in their explicit theoretical frameworks. The analysis of growth paths follows proposition of the model and, subsequently, some policy implications for the possibilities of sustained growth for the developing economies are derived from it in reference to the observation of the realities of Asian economies.

1.3. A Theoretical Model and Growth Paths

Being grounded on the considerations in Section 1.2, I first present a simple growth model designed to represent the main characteristics of the development behavior of the Asian economies: high rates of physical capital accumulation, growing emphasis on accumulation of technological knowledge, and importance of policy efforts by the governments to realize these accumulation, for rapid economic growth.

In order to follow the growth path of per capita income of an economy, I consider an ordinary Cobb-Douglas type production relation that per capita income at t, $y(t)$, is represented by using the stock of physical capital per worker (capital-labor ratios), $k(t)$ and the accumulation of knowledge, $A(t)$, at that time in the following form:

$$y(t) = k(t)^{\alpha} A(t) \tag{1.1}$$

Here, α is a positive constant which is smaller than 1. It varies in the value from country to country according to the development stage and other economic and social conditions. (As I do not pretend to take the traditional neoclassical assumptions of perfect competitiveness to apply in the markets of actual Asian economies, I steer clear of mention that it represents the share of capital.)

One of the essential efforts for developing economies to make take-off towards the sustained growth paths is admittedly the accumulation of knowledge in its broad sense. The knowledge includes general education for people as a fundamental condition necessary for a rise in quality of human capital and more specific vocational knowledge such as engineering and management techniques used in actual production activity. The acquisition of this knowledge is conducted through a variety of channels, but in the case of developing countries aiming to rapid catch-up to the level of advanced industrial countries, it is usually observed that governmental policies play an overwhelmingly important role for it. For the upgrading of the educational standards of the general public, it is inevitable to implement sophisticated social policies including establishment of the comprehensive educational system in the nation, and for the acquisition of new technology, governmental industrial policies have a dominant influence over the behavior of individual firms through subsidizing imports of capital goods embodying new technology, encouraging technology transfer in the form of licenses and foreign training, liberalizing capital movement to introduce direct foreign investment, financially supporting R&D activity, and so forth.

Although governmental policy interventions aiming to the accumulation of knowledge would take different forms depending on actual economic, social, and political circumstances of each country and might change forms according to the situations, the efforts in the aggregate will be measured by government expenses devoted to all what is related to the acquisition of knowledge by the people. What we have to take notice, here, is that the effect of the policy efforts is regarded to depend on the amount per capita rather than the total. (Consider the relation of the total amount of government budget for R&D to the effects between Singapore and China.)

Another thing to be considered in the process of knowledge accumulation is the influence of technological gap between the developing and the developed countries on the rates of the acquisition by the former. It is assumed that if a nation ceases to make efforts to add new technology to its stock, that level measured by a yardstick of the contemporaneous level of the world best-practiced technology decreases at a constant rate, ρ. This is caused by the birth of new technical knowledge in the advanced countries on one hand, and by the continuous decay of old one on the other hand. (Consider one typical example of technological transition from the punched card data processing system to the system of electronic computers which arose in the computer industry in the 1960s. Owing to this technological progress, the programming technique of back pannel wiring in Personal Computer Disk Player (PCDF) was reduced to complete obsolescence.)

From the above consideration, the process of accumulation of knowledge is represented in the following equation

$$\frac{dA(t)}{dt} = u(t)y(t) - \rho A(t), \qquad (1.2)$$

where $u(t)$ means a fraction of national income devoted to the acquisition of knowledge, that is, a tax rate for that purpose.

The process of change in physical capital per worker, $k(t)$, can be constructed on the basis of the macroeconomic relation of gross physical investment being equal to national savings. That is, the net investment to physical capital at time t is written as

$$\frac{dk(t)}{dt} = s(1 - u(t))y(t) - \lambda k(t) \qquad (1.3)$$

Here, s and λ denote national savings ratio and rate of depreciation, respectively, which are both assumed positive constants being smaller than 1. The first term of the right-hand side, $(1 - u(t))y(t)$, is the per capita disposable income net of tax for the acquisition of knowledge and thus the savings ratio has to be understood accordingly.

The rate of obsolescence of technical knowledge in the stock of the developing economies, ρ, is considered to correspond to the rate of technical progress of the world best-practiced technology. From Eqs. (1.1) and (1.3), we can derive the amount of policy efforts necessary for the developing economies not to widen the present technological gap anymore and to keep pace with the progressing level of world technology by using $dA(t)/dt = 0$:

$$u(t) = \frac{\rho}{k(t)^\alpha} \qquad (1.4)$$

This shows that the developing economies having a smaller capital-labor ratio, have to continue the policy efforts more in order to keep pace with the technological standards of the advanced economies. The greater the pace, the more efforts are required, naturally.

In the same way, we can obtain the relation of the stock of knowledge $A(t)$ to the capital-labor ratio, $k(t)$ when $k(t)$ remains constant, $dk(t)/dt = 0$, in the equation

$$A(t) = \frac{\lambda k(t)^{1-\alpha}}{s(1 - u(t))} \qquad (1.5)$$

The above model has the similar expressions to what Karl Shell (1966) presented in his study of relationship between inventive activity and economic growth, which was highly suggestive to my study. The similarity of models takes place from a common nature intrinsic to the accumulation activity of knowledge. Special attention is paid in my analysis, however, to the policy efforts by the governments of developing economies to the growth through transfer of technology from the advanced countries and to the investigation of the initial conditions for take-off towards the sustained growth in relation to these efforts with the use of this model.

Hereafter, as the first step of the study, the policy efforts are assumed to be continued with a certain level by the governments, and thus,

$$u(t) = \bar{u} \tag{1.6}$$

Then, the values of $A(t)$ and $k(t)$ corresponding to $dA(t)/dt = 0$ and $dk(t)/dt = 0$ are determined to be A_* and K_*, respectively, irrelevant to time:

$$A_* = \frac{\lambda k_*^{1-\alpha}}{s(1-\bar{u})} \tag{1.7}$$

$$k_* = \frac{\rho}{\bar{u}} \tag{1.8}$$

As a starting step of the analysis, with the level of the policy efforts being taken to be a time-invariant constant, I attempt to derive the growth equations for $A(t)$ and $k(t)$ to know the behavior of these trajectories according to the initial conditions of the developing economies, and then examine the possibilities of take-off towards their sustained growth by changing the levels of policy efforts in connection to the initial situations.

In order to solve the differential Eqs. (1.2) and (1.3), I try to transform it to a linear system by the Taylor expansion about (A_*, k_*), which makes it possible to analyze the behavior of the growth paths around that point and obtain the approximate expressions for the trajectories. The transformation practiced on Eqs. (1.2) and (1.3) gives the following non-homogeneous linear differential equation system:

$$\frac{dv(t)}{dt} = \lambda w(t) - \ln(k_*) \tag{1.9}$$

$$\frac{dv(t)}{dt} = \alpha\rho v(t) - \lambda(1-\alpha)w(t) - [\ln(A_*) - (1-\alpha)\ln(k_*)], \tag{1.10}$$

where $v(t) = (1/\alpha\rho)\ln(A(t))$, and $w(t) = (1/\lambda)\ln(k(t))$.

For the sake of obtaining a fundamental system of solution for the homogeneous part of the above equation system, I construct the characteristic equation:

$$\psi(\varphi) = \begin{bmatrix} 0 & \lambda \\ \alpha\rho & -\lambda(1-\alpha) \end{bmatrix} - \varphi E = \varphi^2 + \lambda(1-\alpha)\varphi - \alpha\rho\lambda = 0 \tag{1.11}$$

From this, the characteristic roots are obtained as:

$$\varphi_1 = -\frac{1}{2}[\lambda(1-\alpha) + \sqrt{D}] = -\mu \quad (\mu > 0)$$

$$\varphi_2 = \frac{1}{2}[-\lambda(1-\alpha) + \sqrt{D}] = \omega \quad (\omega > 0) \tag{1.12}$$

$$(D = \lambda^2(1-\alpha)^2 + 4\alpha\rho\lambda).$$

Therefore, the characteristic equation of this system has real different roots of opposite signs, and thus the stationary point (A_*, k_*) is a local saddle point. Moreover, as the function $y(t)$ is certainly twice-continuously differentiable with respect to k, that point proves to be a global saddle point.

From the characteristic roots of φ_1 and φ_2, a solution matrix is constructed as:

$$Y = \left(\begin{bmatrix} A_{11} \\ A_{21} \end{bmatrix} e^{\varphi_1 t} \begin{bmatrix} A_{12} \\ A_{22} \end{bmatrix} e^{\varphi_2 t} \right), \tag{1.13}$$

where (A_{1i}, A_{2i}) is a characteristic vector corresponding to φ_i. Now, the Wronskian $|Y|$ is not zero for at least a certain value of t, and thus Y becomes the fundamental system of solution for the homogeneous part of the above differential equation system.

With the use of this fundamental system of solution, the general solution for the original non-homogeneous system is obtained in the form of:

$$\begin{bmatrix} v(t) \\ w(t) \end{bmatrix} = Y(t) \begin{bmatrix} c_1(t_0) \\ c_2(t_0) \end{bmatrix} + Y(t) \int_{t_0}^{t} Y^{-1}(\tau) \begin{bmatrix} f_1 \\ f_2 \end{bmatrix} d\tau, \tag{1.14}$$

having arbitrary constants c_1 and c_2 at the initial stage t_0. Putting the solution matrix $Y(t)$ in this relation, we obtain the explicit expressions for the general solution as:

$$v(t) = A_{11}c_1(t_0)e^{\varphi_1 t} + A_{12}c_2(t_0)e^{\varphi_2 t}$$

$$+ \frac{\lambda}{\varphi_1\sqrt{D}}\left[\ln(A_*) - \left(\frac{\varphi_2}{\lambda}+1-\alpha\right)\ln(k_*)\right] \cdot \{\exp[\varphi_1(t-t_0)] - 1\}$$

$$+ \frac{\lambda}{\varphi_2\sqrt{D}}\left[\ln(A_*) - \left(\frac{\varphi_1}{\lambda}+1-\alpha\right)\ln(k_*)\right] \cdot \{\exp[\varphi_2(t-t_0)] - 1\}$$

$$\tag{1.15}$$

$$w(t) = A_{21}c_1(t_0)e^{\varphi_1 t} + A_{22}c_2(t_0)e^{\varphi_2 t}$$

$$+ \frac{\lambda}{\varphi_1\sqrt{D}}\left[\ln(A_*) - \left(\frac{\varphi_2}{\lambda}+1-\alpha\right)\ln(k_*)\right]$$

$$\times \left(\frac{A_{21}}{A_{11}}\right)\{\exp[\varphi_1(t-t_0)]-1\}$$

$$+\frac{\lambda}{\varphi_2\sqrt{D}}\left[\ln(A_*)-\left(\frac{\varphi_1}{\lambda}+1-\alpha\right)\ln(k_*)\right]$$

$$\times \left(\frac{A_{22}}{A_{12}}\right)\{\exp[\varphi_2(t-t_0)]-1\}. \tag{1.16}$$

Changing $v(t)$ and $w(t)$ into original variables, we have the final expressions for time paths of the stock of knowledge $A(t)$ the capital-labor ratio $k(t)$ in the following way:

$$A(t)=\exp\{\alpha\rho[(g_1+h_1e^{-\varphi_1 t_0})e^{\varphi_1 t}+(g_2+h_2e^{-\varphi_2 t_0})e^{\varphi_2 t}-h_1-h_2]\} \tag{1.17}$$

$$k(t)=\exp\{\varphi_1(g_1+h_1e^{-\varphi_1 t_0})e^{\varphi_1 t}+\varphi_2(g_2+h_2e^{-\varphi_2 t_0})e^{\varphi_2 t}-\varphi_1 h_1-\varphi_2 h_2\}, \tag{1.18}$$

where constant and coefficient terms g_1, g_2, h_1, h_2 are represented as

$$g_1=\left[\frac{\varphi_2\ln(A_0)-\alpha\rho\ln(k_0)}{\alpha\rho(\varphi_2-\varphi_1)}\right]e^{-\varphi_1 t_0} \tag{1.19}$$

$$g_2=-\left[\frac{\varphi_1\ln(A_0)-\alpha\rho\ln(k_0)}{\alpha\rho(\varphi_2-\varphi_1)}\right]e^{-\varphi_2 t_0} \tag{1.20}$$

$$h_1=\frac{\lambda}{\varphi_1\sqrt{D}}\left\{\ln(A_*)-\left(\frac{\varphi_2}{\lambda}+1-\alpha\right)\ln(k_*)\right\} \tag{1.21}$$

$$h_2=\frac{\lambda}{\varphi_2\sqrt{D}}\left\{-\ln(A_*)+\left(\frac{\varphi_1}{\lambda}+1-\alpha\right)\ln(k_*)\right\} \tag{1.22}$$

In the relations (1.19) and (1.20), A_0 and k_0 denote the initial values of $A(t)$ and $k(t)$ at $t=t_0$, respectively. These initial conditions are due to play a crucial role in the future growth paths of the economies, which will be investigated in the next section.

The time paths of $A(t)$ and $k(t)$ obtained here represent no more than the approximation to those implied by the original model postulated in (1.1)–(1.3), but they preserve the fundamental nature inherent in it. Thus, Eqs. (1.17) and (1.18) yield the expressions for the trajectories of growth in an (A, k)-plane by a process of elimination of time t from them in the following form:

$$|\mu\ln[A(t)]+\alpha\rho\ln[k(t)]+\alpha\rho(\mu+\omega)h_2|^\mu$$

$$\times|\omega\ln[A(t)]+\alpha\rho\ln[k(t)]+\alpha\rho(\mu+\omega)h_1|^\omega$$

$$=|\alpha\rho(\mu+\omega)(g_2+h_2e^{-\omega t_0})|^\mu\cdot|\alpha\rho(\mu+\omega)(g_1+h_1e^{-\mu t_0})|^\omega. \tag{1.23}$$

Some computational manipulations make it possible to rewrite this expression in the form

$$\left| \left(\frac{\mu}{\alpha\rho} \right) \ln \left(\frac{A(t)}{A_*} \right) + \ln \left(\frac{k(t)}{k_*} \right) \right|^{\mu} \cdot \left| \left(\frac{\omega}{\alpha\rho} \right) \ln \left(\frac{A(t)}{A_*} \right) + \ln \left(\frac{k(t)}{k_*} \right) \right|^{\omega}$$

$$= |(\mu + \omega)A^{12} y_2(t_0)|^{\mu} \cdot |(\mu + \omega)A^{11} y_1(t_0)|^{\omega}, \tag{1.24}$$

where $A^{11} y_1(t_0)$ and $A^{12} y_2(t_0)$ are obtained from the initial conditions for $A(t)$ and $k(t)$ as expressed in the following way:

$$A^{11} y_1(t_0) = \frac{1}{\mu + \omega} \cdot \left\{ \frac{\omega}{\alpha\rho} \cdot \ln \left(\frac{A_0}{A_*} \right) - \ln \left(\frac{k_0}{k_*} \right) \right\} \tag{1.25}$$

$$A^{12} y_2(t_0) = \frac{1}{\mu + \omega} \cdot \left\{ \frac{\omega}{\alpha\rho} \cdot \ln \left(\frac{A_0}{A_*} \right) + \ln \left(\frac{k_0}{k_*} \right) \right\} \tag{1.26}$$

[See also a mathematical note in Appendix.]

In order to depict the trajectories of the growth paths, it is convenient to express at first the parts enclosed with the absolute value marks in the left-hand side of Eq. (1.24) in the linear form. This can be done by putting

$$x_1(t) = \left(\frac{1}{\alpha\rho} \right) \ln \left(\frac{A(t)}{A_*} \right) \quad \text{and} \quad x_2(t) = \left(\frac{1}{\lambda} \right) \ln \left(\frac{k(t)}{k_*} \right), \tag{1.27}$$

which gives

$$|\mu x_1(t) + \lambda x_2(t)|^{\mu} \cdot |\omega x_1(t) - \lambda x_2(t)|^{\omega}$$

$$= |(\mu + \omega)A^{12} y_2(t_0)|^{\mu} \cdot |(\mu + \omega)A^{11} y_1(t_0)|^{\omega}. \tag{1.28}$$

The trajectories of $x_1(t)$ and $x_2(t)$ are shown in the phase plane of Fig. 1.1. In the laws of motion there, attention must be paid to the properties that the growth of $x_1(t)$ or $x_2(t)$ always becomes zero when a trajectory cuts across the lines

$$x_2(t) = 0 \quad \text{and} \quad \alpha\rho x_1(t) - \lambda(1 - \alpha)x_2(t) = 0.$$

The trajectories approach an asymptotic line,

$$\omega x_1(t) - \lambda x_2(t) = 0,$$

as time goes on, one group expanding and the other dampening. The origin corresponds to the point (k_*, A_*).

After the law of motion in the phase diagram is understood, the growth trajectories of $A(t)$ and $k(t)$ are easily depicted. Since the slope of an asymptotic line extending northeastward is easily ascertained to be greater than that of the line signifying $dx_2(t)/dt = 0$ as shown in Fig. 1.1, the asymptotic curve

$$\left(\frac{\omega}{\alpha\rho} \right) \ln \left(\frac{A(t)}{A_*} \right) - \ln \left(\frac{k(t)}{k_*} \right) = 0 \tag{1.29}$$

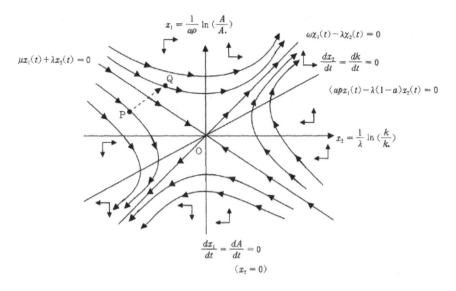

$$x_1 = \frac{1}{\alpha p} \ln\left(\frac{A}{A_*}\right)$$

$$\mu x_1(t) + \lambda x_2(t) = 0$$

$$\omega \chi_1(t) - \lambda \chi_2(t) = 0$$

$$\frac{dx_2}{dt} = \frac{dk}{dt} = 0$$

$$(\alpha p x_1(t) - \lambda(1-a)x_2(t) = 0$$

$$x_2 = \frac{1}{\lambda} \ln\left(\frac{k}{k_*}\right)$$

$$\frac{dx_1}{dt} = \frac{dA}{dt} = 0$$
$$(x_2 = 0)$$

Fig. 1.1.   Phase plane of $(x_1(t), x_2(t))$.

cuts the $dk(t)/dt = 0$ curve at the point $O(k_*, A_*)$ from below to above as it stretches to the northeast. And it has already been found that the crossing point is a saddle point.

In the plane of the growth trajectories, the point O moves according to the change in the value u, policy efforts. This means that policy efforts might switch some growth paths which are to dampen in the future to the other paths and make them go into the trajectories having expanding properties. This possibility is exemplified in Fig. 1.1 by a switch of a trajectory from P to Q. The effects of policy on the growth paths together with the initial conditions are considered in the next section, especially with the East Asian economies in mind.

1.4. Initial Conditions and Policy Efforts

Among the results derived from the above theoretical analysis based on a simple growth model, what seems to be of special significance from the point of view of economic development is the relation between the initial state of an economy as the fundamental conditions for the development and the effects of policy implementation on the possibility of growth.

As mathematical models invented by economists always do so, my model presented in this paper takes into account only the essential properties associated with the problems to be considered. Thus, the discussion here is not concerned with full description about sophisticated aspects in the real economy, but it refers to those to the extent that the model is related to them. The purpose of model-building is to extract essential law of immanent behavior in the reality from its complexity for the cause of better understanding of the actual economy and better policy-making appropriate for it.

As regards the initial conditions of an economy aiming to the take-off for sustained growth, the model typically indicates what amounts of accumulated knowledge A and of physical capital stock per worker k are needed at $t = t_0$. Figure 1.1 shows that in order to get on the paths which are to be led to the sustained growth, the economy must be in the region above the line

$$\mu x_1(t) + \lambda x_2(t) = 0 \qquad (1.30)$$

in the phase plane at the initial time $t = t_0$. This region is formed by an asymptotic curve equivalent to the equation which is given as

$$\frac{\mu}{\alpha\rho} \cdot \ln\left(\frac{A(t)}{A_*}\right) + \ln\left(\frac{k(t)}{k_*}\right) = 0 \qquad (1.31)$$

in the trajectories diagram which is easily graphed out. The economies having the endowments of A and k at the initial time, $A(t_0)$ and $k(t_0)$, which are located in the region under this curve, are on the trajectories going eventually to the state at a low ebb.

This simple theoretical conclusion throws some light on the arguments concerning the growth of Asian economies. As mentioned in Section 1.2, Krugman poured cold water on the popular enthusiasm about Asian rapid economic growth, stating that Asian input-driven growth is an inherently limited process as far as it is not accompanied by an increase in efficiency with which inputs are used. With reference to the above conclusion seen in Fig. 1.1, it seems that Krugman's view is correct no matter how much physical capital is piled up, the economies cannot go into the trajectories eventually heading for the developed state as long as they stay in the region under the boundary curve marked by Eq. (1.31) owing to the absence of efficiency growth, that is, the low level of the accumulation of knowledge A. In that circumstance, it appears that the economies make rapid growth through high rates of the mobilization of resources into production, but as a matter of fact, they may simply move to one of the upper trajectories of the same dampening nature, and then the growth is not sustained actually. In a different situation, however, where the economies have already accumulated a considerable amount of knowledge whilst the stock of physical capital is at an extremely low level, the economies could find a way to go into a sustained growth path towards the developed state. This might be possible by only a small amount of efforts of accumulation of physical capital through the measures like receipt of foreign aids. Otherwise, those economies with a high level of knowledge might ever remain in the sustained growth region above the boundary curve even at a low level of capital stock. This is considered the case with Japan's economy that was immediately after the end of the World War II. Japan had attained to the industrial state near the then Western economies, but the accumulated production facilities were almost completely destroyed by bombardment in wartime. No one can destroy knowledge dwelling in the nation, however, Japan embarked on the reconstruction of its economy after the war, keeping the technological knowledge associated to productive activities accumulated in peacetime before the war and augmented by the government-financed R&D mainly concerned with advanced strategic technology. In the process of the reconstruction, the lack of physical capital was the problem of vital importance for the government to deal with. In order to tackle this problem, it took a bold step called the "priority production system" that the limited amounts of Japan's scarce resources at that time were to be committed mainly to the construction of productive facilities of the fundamental industries such as iron and steel, shipbuilding, and electric power industries. In so doing, Japan's economy could go into the trajectory of rapid and self-sustaining growth in five years after the end of the war. (In addition to such policy efforts, it is commonly admitted that the Korean War in 1950 played a definite role as an engine in sending Japan's economy to the high-growth path.)

As far as the static initial conditions are concerned, Krugman's statement on the limitedness of the economic growth of the newly industrializing countries in the Pacific Rim seems to be correct on the basis of the analyses here. However, Krugman disregards the fact that the continuous efforts of augmenting knowledge or human skills in the nation could change the economy's nature from "One-time changes" by mobilization of inputs to vitalized growth by increases in efficiency. A continuous policy effort to augment knowledge, $u(t) = \bar{u}$, moves the point $O(k_*, A_*)$ as time goes on. If this point moves towards the origin in compliance with the efforts, the dampening region of the economy diminishes accordingly. The behavior of the point O in response to changes in the level of u is shown in Fig. 1.2. Recall that $u(t)$ denotes part of national income devoted to the acquisition of knowledge and is generally considered to be the tax rate for that purpose. However, the accumulation of knowledge is not always implemented by administrative measures based on governmental policies, but it could also be taken place in ordinary behavior of free enterprises or individuals being driven by market competition or a desire to improve oneself. The variable $u(t)$ includes all these activities related to the acquisition of knowledge by the nation.

When the value of u is so small as to be almost zero, the initial conditions for an economy to go along the developing trajectories are highly demanding: the economy has to be equipped with a vast amount of physical capital stock along with a fairly large accumulation of knowledge at the beginning of stage of development since k_* is of almost infinity and A_* is $(\lambda/s)k_*^{1-\alpha}$ at $u = 0$. This can be said to be a contradiction in terms of "development." As $u(t)$ takes a larger value starting from zero, the conditions for growth become less demanding. This stable (zero growth) point O approaches the origin accordingly and the required

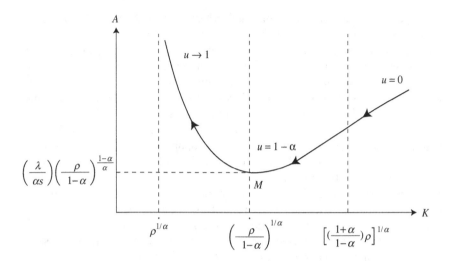

Fig. 1.2. Motion of stable (zero growth) point subject to policy efforts.

accumulation of knowledge corresponding to the smallest value of k_* reaches the minimum $(\lambda/\alpha s)[\rho/(1-\alpha)]^{\frac{1-\alpha}{\alpha}}$. This point M is attained by the level of the policy efforts $u = 1 - \alpha$. After that, the required levels of knowledge at the initial state increase rapidly as u approaches 1. This is a broad outline of changes in the required initial conditions of the economies aiming at self-sustaining growth derived from the motion of the stable point caused by the changes in the level of policy efforts to acquire knowledge. These efforts are not limited to the activities of directly acquiring knowledge through, for instance, government-financed R&D or importation of foreign techniques. Technological knowledge could be accumulated through indirect channels, too, of importing capital goods furnished with highly advanced technology needed for the production of exports under the export promotion strategy.

The analysis shows that policy efforts by the nation could ease the initial conditions required to make the economy grow by changing the state in the poverty region (under the asymptotic curve given by the Eq. (1.31)) to that in the prosperity region (above the curve). This same effect produced by the policy efforts can be explained in the phase diagram of Fig. 1.1 by a switch of a declining path at a point P to a self-sustaining growth path at a point Q. I do not intend here to assert the advantages in economic policy of the selective interventions over the traditional laissez-faire approach. I only would like to indicate that continuous policy efforts can play an important role in improving the initial conditions of the economies which remain in poverty state and cannot find a way to get rid of it. It is taken for granted that whether an economy in the underdeveloped state can actually move to the prosperity region, not taking only an upper growth path in the same poverty region by "one-time changes", depends upon the extent to which the economy can achieve efficiency growth by the accumulation efforts of knowledge of the nation.

1.5. Concluding Remarks

I have tried in this paper to analyze the fundamental structure of the Asian economic growth and to bring to light the basic problem to be considered for the sake of the development of the East Asian economies in the hope of further promoting constructive arguments about them between the popular enthusiasm alleging the "Asia's miracle" and the scholarly skepticism about the Asian supremacy of the growth asserting a lack of efficiency growth in these economies.

Economic growth, as an increase in per capita national income, is achieved through both quantitative and qualitative advances in economic activities: quantitative advances of the economy can be accomplished by mobilization of capital and labor inputs in production processes, while qualitative advances can be caused by efficiency growth in the economy typically through technological improvements. In the light of this consideration, I introduced a simple mathematical model to analyze the fundamental properties of growth paths in relation to the initial state of a country visualizing to enter the take-off stage followed by sustained growth. Growth equations derived from that model show that all the growth trajectories are divided into two groups according to the initial conditions, one of which consists of trajectories having the eventually expanding properties with the other being those of the eventually dampening properties. The phase plane accommodating all the possible growth paths is separated into two parts by an equation signifying an asymptotic curve. One is the area above the curve where all the eventually expanding trajectories exist and the other is the area below the curve having all the eventually dampening ones. I designated the former as the "prosperity region" and the latter as the "poverty region." An economy lying in the poverty region at the initial state will be destined to stay in the situation of low standard of living, if it does not make any policy efforts to accumulate knowledge. On the contrary, the policy efforts could send the economy to one of the growth paths in the prosperity region. From the properties of the poverty region which enlarges or reduces according to the changes in the level of policy efforts, growth policy unaccompanied by increases in efficiency-mobilization of resources without augmentation of knowledge might give the economy only "one-time changes" of the state which move it into one of the upper trajectories in the same region. This may correspond to the case of an inherently limited input-driven growth mentioned by Krugman about Asian rapid economic growth. However, much attention must be paid to the possibility that continuous efforts to augment knowledge by the nation would lead the economy to a sheer self-sustaining growth path by moving it from the poverty region to the prosperity region, or by switching the trajectories from the eventually dampening path to one of the eventually expanding paths. As a matter of fact, Japan has accomplished this switch in growth path through the implementation of sophisticated economic policies characterized by a series of "economic plans" which extended over five decades after the war. South Korea, as well, has made high and sustained growth accompanied by structural transformation through continuous policy efforts strongly led by the government in pursuit of the Japanese model to a great extent (Takashima, 1994).

An economy may differ with another on the forms of policy efforts to accumulate knowledge, depending on the differences of political and economic surroundings between them. In reality, the economies of South-East Asia — Singapore, Thailand, Malaysia, and Indonesia — have taken different strategies to acquire knowledge from those of the North-East Asian forerunners, Japan and South Korea, by opening their markets to foreign direct investment (The Economist, 1995), as compared with these East-Asian peers having striven against it.

It depends on a degree of increases in efficiency whether these East-Asian economies truly have made or can make a growth miracle. At the early-industrial stage when the economy is about to start its industrialization for growth, policy measures like selective interventions and coerced mobilization of resources might prove effective for structural transformation and produce a rapid growth. But the quantitative mobilization of resources inevitably reduces the economy to the state of decreasing returns. The sheer self-sustaining growth can be achieved only by continuous efficiency growth through accumulation of knowledge, typically speaking, technological advance in the broad sense of the word, which can realize increasing returns in production. And this cannot be made by government regulations and protectionism, but can be progressed only by continuous development of creativity inspired in the nation by the free competitive environment.

Mathematical Appendix

In this Appendix, I provide another method of calculations for the solutions of the non-homogeneous differential Eqs. (1.2) and (1.3), which proves to give the same result as (1.23).

I start with the non-homogeneous linear differential system, Eqs. (1.9) and (1.10), obtained by the Taylor expansion of the original system about zero-growth point (A_*, k_*). This system can be reduced to the form of a linear homogeneous system of differential equations

$$\frac{\mathrm{d}x_1}{\mathrm{d}t} = \lambda x_2 \tag{A.1}$$

$$\frac{\mathrm{d}x_2}{\mathrm{d}t} = \alpha\rho x_1 - \lambda(1-\alpha)x_2 \tag{A.2}$$

by replacing $v(t)$ and $w(t)$ with new variables $x_1(t)$ and $x_2(t)$ having the relations

$$x_1(t) = v(t) - (1/\alpha\rho) \cdot \ln(A_*)$$

$$= (1/\alpha\rho) \cdot \ln(A(t)/A_*) \tag{A.3}$$

$$x_2(t) = w(t) - (1/\lambda) \cdot \ln(k_*)$$

$$= (1/\lambda) \cdot \ln(k(t)/k_*) \tag{A.4}$$

Thus, the differential system can be written in vector form as follows

$$\begin{pmatrix} dx_1(t)/dt \\ dx_2(t)/dt \end{pmatrix} = \begin{bmatrix} 0 & \lambda \\ \alpha\rho & -\lambda(1-\alpha) \end{bmatrix} \cdot \begin{pmatrix} x_1(t) \\ x_2(t) \end{pmatrix} \tag{A.5}$$

Considering a certain linear transformation

$$y = A_1 x_1 + A_2 x_2 \quad \text{and} \quad \frac{dy}{dt} = \phi y, \tag{A.6}$$

next relation can be obtained from Eqs. (A.1) and (A.2):

$$A_1(\lambda x_2) + A_2[\alpha\rho x_1 - \lambda(1-\alpha)x_2] = \phi(A_1 x_1 + A_2 x_2) \tag{A.7}$$

(Here, notations y and A_i have no conceptual relation with the variables denoting per capita income and level of knowledge in the original model of the text, respectively.) Since the variables x_1 and x_2 are to take arbitrary values in Eq. (A.6), Eq. (A.7) yields

$$-\phi A_1 + \alpha\rho A_2 = 0 \tag{A.8}$$

$$\lambda A_1 + [-\lambda(1-\alpha) - \phi]A_2 = 0 \tag{A.9}$$

In these equations, the next relation must be established in order for the non-zero solutions for A_1 and A_2 to exist

$$\begin{vmatrix} -\phi & \alpha\rho \\ \lambda & -\lambda(1-\alpha) - \phi \end{vmatrix} = \begin{vmatrix} -\phi & \lambda \\ \alpha\rho & -\lambda(1-\alpha) - \phi \end{vmatrix} = 0 \tag{A.10}$$

This is nothing else but the characteristic equation for the coefficient matrix of the homogeneous differential system Eq. (A.5).

The characteristic roots ϕ_1 and ϕ_2 of this equation were given in the text as Eq. (1.12) and proved to be real and different, having opposite signs. Therefore, characteristic vectors (A_{i1}, A_{i2}) are obtained from Eq. (A.8) or Eq. (A.9) corresponding to $\phi_i (i = 1, 2)$. (One of the Eqs. (A.8) and (A.9) is derived from the other one along with the above characteristic equation which gives the existence conditions for the solution.) From $\phi_1 \neq \phi_2$ and the second relation of Eq. (A.6), y_1 and y_2 are found to form a system of linear independence.

With the characteristic roots ϕ_1 and ϕ_2 having real different values of opposite signs, the second relation of Eq. (A.6) is written as a system of two equations, each corresponding to one of the roots:

$$\begin{pmatrix} dy_1(t)/dt \\ dy_2(t)/dt \end{pmatrix} = \begin{bmatrix} \phi_1 & 0 \\ 0 & \phi_2 \end{bmatrix} \cdot \begin{pmatrix} y_1(t) \\ y_2(t) \end{pmatrix} \tag{A.11}$$

Thus, the system can easily be solved in the following way:

$$y_1(t) = y_1(t_0) \exp[\phi_1(t - t_0)] \tag{A.12}$$

$$y_2(t) = y_2(t_0) \exp[\phi_2(t - t_0)], \tag{A.13}$$

where negative root ϕ_1 and positive one ϕ_2 are rewritten with the use of positive notations and as μ and ω as $\phi_1 = -\mu$ and $\phi_2 = \omega$, respectively.

Using the two variables y_1 and y_2 corresponding to those two different characteristic roots, the full linear transformation Eq. (A.6) between x_i and y_i is written in the form

$$\begin{pmatrix} y_1 \\ y_2 \end{pmatrix} = \begin{bmatrix} A_{11} & A_{12} \\ A_{21} & A_{22} \end{bmatrix} \cdot \begin{pmatrix} x_1 \\ x_2 \end{pmatrix} \tag{A.14}$$

Here, the first row in the matrix A_{ij} represents the characteristic vector of the coefficient matrix of the system Eq. (A.5) corresponding to the first characteristic root ϕ_1 and the second row is that corresponding to the second root ϕ_2. Then, the solutions of Eqs. (A.12) and (A.13) and can be transformed into those of $x_1(t)$ and $x_2(t)$ in the following expressions:

$$x_1(t) = A^{11} y_1(t_0) e^{-\mu(t-t_0)} + A^{12} y_2(t_0) e^{\omega(t-t_0)} \tag{A.15}$$

$$x_2(t) = A^{21} y_1(t_0) e^{-\mu(t-t_0)} + A^{22} y_2(t_0) e^{\omega(t-t_0)}, \tag{A.16}$$

where A^{ij} is an (i, j) element of the inverse matrix of (A_{ij}) in Eq. (A.14). The relations between A^{ij}s and the coefficients of the original system are obtained by putting the above solutions into Eqs. (A.1) and (A.2), which yields

$$\mu A^{11} + \lambda A^{21} = 0 \quad \text{and} \quad \omega A^{21} - \lambda A^{22} = 0 \tag{A.17}$$

$$\alpha \rho A^{11} + [\mu - \lambda(1 - \alpha)]A^{21} = 0 \quad \text{and} \quad \alpha \rho A^{12} + [-\omega - \lambda(1 - \alpha)]A^{22} = 0. \tag{A.18}$$

Equations (A.17) and (A.18) are not independent because the first relation of Eq. (A.18) can be derived from the first relation of Eq. (A.17) with the help of the relation expressed in the characteristic equation and the second relation of Eq. (A.18) can be obtained from the second relation of Eq. (A.17) exactly the same way.

Through a process of elimination of t, Eqs. (A.15) and (A.16) yield the general equation of trajectories of $(x_1(t), x_2(t))$ in the following form

$$|\mu x_1(t) + \lambda x_2(t)|^\mu \cdot |\omega x_1(t) - \lambda x_2(t)|^\omega$$
$$= |(\mu + \omega)A^{12}y_2(t_0)|^\mu \cdot |(\mu + \omega)A^{11}y_1(t_0)|^\omega \qquad \text{(A.19)}$$

which was given in Eq. (1.28) in the text. The motion of these trajectories is depicted in the phase plane of Fig. 1.1. This equation can be rewritten into the expression of the original variables $A(t)$ and $k(t)$ with the use of the relations (A.3) and (A.4) as

$$\left| \left(\frac{\mu}{\alpha\rho} \right) \ln \left(\frac{A(t)}{A_*} \right) + \ln \left(\frac{k(t)}{k_*} \right) \right|^\mu \cdot \left| \left(\frac{\omega}{\alpha\rho} \right) \ln \left(\frac{A(t)}{A_*} \right) - \ln \left(\frac{k(t)}{k_*} \right) \right|^\omega$$
$$= |(\mu + \omega)A^{12}y_2(t_0)|^\mu \cdot |(\mu + \omega)A^{11}y_1(t_0)|^\omega, \qquad \text{(A.20)}$$

which was Eq. (1.24) in the text. The behavior of growth paths are easily depicted in $(A(t), k(t))$-plane.

Individual growth equations of $A(t)$ and $k(t)$ are obtained from Eqs. (A.15) and (A.16) by changing variables, using Eqs. (A.3) and (A.4). That is,

$$A(t) = A(t_0) \exp[(A^{11}y_1(t_0)e^{-\mu(t-t_0)} + A^{12}y_2(t_0)e^{\omega(t-t_0)})\alpha\rho] \qquad \text{(A.21)}$$

$$k(t) = k(t_0) \exp(-\mu A^{11}y_1(t_0)e^{-\mu(t-t_0)} + \omega A^{12}y_2(t_0)e^{\omega(t-t_0)}). \qquad \text{(A.22)}$$

These equations give us the unknown constants, $A^{11}y_1(t_0)$ and $A^{12}y_2(t_0)$ in Eqs. (A.19) and (A.20) in consideration of the initial conditions, $A(t_0)$ and $k(t_0)$, as Eqs. (1.25) and (1.26) in the text.

In the phase plane of $(x_1(t), x_2(t))$, the asymptotic lines for the trajectories of Eq. (A.19) are found to be

$$\mu x_1(t) + \lambda x_2(t) = 0 \quad \text{and} \quad \omega x_1(t) - \lambda x_2(t) = 0, \qquad \text{(A.23)}$$

which leads to the asymptotic curves for growth paths of Eq. (A.20) in the form

$$\left(\frac{\mu}{\alpha\rho} \right) \ln \left(\frac{A(t)}{A_*} \right) + \ln \left(\frac{k(t)}{k_*} \right) = 0$$

and

$$\left(\frac{\omega}{\alpha\rho} \right) \ln \left(\frac{A(t)}{A_*} \right) - \ln \left(\frac{k(t)}{k_*} \right) = 0. \qquad \text{(A.24)}$$

These play a crucial role in characterizing the behavior of trajectories in both planes of $(x_1(t), x_2(t))$ and $(A(t), k(t))$, as explained in the text.

References

Amsden, AH and A Singh (1994). Growth in developing countries: lessons from East Asian countries — the optional degree of competition and dynamic efficiency in Japan and Korea. *European Economic Review*, 38, 941–951.

Chen, EKY (1979). *Hyper Growth in Asia Economics A Comparative Study of Hong Kong, Japan, Korea, Singapore and Taiwan*, London: Macmillan.

Dornbusch, R, S Fischer and PA Samuelson (1977). Comparative advantage, trade, and payments in a Ricardian model with a continuum of goods. *American Economic Review*, 67, 823–839.

Edwards, S (1992). Trade orientation, distortions and growth in developing countries. *Journal of Development Economics*, 39, 31–57.

Gognon, JE and AK Rose (1995). Dynamic persistence of industry trade balance: how pervasive is the product cycle? *Oxford Economic Papers*, 47, 229–248.

Grossman, GM and E Helpman (1991). Quality ladders and product cycle. *Quarterly Journal of Economics*, 106, 557–588.

Jones, R (1970). The role of technology in the theory of international trade. In *The Technology Factor in International Trade*, R Vernon (ed.), New York: NBER.

Kim, J-II and LJ Lau (1994). The sources of economic growth of the East Asian newly industrialized countries. *Journal of the Japanese and International Economics*, 8, 235–271.

Krugman, PR (1979). A model of innovation, technology transfer, and the world distribution of income. *Journal of Political Economy*, 87, 253–266.

Krugman, PR (1987). The narrow moving band, the Dutch disease, and the competitive consequences of Mrs. Thatcher. *Journal of Development Economics*, 27, 41–55.

Krugman, PR (1994a). Does third world growth hurt first world prosperity? *Harvard Business Review*, July–August, 113–121.

Krugman, PR (1994b). The myth of Asia's miracle. *Foreign Affairs*, 73 November/December, 63–78.

Lau, ML and H Wan Jr (1993). On the mechanism of catching up. *European Economic Review*, 38, 952–963.

Lucas Jr, RE (1988). On the mechanics of economic development. *Journal of Monetary Economics*, 22, 3–42.

Lucas Jr, RE (1993). Making a miracle. *Econometrica*, 61, 251–272.

Maddison, A (1979). Per capita output in the long run. *Kyklos*, 32, 412–429.

Matsuyama, K (1991). Increasing returns, industrialization, and indeterminacy of equilibrium. *Quarterly Journal of Economics*, 106, 617–850.

Murakami, Y (1982). *Political Economy of Anti-Classical* (in Japanese). Tokyo: Chuou-Kouron sha.

Muscatelli, V *et al.* (1995). Modeling aggregate manufactured exports for some Asian newly industrialized economies. *Review of Economics and Statistics*, 77, 147–155.

Park, SR and JK Kwon (1995). Rapid economic growth with increasing returns to scale and little or no productivity growth. *Review of Economics and Statistics*, 77, 332–351.

Posner, MV (1961). International trade and technical change. *Oxford Economic Papers*, 13, 323–341.

Romer, PM (1986). Increasing returns and long run growth. *Journal of Political Economy*, 94, 1002–1037.

Rostow, WW (1983). Korea and the fourth industrial revolution, 1960–2000, Proc. the Federation of Korean Industries.

Shell, K (1966). Toward a theory of inventive activity and capital accumulation. *American Economic Review*, 56, 62–68.

Song, BN (1990). *The Rise of the Korean Economy*. Hong Kong: Oxford University Press.

Stokey, NL (1988). Learning by doing and the introduction of new goods. *Journal of Political Economy*, 96, 701–717.

Stokey, NL (1991a). Human capital, product quality, and growth. *Quarterly Journal of Economics*, 106, 587–616.

Stokey, NL (1991b). The volume and composition of trade between rich and poor countries. *Review of Economic Studies,* 58, 63–80.

Takashima, M (1994). Economic growth of Japan and South Korea (translated into Korean). Paper presented at the First Conference on North-East Asian Economics at the Korea: Incheon City University.

The Economist (1995). Asia's competing capitalisms (24 June Leader). *The Economist*, 336, 13.

The World Bank (1991). *World Development Report 1991 — The Challenge of Development*, Oxford: Oxford University Press.

The World Bank (1993). *The East Asian Miracle Economic Growth and Public Policy.* Oxford: Oxford University Press.

Tsao, Y (1985). Growth without productivity; Singapore manufacturing in the 1970s. *Journal of Development Studies*, 18, 25–38.

Tsao, Y (1986). Sources of growth accounting for the Singapore economy. In *Singapore Resources and Growth*, CY Lim and PJ Lloyd (eds.), New York: Oxford University Press, pp. 17–44.

Vernon, R (1966). International investment and international trade in the product cycle. *Quarterly Journal of Economics,* 80, 190–207.

Wong, KP (1986). Savings, capital flow and capital formation. In *Singapore; Resources and Growth*, CY Lim and PJ Lloyd (eds.), New York: Oxford University Press.

Young, A (1992). A tale of two cities: factor accumulation and technical change in Hong Kong and Singapore. In *NBER Macroeconomics Annual*, OJ Blanchard and S Fischer (eds.), Cambridge: MIT Press.

Young, A (1994a). The tyranny of numbers: confronting the statistical realities of the East Asian growth experience. NBER Working Paper No. 4680.

Young, A (1994b). Lessons from the East Asian NICS a contrarian view. *European Economic Review*, 38, 964–973.

CHAPTER 2

POPULATION AND POVERTY: A GENERAL EQUILIBRIUM APPROACH

Mats Lundahl

University of Stockholm, Sweden

Knut Wicksell's writings on poverty and population are not considered to belong to his most original pieces (Fong, 1976, p. 314; Gårdlund, 1996; Gustafsson, 1961, pp. 203, 226; Henriksson, 1991, p. 40; Pålsson Syll, 2002, p. 241; Uhr, 1951, pp. 832–834; 1962, p. 3, pp. 59–60, pp. 328–329; 1991a). If we caricature a little, the way Wicksell's views on population and to poverty are usually conceived of is the following. The sex drive of mankind leads it to reproduce in geometric progression, as hypothesized by Malthus. Food production, on the other hand, only increases in arithmetic progression, also à la Malthus. This is an impossible situation, which can go on for a limited time only. People get poorer and then attempt to emigrate if they can. For those who fail, the vices of drunkenness and prostitution lurk around the corner. The only escape goes through the systematic use of contraceptives within the marriage. The optimum population is the one that maximizes the economic well-being of the population. "The optimum population theory is the core of Wicksell's population theory," summarized Fong (1976, p. 315), and this is usually the only credit he receives when his writings on population are mentioned (Fong, 1976, p. 314; Gottlieb, 1945, pp. 291–292; Hutchinson, 1967, p. 391; Lindahl, 1958, p. 35; Pitchford, 1974, p. 87; Robbins, 1927: p. note, p. 118; Schumpeter, 1954, p. 582; Sommarin, 1926–27, p. 29; Spengler, 1983).

This treatment is not fair to Wicksell. In his foreword to *Value, Capital and Rent* Shackle (1954, p. 7) makes the following characteristic of Wicksell's scientific contribution, "Wicksell's work was like a mountain from whose flanks divergent streams run down and bring fertility to widely separate fields, only to merge again later into a single broad river." This statement describes his views on poverty and population very well. However, also in this context there is a great deal more originality in Wicksell than what is commonly realized. He developed his ideas in a large number of published and unpublished writings all the way from 1880 until his death in 1926, and once you put the writings next to each other they form a coherent general equilibrium system of the interplay between population growth and poverty, trade and factor movements. As early as 1891 (Wicksell, 1891) he had sketched the first outline of what would 80 years later be formalized as the specific factors model of international trade by Jones (1971) and Samuelson (1971a, b). It is mainly here, and less in his insistence on Malthusian characteristics or in his discussion of the optimum population, that Wicksell's original contribution to the analysis of poverty and population lies. The present essay will be devoted to an examination of his theory.[1] We will then begin with its core element: diminishing returns.

2.1. Diminishing Returns and Technological Pessimism

Population growth tends to depress both per capita income and wages, because diminishing returns prevail in the economy. A strong population increase increases the demand for food and production is displaced to even more marginal lands. In the process, wages will fall (Wicksell, 1892, p. 309). Agricultural output can always be increased by capital accumulation and labor force growth, but not to the corresponding extent (Wicksell, 1914, p. 4), and mere population growth simply depresses the wage rate and increases land rents and the return to capital.

Agriculture is not the only branch subject to diminishing returns. Industrial production is based on natural resources, which will be exhausted in the longer run (Wicksell, 1902, pp. 548–549), and it is intimately connected with agriculture on the input side (Wicksell, 1914, p. 7). Hence, whenever diminishing returns are present in agriculture they are also present in manufacturing. Infrastructure displays diminishing returns as well. The satisfaction of an increasing demand for foodstuffs, in the "countries of old culture," Wicksell argues, is not possible without infrastructural development (Wicksell, 1999c, p. 121), but the latter is subject to diminishing returns, which in turn tends to create unemployment and reduce demand in the economy.

It is often argued that over time technological progress will counteract and overtake diminishing returns and hence raise incomes. Wicksell, however, contended that all that this would lead to would be a temporary upward shift in the marginal productivity curve, and that diminishing returns would thereafter take

---

[1] For a more detailed exposition of the individual elements of Wicksell's theory, see Lundahl (2005a, b).

over once more, albeit from a higher level (Wicksell, 1903, p. 173). The few inventions that occur mainly tend to increase the population since they make it easier to get a job. Therefore, in the end, the only thing that inventions can do is to sustain a given population, but not its increase over a longer period of time (Wicksell, 1999a, p. 97).

Mechanization does not necessarily increase wages (Wicksell, 1958, p. 102). Discoveries that introduce new power sources or make it possible to cultivate new fields benefit the workers, but inventions may also save on labor without, for example, bringing new natural resources into production (Wicksell, 1958, pp. 102–103; 1934, p. 164). As is well known, in one of the most celebrated passages of his *Lectures*, Wicksell stresses that capital accumulation will generally lead to a wage increase, whereas technological progress may not (Wicksell, 1934, p. 164).

2.2. Overpopulation

Wicksell's technological pessimism and his insistence on the severity of diminishing returns led him to the conclusion that Europe was overpopulated. Relative overpopulation is present when the population has increased faster than the available means of nutrition, and Wicksell argued that this was the case both in his native Sweden in the 1870s and in the rest of Europe (Wicksell, 1882, p. 99). He had good reasons for this. When Wicksell began his investigation of the population problem, Sweden was characterized by a high natural population growth, increasing numbers of surviving children in the families, low living standards and terrible housing conditions among the working classes, and rural–urban migration and emigration especially to the United States. A strong recession towards the end of the 1870s exacerbated these trends (Kock, 1944, p. 81). The decline in mortality that had taken place had accelerated the rate of population growth to an all-time high, and Wicksell concluded that fertility had to be reduced with at least one-third in order to restore the balance between death and birth rates (Wicksell, 1887a, p. 25).

As Wicksell saw it, population growth also led to war (Wicksell, 1891, p. 297; 1979, p. 149). Unless the economy flourished, not only at home, but in neighboring countries as well, feeding growing populations might be impossible, and the result might be war (Wicksell, 1891, p. 297). In an economic analysis of World War I, he (Wicksell, 1978, p. 246) states that all wars were ultimately driven by the lack of space to feed the population. Wars and population growth tended to form a vicious circle. Overcrowding easily leads to war, and a large population is a prerequisite for victory. Therefore, the military and the ruling classes will be against decreasing birth rates (Wicksell, 1978, p. 247). On the other hand, if war and population growth interact in a vicious circle, then there is of course no reason why peace and population control should not do the same in a virtuous one.

2.3. Trade and Emigration

Wicksell argued that the European colonization of overseas territories had led to a division of labor, which allowed western Europe to trade its manufactures for foodstuffs from overseas and from eastern Europe (Wicksell, 1999d, p. 148). The extensive trade of industrial goods for food, he, however, considered dangerous. In the first place, the overseas food producers would also run into diminishing returns to labor in agriculture and therefore be forced to move labor into manufacturing. In the end, they would consume most of their agricultural produce themselves and leave little for exports (Wicksell, 1891, p. 180; 1999d, pp. 148–149).

This sequence of events would be reinforced by the introduction of tariffs on manufactures in overseas countries that would restrict the entry for western European industrial producers and make it diffcult for Europe to use imports to satisfy its demand for food. The direct cause of protectionism was the growth of the population. Wicksell (1999b, p. 64) stressed that tariffs would be introduced as soon as the population had grown large enough for rent to appear on a major scale in agriculture. The tariff would then increase wages at the expense of rent.

Wicksell also pointed to a second problem with specialization and trade: that minerals and fossil fuels would be available only at a cost that would be rising faster than what material-saving technological progress would be able to compensate for (Wicksell, 1999d, p. 149). The third obstacle to continued international trade that Wicksell saw was that the population of the food-exporting countries would increase and consume its former food surplus while ceasing to demand western European manufactures (Wicksell, 1979, p. 148).

Wicksell considered the golden age of factor-proportions-based trade to be an exceptional episode in economic history (Wicksell, 1926, p. 265). The exchange of manufactures for food staples was not sustainable in the long run. Diminishing returns to a rapidly growing population would ensure this (cf. Uhr, 1962, pp. 328–329). In the end, Europe would have to produce its own primary products but that would be impossible unless the population could be reduced.

One way of obtaining a reduction of the population was emigration. At least 100,000 Swedes left their mother country during 1880 and 1881, the vast majority for the United States, a figure which Wicksell considered large for a country of 4.5 million inhabitants (Wicksell, 1882). Emigration, he argued, reduces the competition among the workers for the available jobs and hence increases wages, and the reduction of the number of consumers will serve as a brake on prices. This, from the distributional point of view, would be positive (Wicksell, 1882, p. 19). Wicksell was, however, not prepared to endorse the idea that labor migration is an unmitigated blessing. The reason was the cost of education incurred by the home country and the failure to match this with a contribution to GDP by the emigrants (Wicksell, 1882, pp. 23–24). This, however, assumes that the prospective emigrants can be employed at home. Should this not be the case, their departure is simply a way of writing off the loss that has already been incurred by their home country.

2.4. Towards the Optimum Population

Wicksell (1882, p. 47) emphasized that there was a close connection between the economic situation in Sweden and the rate of emigration. The cause of emigration, he argued, must be sought in the excessive growth of the Swedish population (Wicksell, 1882, p. 55). Wicksell saw a potentially Malthusian situation building up, where neither the growth of agriculture nor the growth of manufacturing industry could serve to accommodate five new families instead of four. The land could not be subdivided indefinitely, so the agricultural sector would have to shed labor to industry and commerce with lower wages and living standards as the main consequence (Wicksell, 1882, p. 61). Thus, Wicksell was forced to conclude that no obstacles should be put in the way of migration (Wicksell, 1999d, p. 146). He hastened to stress that the *real* emigration issue is connected with population growth. To argue that the size of the population should be expanded was simply foolish (Wicksell, 1999d, p. 155).

The issue was the optimum size of population, "the number that in the given conditions is best suited to the available natural resources and is therefore most compatible with the achievement of material well-being, which is after all the necessary basis for all other culture" (Wicksell, 1999d, p. 157). In Sweden, the optimum figure was far below the actual one according to Wicksell, and he was convinced that this was the situation in the rest of Europe as well (Wicksell, 1979, p. 146).

It might be impossible to reduce the population to the extent needed without increasing the rate of emigration substantially (Wicksell, 1999d, p. 160). In the near future, however, as Wicksell saw it, emigration would become much more difficult than in the past (Wicksell, 1887a, p. 26). Not least, the agricultural frontier in the United States was almost closed (Wicksell, 1887a, p. 27). Finding a place for the surplus population would become increasingly hard, and Wicksell came up with the not too realistic proposal that Siberia could provide an outlet (Wicksell, 1999d, p. 161).

When the population grows, diminishing returns tend to lower per capita income, but against this we have to put economies of scale, increased division of labor, improved organization forms, etc. Where these two tendencies match each other is where the optimum population is found (Overbeek, 1973, p. 510).

As time went by, Wicksell, who at the beginning of the 1880s had recommended a slow increase of the Swedish population, became more and more convinced that the population had to be stationary instead (Wicksell, 1924/25, p. 260).

When it came to the methods for reducing the size of the population, Wicksell was opposed to postponing the age when marriage is contracted, since that would put an unnatural brake on the sex lives of young people. The only remedy was the neo-Malthusian one (Wicksell, 1979, p. 150). Early marriages were not feasible without anti-contraceptive devices (Wicksell, 1887b, p. 49). Later in his life, Wicksell went on to argue that abortion would be permissible as well, under reasonable circumstances (Wicksell, 1925).

2.5. A Formalization of the Wicksellian System

Wicksell's discussion of the effects of population growth is carried out within an implicit framework that closely resembles the modern general equilibrium approach to international trade and factor movements, as this was developed in the 1970s. Time after time, he comes back to the interplay between events in Europe and overseas. In the present context, we will label these two regions "The Old World" and "The New World," respectively. The production structure that Wicksell worked with is almost completely symmetric. Both regions produce agricultural goods on the one hand and manufactures on the other. (Below we will come back to the main difference: the temporary existence of an agricultural frontier in the New World.) Let us begin by portraying the Old World.

The production functions of the Old World are:

$$A_O = A_O(L_{OA}, T_O, K_{OA}) \tag{2.1}$$

$$M_O = M_O(L_{OM}, R_O, K_{OM}) \tag{2.2}$$

linearly homogeneous, with diminishing returns to all production factors, but with positive cross-derivatives. Production of agricultural goods (A_O) takes place with the aid of labor (L_{OA}), land (T_O) and capital (K_{OA}), while manufacturing (M_O) uses labor (L_{OM}), a natural resource (R_O), and capital (K_{OM}). Labor is mobile between the two sectors, and there is full employment of the labor force (L_O):

$$L_{OA} + L_{OM} = L_O \tag{2.3}$$

Land is a fixed production factor. So is the natural resource. Wicksell kept insisting on the exhaustibility of natural resources everywhere. He did not deal with mobility of capital anywhere in his writings on population and poverty. In fact, the importance of capital in agriculture is played down almost everywhere except in his discussion of technological progress. This makes it natural to treat the two capital stocks as sector-specific. It is thus obvious that Wicksell's production framework essentially corresponds to the specific factors model of Jones (1971) (cf. also Samuelson, 1971a, b), with a single mobile factor: labor.

With profit-maximizing producers in both sectors, the production factors are rewarded with the value of their respective marginal products. If we choose to use manufactures as our *numéraire*, i.e., set $P_M = 1$ and $P = P_A/P_M$, we must have that

$$w_O = PA_O^L \qquad (2.4)$$

$$w_O = M_O^L \qquad (2.5)$$

for the wage rate.

With sector-specific factors there will be no factor price equalization between countries. The easiest way to see this is by borrowing a diagram from the original Jones (1971) article.

In Fig. 2.1, we have put the two Old World curves for the value of the marginal productivity (VMPL) in agriculture and manufacturing back to back. Labor use in agriculture is measured leftwards from O and labor use in manufacturing rightwards from the same point. Assume that the total labor force available is AB. Dividing this between the two sectors so as to equalize the VMPL, yields an Old World wage rate equal to OE. The figure has been drawn on the assumption of given capital stocks, land, and natural resources. Assume next that the New World has exactly the same technology and endowments of the fixed factors as the Old World, so that the same VMPL curves apply, but a labor force which is only equal to A'B'. This will then give rise to a higher wage rate: OF. Thus, as long as migration is not free, neither the wages nor the returns to the specific factors will be equalized. We, hence, need to operate with one wage rate (w_O) for the Old World and one (w_N) for the New World.

Turning to the returns to the specific factors we have

$$r_{OA} = PA_O^T \qquad (2.6)$$

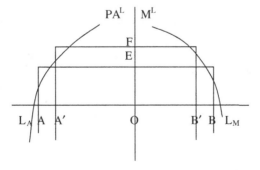

Fig. 2.1. Wage determination in the specific factors model.

for the land rent,

$$r_{OM} = M_O^R \tag{2.7}$$

for the natural resource rent, and

$$i_{OA} = PA_O^K \tag{2.8}$$

$$i_{OM} = M_O^K \tag{2.9}$$

for the returns to the two capital stocks.

The outputs of the two commodities can also be stated as functions of their relative price (P) and a shift parameter (α), to symbolize exogenous influences on production, like changes in factor endowments and technology:

$$A_O = A_O(P, \alpha) \tag{2.10}$$

$$M_O = M_O(P, \alpha) \tag{2.11}$$

Wicksell discusses changes in demand and relative commodity prices, i.e., he works with the assumption of two "large" economic regions whose actions together determine international prices. This means that we have to specify the demand side as well. The total income of the Old World (Y_O) is given by:

$$Y_O = PA_O + M_O \tag{2.12}$$

This entire income is spent on consumption of the two goods (D_{OA} and D_{OM}):

$$Y_O = PD_{OA} + D_{OM} \tag{2.13}$$

The demand for agricultural goods in the Old World is a function of relative commodity prices, income, and preferences (symbolized by the shift parameter β):

$$D_{OA} = D_{OA}(P, Y_O, \beta) \tag{2.14}$$

This finishes our description of the Old World. The economic structure of the New World is completely analogous (cf., however, below for the case of the agrarian frontier) but for the separate shift parameters, γ (production) and δ (demand) (and hence the equations (not spelled out) are numbered analogously: $(2.1')$–$(2.14')$.

What remains to be done is to close the system. Wicksell assumes that the Old World trades freely with the New World (while factor movements are regulated). Thus, we may use the equilibrium condition for the market for agricultural goods:

$$D_{OA} - A_O = A_N - D_{NA} \tag{2.15}$$

where the Old World is a net importer and the New World a net exporter. No corresponding equation is needed for the market for manufactures, since according to Walras' Law, if all the markets except one are in equilibrium, then the last one must be so too.

The system (2.3)–(2.4), (2.3′)–(2.14′), and (2.14) has 25 equations and 25 unknowns (A_O, M_O, L_{OA}, L_{OM}, w_O, r_{OA}, r_{OM}, i_{OA}, i_{OM}, Y_O, D_{OA}, D_{OM}, the corresponding New World variables and P). This system can be used for studying the parameter changes in Wicksell's system, and the production functions (2.1)–(2.2) and (2.1′)–(2.2′) can be used for solving for output changes at the given commodity prices.

2.6. The Effects of Population Growth in the Old World

The trigger that puts the Wicksellian system in motion is the human sex drive, which results in the growth of the population and the labor force in the Old World. With the given relative commodity prices, this will serve to increase employment and production in both sectors, lower the wage rate, and increase the returns to all the fixed factors. To see this, we employ Eqs. (2.3)–(2.5) to solve for changes in employment and wages, Eqs. (2.1) and (2.2) to solve for output changes, and finally Eqs. (2.6)–(2.9) to find the changes in the rewards of the specific factors.

Differentiating Eqs. (2.3)–(2.5) and solving for the changes in labor use yields:

$$dL_{OA} = -(1/\Delta)M_O^{LL}dL_O > 0 \qquad (2.16)$$

$$dL_{OM} = -(1/\Delta)PA_O^{LL}dL_O > 0 \qquad (2.17)$$

where

$$\Delta = -(M_O^{LL} + PA_O^{LL}) > 0 \qquad (2.18)$$

and $dw_O < 0$, from Eq. (2.4) or Eq. (2.5). Consequently, the production of both commodities increases in the Old World.

These changes portray the basic Malthusian mechanism. When the population and the labor force grow, at constant commodity prices, both agriculture and manufacturing increase their employment of labor, but only at a falling wage rate in terms of manufactures, and hence increase their output as well. It is easily demonstrated that this simultaneously increases the returns to the fixed factors, e.g., the land rent. Differentiating Eq. (2.6) gives:

$$dr_{OA} = PA_O^{TL}dL_{OA} > 0 \qquad (2.19)$$

This is what Wicksell meant when he stated that the rich in society — the owners of fixed assets — had an interest in maintaining a high rate of population growth, while at the same time this served to depress the living standard of the workers, i.e., to increase their poverty. That, in turn, was what led to drunkenness and other social evils.

2.7. Technological Progress

As we have found, Wicksell did not believe that technological progress could serve to overcome the effects of diminishing returns. Let us see what the effects of technological progress may be with the given commodity prices. This makes it possible to compare directly with the effects of population growth. Differentiating Eqs. (2.3)–(2.5) with a constant population and labor force and solving for the changes in labor use and wages gives:

$$dL_{OA} = (1/\Delta)(PA_O^{L\alpha} - M_O^{L\alpha})d\alpha \tag{2.20}$$

$$dL_{OM} = (1/\Delta)(M_O^{L\alpha} - PA_O^{L\alpha})d\alpha = -dL_{OA} \tag{2.21}$$

$$dw_O = -(1/\Delta)P(A_O^{LL}M_O^{L\alpha} + M_O^{LL}A_O^{L\alpha})d\alpha > 0 \tag{2.22}$$

where $d\alpha$ symbolizes technological progress, $A_O^{L\alpha}$ and $M_O^{L\alpha}$ measure the impact of technological progress on the marginal productivity of labor in agriculture and manufacturing, respectively, and where Δ is Eq. (2.18).

We find that provided that both marginal productivities are increased by technological progress, the wage rate must rise. Whether labor moves in or out of agriculture (manufacturing) in the "normal" case where both marginal products are increased by technological progress depends on which of the two productivity-increasing effects is the stronger one.

We can now also compare the effects of diminishing returns on the wage rate with those of technological progress. This is done using Eq. (2.22) where both the growth of the labor force and technological progress have been incorporated:

$$dw_O = -(1/\Delta)P[A_O^{LL}M_O^{LL}dL_O + (A_O^{LL}M_O^{L\alpha} + M_O^{LL}A_O^{L\alpha})d\alpha] \tag{2.23}$$

What Wicksell argues is that the first term within the square brackets is larger than the second. The size of the labor force growth, dL_O, and the strength of the diminishing returns A_O^{LL} and M_O^{LL} are strong enough to outweigh the productivity-raising influences of technological progress $M_O^{L\alpha}$ and $A_O^{L\alpha}$.

Assuming that the above sequence is generalized to the entire Old World, it is bound to have an impact on relative commodity prices as well. In order to find the direction of the price change, however, we must make use of the larger general equilibrium system above. We then need the supply functions for the two goods in the Old and the New World, Eqs. (2.10) and (2.11) and Eqs. (2.10′)–(2.11′), the two regional income expressions (2.12) and (2.12′), the two demand functions for agricultural goods, (2.14) and (2.14′), and, finally, the equilibrium condition for the market for agricultural goods: Eq. (2.15). This system of nine equations can be solved for changes in the nine unknowns A_O, M_O, A_N, M_N, Y_O, Y_N, D_{OA}, D_{NA}, and P. Differentiating the system, assuming that no technological change takes place, so that $d\alpha$ symbolizes labor force growth only, and that there is no exogenous change in the New World, and solving for dP yields:

$$dP = -(1/\Delta^*)[D_{OA}^{\beta}d\beta - D_{OA}^{Y}P(A_O^{\alpha}M_O^{LL} + M_O^{\alpha}A_O^{LL})(1/\Delta)dL_O$$
$$+ PA_O^{\alpha}M_O^{LL}(1/\Delta)dL_O] \qquad (2.24)$$

where

$$\Delta^* = D_{OA}^{P} + D_{OA}^{Y}A_O + D_{OA}^{Y}(PA_O^{P} + M_O^{P}) + D_{NA}^{P} + D_{NA}^{Y}A_N$$
$$+ D_{NA}^{Y}(PA_N^{P} + M_N^{P}) - A_O^{P} - A_N^{P} < 0 \qquad (2.25)$$

where we have used Eqs. (2.15) and (2.16), and $\Delta > 0$ is Eq. (2.17).

The denominator of (2.24) must be negative. This is nothing but the partial derivative of the excess demand for agricultural goods with respect to their price, and if our model is to be stable in the sense of Walras, this must be negative. The numerator in turn contains three terms. The first is the change in the demand for agricultural goods in the Old World that results for a change in preferences at given incomes and commodity prices when the population grows. Wicksell envisaged an increased demand for food (agricultural goods) when the population grew. This he made explicit in the case of the New World, where it "also" took place, and it is clear that he had the same mechanism in mind for the Old World. Hence, this term is positive.

The second term is the increased demand for agricultural goods that emanates from the increase of the total income of the Old World when the labor force grows and more of both commodities is produced at given prices. Assuming that agricultural goods are not inferior, this term should be positive as well. The third term is the increase in the production of agricultural goods that takes place when the labor force grows as a result of population growth. Whether the relative price of agricultural goods rises or falls then depends exclusively on whether the demand for agricultural goods increases faster than the supply of it when the population grows in the Old World. Wicksell assumed that the demand effect was the strongest one. Thus, population growth at home tends to turn the terms-of-trade against the Old World.

2.8. Problems of Foreign Trade

Wicksell did not believe that a specialization according to comparative advantage would contribute to solving the population problem in the Old World. On the contrary, he argued, there were at least three problems connected with international trade that would preclude it from working as an engine (Robertson, 1938), or even as a "handmaiden" (Kravis, 1970) of growth, to use two latter-day terms. The first was the tendency for manufacturing output to stagnate in the Old World when natural resources were depleted. The second was the tariff policy of the New World (read: the United States). The third was the population growth and demand changes in the New World. Let us see how this works in terms of our model.

The depletion of natural resources can be expressed as a reduction of R_O, i.e., $dR_O < 0$. Differentiating Eqs. (2.3)–(2.5) once more, but this time with a given labor force and given commodity prices, and solving for the resulting changes in labor use and wages yields:

$$dL_{OA} = -dL_{OM} = -(1/\Delta)M_O^{LR}dR_O > 0 \qquad (2.26)$$

$$dw_O = -(1/\Delta)PA_O^{LL} \cdot M_O^{LR}dR_O < 0 \qquad (2.27)$$

where $dR_O < 0$ and Δ still is Eq. (2.17).

When the natural resource shrinks, the marginal productivity of labor is reduced in manufacturing, and this sector hence starts to shed workers, who can only be reabsorbed in the economy — some of them in agriculture — at a lower wage rate. This also means that manufacturing output must contract while agricultural output expands:

$$dM_O = M_O^R dR_O + M_O^L dL_{OM} < 0 \qquad (2.28)$$

$$dA_O = A_O^L dL_{OA} = -A_O^L dL_{OM} > 0 \qquad (2.29)$$

At the same time, with given commodity prices, Y_O must fall, since the total factor endowment of the Old World has shrunk:

$$dY_O = -PA_O^L dL_{OM} + M_O^R dR_O + M_O^L dL_{OM} \qquad (2.30)$$

but since the values of the marginal products of labor must be equal, this reduces to

$$dY_O = M_O^R dR_O < 0 \qquad (2.31)$$

Provided that none of the two goods is inferior, the demand for both manufactures and agricultural goods must shrink as income shrinks, i.e., the relative price of agricultural goods, whose production has increased, must fall in relation to that of manufactures. As Wicksell predicted, the depletion of natural resources tends to reduce the demand for imports in the Old World, since this region can now afford to buy less. This in turn interacts with the changes on the supply side to reduce the relative price of agricultural goods in the world market.

The second problem for the Old World when it comes to using international trade to mitigate the consequences of population growth according to Wicksell was the tendency for the New World countries (notably the United States) to use tariffs to protect their manufacturing sectors. Tariffs drive a wedge between relative commodity prices in the domestic market in the New World and world market prices (still adhered to in the Old World). We may denote the former by P_N, while retaining P for the relative world market price of agricultural goods. This means that we have to add an equation to our general equilibrium system:

$$P_N = P_A/P_M(1 + t) = P/(1 + t) \tag{2.32}$$

where t is the tariff on manufactures in the New World. Let us next find out what the introduction of the tariff will do to P_N and P, respectively.

Let us begin with the former. We then need Eqs. (2.10)–(2.12), (2.14), (2.10′)–(2.12′), (2.14′) — the latter modified so as to incorporate P_N instead of P — plus Eqs. (2.15) and (2.32). Differentiating this system, assuming that initially $P_N = P$, and $t = 0$, and solving for dP_N yields:

$$dP_N = (1/\Delta^*)P[A_O^P - D_{OA}^P - D_{OA}^Y A_O - D_{OA}^Y(PA_O^P + M_O^P)]dt < 0 \tag{2.33}$$

where $\Delta^* < 0$, is Eq. (2.25) above. The introduction of the tariff on manufactured goods raises the relative price of these goods in the New World, i.e., it lowers the price of agricultural goods in terms of manufactures. Expression (2.33) shows that when the tariff on manufactures is introduced in the New World, if we keep P_N constant, the relative price of agricultural goods must increase in the world market (cf. Eq. (2.32)). Old World producers then react by increasing their production and Old World consumers reduce their demand (while New World consumers and producers, who are facing P_N, not P, do not react at all). An excess supply is created, which serves to lower the price of agricultural goods in the New World.

To find out what happens to the world market price, P, we again use Eq. (2.32) together with the other equations employed in the derivation of Eq. (2.33). This yields:

$$dP = (1/\Delta^*)P[D_{NA}^P + D_{NA}^Y A_N + D_{NA}^Y(PA_N^P + M_N^P) - A_N^P]dt > 0 \tag{2.34}$$

in analogy with Eq. (2.33). This expression must be positive, since the denominator is negative and the numerator is the partial derivative of the excess *demand* for agricultural goods with respect to its price, which for stability reasons must be negative. Thus, a tariff on manufactured goods in the New World will lower its relative price in the world market, i.e., increase the relative price of agricultural goods.

When the tariff is introduced, if we keep P constant, the relative domestic price of agricultural goods in the New World falls (cf. Eq. (2.32)). New World consumers increase their demand and producers reduce their supply. An excess demand is created in the world market and the international price of agricultural goods rises.

Together, Eqs. (2.33) and (2.34) express a standard result: When a tariff is introduced, this serves to increase the domestic price of the good subject to the tariff, while it will lower its price in the world market. The tariff pulls resources out of agriculture into manufacturing in the New World, and hence reduces the world-wide supply of agricultural goods.

The third of Wicksell's obstacles to international trade is the rising demand for agricultural goods that accompanies the growth of the population in the New World. This is obtained by differentiating Eq. (2.14') with commodity prices and incomes held constant:

$$dD_{NA} = D_{NA}^{\delta} d\delta \qquad (2.35)$$

This works exactly as $D_{OA}^{\beta} d\beta$ in Eq. (2.24). It serves to increase the relative price of agricultural goods in the world market, i.e., it tends to turn the terms-of-trade against the Old World. It should, however, be noted that it does not work in isolation but is a result of the growth of the population in the New World, which means that its effects, and the effects of rising New World income, must be weighed against the effects of increased New World production of agricultural goods when the labor force of the New World grows. Let us next turn to the investigation of these effects, but then we must also introduce emigration from the Old to the New World.

2.9. Migration from the Old to the New World

The fall in the wage rate in the Old World when the population there grows is what for Wicksell triggers emigration. The effect of this is to increase the population in the New World instead of in the Old. Hence, it is part of the sequence we have just discussed. In the New World, it increases the demand for agricultural goods at given commodity prices and incomes, it increases the production of agricultural goods and it increases income and hence the demand for agricultural goods at constant commodity prices.

In his discussion of agricultural production in the New World, Wicksell, kept coming back to the issue of the land frontier. This, he argued, was rapidly being closed, at least in the United States, while it might still be in existence elsewhere in the New World. Our general equilibrium model can be used to examine both the situations. Let us begin with the situation where emigrants who arrive in the New World can put virgin land under the plow.

For the sake of simplicity, let us assume that the entire addition to the Old World population can emigrate to the New World. (This allows us to disregard production effects in the Old World.) When the emigrants arrive at their new destination they can either work in the manufacturing sector or in agriculture, on the existing agricultural land. They may also, however, extend the land frontier. In the present context, we will draw on the Findlay (1996) model, of the territorial expansion of empires, where it is the use of labor (an army) that extends the territory. Here, we may think of a land-clearing "brigade" (L_{NT}) instead, since this is clearly how Wicksell conceived the situation.

The introduction of an endogenous land frontier changes the production function for agricultural goods in the New World to

$$A_N = A_N[L_{NA}, T_N(L_{NT}), K_{NA}] \qquad (2.1'')$$

Labor now has to be divided among three different uses:

$$L_{NA} + L_{NM} + L_{NT} = L_N \qquad (2.2'')$$

and to the two wage Eqs. (2.4′) and (2.5′) we have to add a third one:

$$w_N = PA_N^T T^L \qquad (2.36)$$

The "land-clearing brigade" extends the frontier of cultivation, and its marginal product is valued at a shadow price equal to the value of the marginal product of land in agriculture. We will furthermore assume that the frontier land can be obtained only at an increasing cost in terms of labor, i. e., that the clearing of land is subject to diminishing returns ($T^L > 0$, $T^{LL} < 0$).

Differentiating (2.2″), (2.4′), (2.5′), and Eq. (2.36), and solving for the changes in labor use and wages as new emigrants arrive, yields:

$$dL_{NA} = (1/\Delta^{**})PM_N^{LL}[A_N^{TT}(T^L)^2 + A_N^T T^{LL} - A_N^{TL} T^L)dL_N > 0 \qquad (2.37)$$

$$dL_{NM} = (1/\Delta^{**})P^2\left\{(T^L)^2[A_N^{TT}A_N^{LL} - (A_N^{TL})^2] + A_N^T T^{LL}A_N^{LL}\right\}dL_N > 0 \quad (2.38)$$

$$dL_{NT} = (1/\Delta^{**})PM_N^{LL}(A_N^{LL} - A_N^{TL}T^L)dL_N > 0 \qquad (2.39)$$

$$dw_N = (1/\Delta^{**})P^2 M_N^{LL}\left\{(T^L)^2[A_N^{TT}A_N^{LL} - (A_N^{TL})^2]\right.$$
$$\left. + A_N^{LL}A_N^T T^{LL}\right\}dL_N < 0 \qquad (2.40)$$

where

$$\Delta^{**} = PM_N^{LL}\left[A_N^{TT}(T^L)^2 + A_N^T T^{LL} + A_N^{LL} - 2A_N^{TL}T^L\right]$$
$$+ P^2\left\{A_N^{LL}A_N^T T^{LL} + (T^L)^2[A_N^{TT}A_N^{LL} - (A_N^{TL})^2]\right\} \qquad (2.41)$$

and where we have used the fact that when production functions are linearly homogeneous $A_N^{TL} = A_N^{LT}$.

The Δ^{**} is positive. The first term is positive, so is the first part of the second, and we can prove that the last part is positive as well. For this we use Euler's theorem. With linearly homogeneous production functions we have that

$$A_N^{TT}T_N + A_N^{LT}L_{NA} + A_N^{KT}K_{NA} \equiv 0 \qquad (2.42)$$

$$A_N^{TL}T_N + A_N^{LL}L_{NA} + A_N^{KL}K_{NA} \equiv 0 \qquad (2.43)$$

Equations (2.42) and (2.43) may be solved for A_N^{TT} and A_N^{LL}, respectively:

$$A_N^{TT} = -A_N^{LT}(L_{NA}/T_N) - A_N^{KL}(K_{NA}/T_N) \tag{2.44}$$

$$A_N^{LL} = -A_N^{TL}(T_N/L_{NA}) - A_N^{KL}(K_{NA}/L_{NA}) \tag{2.45}$$

These expressions can now be substituted into the last term of Eq. (2.41) and the expression within the second squared brackets may be developed to yield

$$A_N^{TT}A_N^{LL} - (A_N^{TL})^2 = A_N^{TL}A_N^{KL}(K_{NA}/T_N) + A_N^{KT}A_N^{TL}(K_{NA}/L_{NA})$$
$$+ A_N^{KT}A_N^{KL}(K_{NA}/T_N)(K_{NA}/L_{NA}) > 0 \tag{2.46}$$

Thus, Eq. (2.41) is positive.

What happens when the emigrants arrive in the New World is that they go into all three employments: directly into agriculture, into manufacturing, and indirectly into agriculture, by developing the marginal land so that the latter may be put under the plow. They can be absorbed, however, only at the cost of a falling wage rate.

It is also interesting to investigate what will happen to the land rent on the frontier. The land rent is given by (6′). Differentiating this, and keeping in mind that

$$T_N = T_N(L_{NT}) \tag{2.47}$$

yields

$$dr_{NA} = P(A_N^{TL}dL_{NA} + A_N^{TT}T^L dL_{NT}) \tag{2.48}$$

Inserting the expressions for the change in labor use, Eqs. (2.37) and (2.39) give us

$$dr_{NA} = (1/\Delta^{**})P^2 M_N^{LL}\left\{T^L\left[A_N^{TT}A_N^{LL} - (A^{TL})^2\right] + A_N^{TL}A_N^T T^{LL}\right\}dL_N \tag{2.49}$$

The land rent may fall in the New World when immigrants arrive and cultivation is extended, unless diminishing returns to extension are strong. According to Wicksell, the frontier is virtually closed, so the latter is precisely what we should expect, and once the frontier is closed we are back in our original general equilibrium system. The analogy with Eqs. (2.20)–(2.22) is perfect, with the one difference that the New World has a higher endowment of land, which should mean that the existing wage rate is higher there than in the Old World, as pointed out by Wicksell and illustrated in Fig. 2.1. Emigration should thus be beneficial for those who undertake it. Also, as far as the development of relative commodity prices is concerned, Eq. (2.24) may be used, substituting N (the New World) for O (the Old World). Presumably, however, the tendency for population growth to increase the relative price of agricultural goods is weaker when the population grows in the New World instead of in the Old, since the additional agricultural outputs generated should be higher and the shift in consumer preferences weaker. But Wicksell argued that this was only a temporary blessing, since as the population kept growing the structure of the New World economy would gradually approximate that of the Old World.

The next parameter shift to be discussed is one mentioned more *en passant* by Wicksell: capital movements. What we have to compare is the effects of a growth of capital stocks in the Old World with the growth of those of the New World, assuming that capitalists are free to decide where they want accumulation to take place. We then want to focus on the development of the two wage rates. Let us start in the Old World. Again we differentiate Eqs. (2.3)–(2.5) at constant commodity prices and with a given labor force. The exogenous change is the increase in K_{OA} and K_{OM}.

Differentiating the system and solving for the change in the wage rate yields:

$$dw_O = -(1/\Delta)\big(P(A_O^{LK}M_O^{LL}dK_{OA} + M_O^{LK}A_O^{LL}dK_{OM}\big) > 0 \qquad (2.50)$$

Regardless of which of the two capital stocks (probably both) that grows, the wage rate will increase. Whether labor will move from manufacturing to agriculture or vice versa depends on the differences in capital accumulation on the one hand and on the impact of additional capital on the marginal productivities of labor on the other:

$$dL_{OA} = -dL_{OM} = (1/\Delta)\big(PA_O^{LK}dK_{OA} - M_O^{LK}dK_{OM}\big) \qquad (2.51)$$

Wicksell implicitly compared Eqs. (2.50) and (2.51) with the analogous expressions for capital accumulation in the New World, arguing that from the point of view of the prospective emigrants, capital formation overseas would be preferable, i.e., for

$$dK_{NA} = dK_{OA} \text{ and } dK_{NM} = dK_{OM}, \quad A_N^{LK} > A_O^{LK} \text{ and } M_N^{LK} > M_O^{LK}. \qquad (2.52)$$

The only parameter change in the Wicksellian system that we have not investigated so far is war. As we know, Wicksell was constantly worried that overpopulation would result in territorial aggression. How can this be handled in the model? If we stick to the sequence that Wicksell obviously had in mind, war is triggered by population growth, and the short-run effect of war is a reduction of the population of the nations involved in the war, both as a result of the belligerent activities *per se* and as a result of starvation, etc., that follows in the footsteps of war. This, then, would reverse all sequences that we have already dealt with that are triggered by population growth. However, according to Wicksell, war "solves" the population problem only in the short run, because at some point after the termination of the war activities there will again be a drive to increase the population, possibly triggered by the rulers, politicians, and militaries of the countries that have suffered, and then we are of course back where we began our analysis in this chapter.

2.10. Conclusions

The present essay has been devoted to the exercise of putting all the bits and pieces of Wicksell's scattered analysis of population growth together. The result is astonishing. Far from confirming the conventional wisdom that what he wrote on the population question was mechanical and simplistic, it turns out that the exercise results in a coherent general equilibrium framework which very much resembles the specific factors model of international trade foreshadowed by Haberler (1936) and formalized by Jones (1971) and Samuelson (1971a, b). Within this setting, Wicksell handled factor growth (population, natural resources, and capital), technological progress, tariffs, and factor movements. In this, he stands out as a precursor of the modern theory of international trade. It is here then, rather than in the use of the optimum population concept, that Wicksell's original contribution to the analysis of population growth lies.

References

Findlay, R (1996). Towards a model of territorial expansion and the limits of empire. In *The Political Economy of Conflict and Cooperation*, MF Garfinkel and S Skaperdas (eds.), New York: Cambridge University Press, pp. 41–56.

Fong, MS (1976). Knut Wicksell's "The Two Population Problems". *History of Political Economy*, 8, 172–188.

Gårdlund, T (1996). *The Life of Knut Wicksell*. Cheltenham, UK and Brookfield VT: Edward Elgar, p. 355.

Gottlieb, M (1945). The theory of optimum population for a closed economy. *Journal of Political Economy*, 53, 289–316.

Gustafsson, B (1961). Svensk ekonomisk teori — Knut Wicksell 1851–1926. *Vår Tid*, 17, 601.

Haberler, G (1936). *The Theory of International Trade*. Edinburgh: William Hodge, p. 408.

Henriksson, RGH (1991). The facts on Wicksell on the facts: Wicksell and economic history. In *The Vital One: Essays in Honour of Jonathan R.T. Hughes. Research in Economic History*, J Mokyr (ed.), JAI Press, Conn: USA, pp. 56–71.

Hutchinson, EP (1967). *The Population Debate. The Development of Conflicting Theories up to 1900*. Boston: Houghton Mifflin, p. 188.

Jones, RW (1971). A three-factor model in theory, trade, and history. In *Trade, Balance of Payments and Growth: Papers in International Economics in Honor of Charles P. Kindleberger*. JN Bhagwati *et al.* (eds.), Amsterdam: North-Holland, pp. 3–21.

Kock, K (1944). Nymalthusianismens genombrott i sverige. In *Studier i ekonomi och historia tillägnade Eli F. Heckscher på 65-årsdagen den 24 november 1944*. Uppsala: Almqvist & Wiksells Boktryckeri, pp. 73–88.

Kravis, IB (1970). Trade as a handmaiden of growth: similarities between the nineteenth and twentieth centuries. *Economic Journal*, 80, December, 850–872.

Lindahl, E (1958). Introduction: Wicksell's life and work. In *Selected Papers on Economic Theory*, K Wicksell (ed.), London: George Allen & Unwin.

Lundahl, M (2005a). *Knut Wicksell on Poverty: No Place Is Too Exalted for the Preaching of These Doctrines*. London and New York: Routledge, p. 122.

Lundahl, M (2005b). Knut Wicksell and the causes of poverty: population growth and dininishing returns. In *Economists and Poverty: From Adam Smith to Amartya Sen*, D Rauhut, N Hatti and C Olsson (eds.), New Delhi: Vedams, pp. 138–176.

Overbeek, J (1973). Wicksell on population. *Economic Development and Cultural Change*, 21(2), 205–211.

Pålsson Syll, L (2002). *De ekonomiska teoriernas historia*, 3rd Ed. Lund Studentlitteratur, p. 299.

Pitchford, JD (1974). *Population in Economic Growth*. Amsterdam: North-Holland, p. 280.

Robbins, L (1927). The optimum theory of population. In *London Essays in Economics: In Honor of Edwin Cannan*, TE Gregory and H Dalton (eds.), London: Routledge, pp. 103–136.

Robertson, DH (1938). The future of international trade. *Economic Journal*, 48, 1–14.

Samuelson, PA (1971a). An exact Hume-Ricardo-Marshall model of international trade. *Journal of International Economics*, 1(1), 1–18.

Samuelson, PA (1971b). Ohlin was right. *Swedish Journal of Economics*, 73, 365–389.

Schumpeter, JA (1954). *History of Economic Analysis*. New York: Oxford University Press.

Shackle, GLS (1954). Foreword to the English translation. In *Value, Capital and Rent*, K Wicksell (ed.), London: George Allen & Unwin.

Sommarin, E (1926–27). Minnesord över professor Knut Wicksell. In Kungliga Humanistiska Vetenskapssamfundet i Lund: Årsberättelse1926/27. Lund.

Spengler, J (1983). Knut Wicksell, father of the optimum. Atlantic Economic Journal, 11(4), 1–5.

Uhr, CG (1951). Knut Wicksell — a centennial evaluation. American Economic Review, 41(5), 829–860.

Uhr, CG (1962). Economic Doctrines of Knut Wicksell. Berkeley and Los Angeles: University of California Press, p. 356.

Uhr, CG (1991). Knut Wicksell, neoclassicist and iconoclast. In The History of Swedish Economic Thought, B Sandelin (ed.), London and New York: Routledge, pp. 76–120.

Wicksell, K (1882). Om utvandringen. Dess betydelse och orsaker. Stockholm: Albert Bonniers Förlag.

Wicksell, K (1887a). Om folkökningen i Sverge och de faror den medför för det allmänna välståndet och för sedligheten, Stockholm: Kungsholms Bokhandel.

Wicksell, K (1887b). Om prostitutionen. Huru mildra och motverka detta samhällsonda? Två föredrag, Stockholm: Kungsholms Bokhandel.

Wicksell, K (1891). La population, les causes de ses progrès et les obstacles qui en arrêtent l'essor. Pièce destinée ou concours Rossi, 1891. Manuscript. Paris: Académie des sciences morales et politiques de l'Institut de France.

Wicksell, K (1892). Normalarbetsdag. In Att uppfostra det svenska folket. Knut Wicksells opublicerade manuskript, L Jonung, T Hedlund-Nyström and C Jonung (eds.), (2001), Stockholm: SNS Förlag, pp. 190–193.

Wicksell, K (1902). Professor Fahlbeck om nymalthusianismen. Ekonomisk Tidskrift, 4, 543–560.

Wicksell, K (1903). Om begreppen produktivitet, rentabilitet och relativ avkastning inom jordbruket. Ekonomisk Tidskrift, 5, 485–507.

Wicksell, K (1914). Allvarliga farhågor. Stockholm: Sällskapet för Humanitär Barnalstring.

Wicksell, K (1924/25). Befolkningsfrågan och sunda förnuftet, Att uppfostra det svenska folket. Knut Wicksells opublicerade manuskript, L Jonung, T Hedlund-Nyström and C Jonung (eds.), (2001), Stockholm: SNS Förlag.

Wicksell, K (1925). Barnalstringsfrågan: Föredrag, hållet vid Nymalthusianska sällskapet. Stockholm: Federativs Förlag.

Wicksell, K (1926). Befolkningsfrågan och världsfreden, Att uppfostra det svenska folket. Knut Wicksells opublicerade manuskript, L Jonung, T Hedlund-Nyström and C Jonung (eds.), (2001), Stockholm: SNS Förlag.

Wicksell, K (1934). *Lectures on Political Economy. Volume One: General Theory.* London: George Routledge and Sons, p. 121.

Wicksell, K (1958). Marginal productivity as the basis of distribution in Economics. In *Selected Papers on Economic Theory.* London: George Allen & Unwin, pp. 121–130.

Wicksell, K (1978). The World War: an economist's view. *Scandinavian Journal of Economics,* 80(2), 233–235.

Wicksell, K (1979). The theory of population, its composition and changes. In *The Theoretical Contributions of Knut Wicksell,* S Strøm and B Thalberg (eds.), London and Basingstoke: Macmillan, pp. 683–717.

Wicksell, K (1999a). A few remarks on the chief cause of social misfortunes and the best means to remedy them, with particular reference to drunkenness. In *Knut Wicksell: Selected Essays in Economics,* B Sandelin (ed.), Vol. 2, London and New York: Routledge, pp. 83–116.

Wicksell, K (1999b). Can a country become underpopulated? In *Knut Wicksell: Selected Essays in Economics,* B Sandelin (ed.), Vol. 2, London and New York: Routledge, pp. 125–135.

Wicksell, K (1999c). Overproduction — or overpopulation? In *Knut Wicksell: Selected Essays in Economics,* B Sandelin (ed.), Vol. 2, London and New York: Routledge, pp. 117–124.

Wicksell, K (1999d). From *The Emigration Inquiry,* Appendix 18. In *Knut Wicksell: Selected Essays in Economics,* B Sandelin (ed.), Vol. 2, London and New York: Routledge, pp. 136–170.

CHAPTER 3

IMMIGRATION, OUTPUT, AND WELFARE
IN A GROWTH MODEL

Partha Sen

Delhi School of Economics, University of Delhi, India

3.1. Introduction

Immigration, or more generally, population growth, has been seen by some commentators as a blessing and by others as a curse. Indeed, it can be both depending on the circumstances. In overpopulated labor-surplus economies, population growth can hardly ever be an unmitigated blessing. But in areas of labor shortages — the domain of growth theory with its assumption of full employment — a higher population growth should be welcome.

In models of economic growth before endogenous growth theory became the rage, an economy's long-run growth rate was said to depend on exogenous factors — population growth, disembodied technical change etc. In these models, while population growth rate raised the growth rate of the economy, it lowered output per capita and welfare (or, equivalently in descriptive models, per capita consumption). This is true of all exogenous growth models which exhibit dynamic efficiency.[1]

The available empirical evidence flies in the face of these predictions. Wherever full employment has prevailed — and all these models were full employment models — be it the US in the 19th century, or the post-Second-World-War "golden age" of capitalism in Europe — the immigration of unskilled workers surely raised the welfare of the average host country resident (and of the immigrant). Let us look at the summary statistics for three of the big immigrant-receiving countries over a period of a century presented in Table 3.1.

---

[1] See e.g., Buiter (1981). Dynamic inefficiency occurs when the interest rate is less than the population growth rate (or, equivalently, profits are less than investment).

51

Table 3.1.

Country	Period	Total Products	Population	Per capita product
USA	1834–43 to 1963–67	42.4	21.2	17.5
Australia	1861–67 to 1963–67	36.4	23.7	10.2
Canada	1870–74 to 1963–67	41.3	19.0	18.7

Source: Kuznets (1971), pp. 11–14.
Note: The last three columns are growth rates per decade.

Both migration and fertility have spawned large literatures. Djajic (1986); Quibria (1989); Rivera-Batiz (1989); Galor (1986); Galor and Stark (1990); Karayalcin (1994) and Kemp and Kondo (1989) analyze the international migration problem. Razin and Yuen (1999) discuss the role of factor mobility in the development process. Ehrlich and Lui (1997) review the role of fertility in growth models. Also, the ethical dimension of population growth has received some attention (see for e.g., Broome, 1996; Ng, 2002).

In this paper, I try and reconcile the facts cited above with theory by constructing a model and analyzing the effect of an increase in the growth rate of population on output and steady-state welfare. The model is a two-sector-two-period overlapping generations model.[2] Unlike a one-sector model, the presence of two sectors model allows one of the sectors to contract, while allowing the other sector to expand with a given capital-labor ratio — i.e., it allows relocation across sectors in addition to capital accumulation to determine factor prices, and hence welfare. In a typical two-sector model in closed economy setting, the two sectors are called consumption and investment and the two inputs as capital and labor. In an economy with an abundant supply of land, we interpret arable land as capital, and the clearing of land for cultivation and activities such as the laying of railway tracks as investment. The consumption good is mainly agricultural, which is very land-intensive, and the clearing and draining of land (or the laying of railway lines) relatively labor-intensive. The consumption good is, therefore, assumed to be capital-intensive (i.e., land-intensive).[3]

In such a setup, population growth could be welfare improving in an economy that satisfies the usual condition for dynamic efficiency viz., rate of interest exceeds

---

[2]In doing this, I build on Sen (2006).

[3]Over time, as the economy industrializes, physical and then human capital accumulation become the dominant features of growth, and change factor intensity rankings of sectors and, indeed, the products themselves (see Galor and Moav, 2002). My exposition is in terms of immigration in an agrarian economy, rather than the post-Second-World-War Europe or Hong Kong. In these countries, openness played a role that I want to abstract from.

the population growth rate. A rise in the population growth rate calls forth a higher level of investment (clearing of land, laying of rail tracks etc.). Investment rises but capital (land) per worker falls. A higher level of investment requires higher savings. An increase in savings here is caused by an increase in wages and output, which raises welfare.[4]

3.2. The Model

The (closed) economy model consists of overlapping generations of individuals or households. Each household with two-period lives, supplies one unit of labor in the first period of its life and in the second period consumes the saving from the first period plus the return on these savings. There are no bequests or inheritances. The population is growing at a constant rate. Production technologies in both the sectors are assumed to be Leontief.

The representative household born in time period t maximizes the utility function (Eq. (3.1)) subject to its lifetime budget constraint (Eq. (3.2)). The utility function U is strictly concave with positive marginal utilities from consumption in both periods. I assume further that $U(.)$ is homothetic. The demand functions are given in Eqs. (3.3) and (3.4).

$$U_t = (C_t^1, C_{t+1}^1) \tag{3.1}$$

$$W_t = C_t^1 + (1 + r_{t+1})^{-1} \cdot C_{t+1}^2 \tag{3.2}$$

$$C_t^1 = c^1 (1 + r_{t+1}) W_t \tag{3.3}$$

and

$$C_{t+1}^1 = c^2 (1 + r_{t+1}) W_t \tag{3.4}$$

where C_{t+1}^i is the consumption in period $i(i = 1, 2)$ of a household born in t, W_t is the wage rate in time period t and r_{t+1} the own interest rate on one period consumption loans between t and $t + 1$.

The saving function, then, is given by

$$s(1 + r_{t+1}) W_t \equiv W_t - c^1 (1 + r_{t+1}) W_t \tag{3.5}$$

It is assumed, as is normal, the substitution effect of an interest rate increase dominates the income effect on saving.

The production side of the economy is represented by the two cost-equal-to-price equations. The consumption good (C) and the investment good (I) are produced under constant returns to scale using capital (K) and labor (L). In our

---

[4]My results depend both on the assumed capital-intensities and the short-run dynamics — these are discussed in detail in the following section.

interpretation, K is arable land, C is the production of food, and I the clearing and draining of land. Both inputs are mobile between sectors instantaneously. Capital is assumed to depreciate completely in the process of production.[5]

$$a_{LC} \cdot W_t + a_{KC} \cdot R_t = I \tag{3.6}$$

$$a_{LI} \cdot W_t + a_{KI} \cdot R_t = p_t \tag{3.7}$$

a_{ij} is the requirement of input i ($i = K, L$) in the production of good j ($j = C, I$), and p is the relative price of the investment good in terms of the numeraire good C and R is the return on capital. Since we assume capital depreciates completely in the process of production, we have in equilibrium: $(1 + r_{t+1}) = R_{t+1}/p \equiv \rho_{t+1}$. The a_{ij}'s are generally functions of the relative factor prices but not here because the production technology is Leontief.

There are two goods markets (for C and I) and two factor markets (for L and K). By Walras' law, if three of these are in equilibrium in any period, then so is the fourth one. We thus have (all magnitudes are per worker)

$$a_{LC} \cdot C_t + a_{LI} \cdot I_t = I \tag{3.8}$$

$$a_{KC} \cdot C_t + a_{KI} \cdot I_t = k_t \tag{3.9}$$

Equations (3.8) and (3.9) are the market-clearing conditions for the labor and capital — the equilibrium condition for the investment goods market is given in Eq. (3.10). The variables C_t, I_t and k_t are respectively, the output of the consumption good, the investment good, and the capital stock (all in period t).

Finally, the dynamics of the economy is represented by the two (implicit) difference equations

$$p_t \cdot I_t = S(\rho_{t+1})W_t \tag{3.10}$$

$$(1 + n) \cdot k_{t+1} = I_t \tag{3.11}$$

where n is the population growth rate with $1 + n > 0$. Later, we will use $N \equiv (1 + n)$, the population growth factor. Equation (3.10) is the saving equal to investment relation — since the former depends on the expected returns from capital in the next period, it is a forward-looking relationship. Equation (3.11) implies that in the presence of cent percent depreciation, this period's investment is the next period's capital stock (expressed in per worker terms in Eq. (3.12)). To focus on a tractable case, I shall assume that the production structure is Leontief, although I shall discuss below the case when this is not so.

---

[5]Durability requires capital gains on the sale of capital to be part of the return to holding of capital. That leaves the steady-state, where there are no capital gains, unaffected. Under some weak conditions, the dynamics is also qualitatively the same as reported in this paper. Note that under our assumption, land is no longer a durable (non-depreciating) input — which is the usual interpretation given to it.

Equations (3.6) and (3.7) yield by logarithmic differentiation

$$\theta_{LC} \cdot \hat{W}_t + \theta_{KC} \cdot \hat{R}_t = 0 \tag{3.12}$$

$$\theta_{LI} \cdot \hat{W}_t + \theta_{KI} \cdot \hat{R}_t = \hat{p}_t \tag{3.13}$$

where θ_{ij} is the share of input i in the price of sector j (e.g., $\theta_{LI} \equiv W \cdot a_{LI}/p$) and a hat over a variable denotes a percentage change (e.g., $\hat{W} = dW/W$).

From Eqs. (3.12) and (3.13), we can solve for $\hat{p}_t$ and $\hat{R}_t$ in terms of $\hat{W}_t$ (the Stolper–Samuelson effects):

$$\eta_{Wp} \equiv \hat{W}_t/\hat{p}_t = -\theta_{KC}/\Delta \tag{3.14}$$

$$\eta_{Rp} \equiv \hat{R}_t/\hat{p}_t = -\theta_{LC}/\Delta \tag{3.15}$$

where $\Delta \equiv \theta_{LC} - \theta_{LI} = \theta_{KI} - \theta_{KC}$ and η_{ij} is the (partial) elasticity of variable i with respect to j. From Eqs. (3.14) and (3.15), we see that $\hat{R}_t/\hat{p}_t$ and $\hat{W}_t/\hat{p}_t$ depend on capital intensities. Given that we have assumed that the consumption good (the growing of food) is land-intensive (while investment activity consisting of clearing, draining of land etc. is labor-intensive), we have $\Delta < 0$ (and $\Omega < 0$ below).

Similarly, by logarithmically differentiating Eqs. (3.8) and (3.9) we then have

$$\lambda_{LC} \cdot \hat{C}_t + \lambda_{LI} \cdot \hat{I}_t = 0 \tag{3.16}$$

$$\lambda_{KC} \cdot \hat{C}_t + \lambda_{KI} \cdot \hat{I}_t = \hat{k}_t \tag{3.17}$$

λ_{ij} is the share of sector j in the total employment of input i.

From Eqs. (3.16) and (3.17), we have the Rybczinski effect of an increase in the capital stock on the output of the investment good (which depends on assumed capital intensities)

$$\eta_{Ik} \equiv \hat{I}_t/\hat{k}_t = \lambda_{LC}/\Omega < 0 \tag{3.18}$$

where $\Omega \equiv \lambda_{LC} - \lambda_{KC} < 0$.

Logarithmically, differentiate Eq. (3.10) and substitute for η_{Wp}, η_{Rp}, and η_{Ik}, from Eqs. (3.14), (3.15), and (3.18), to express $\hat{p}_t$ in terms of $\hat{p}_t$ and $\hat{k}_t$.

$$\eta_{Sp}\eta_{Rp}\hat{p}_t+ = (1 + \eta_{Sp} - \eta_{Wp})\hat{p}_t + \eta_{ik}\hat{k}_i \tag{3.19}$$

Similarly, Eq. (3.11) can be written as (given the Leontief assumption)

$$\hat{N} + \hat{k}_{t+1} = \eta_{Ik}\hat{k}_t \tag{3.20}$$

The two roots of the dynamic system in Eqs. (3.19) and (3.20) are $\mu_1 \equiv \eta_{Ik}$ and $\mu_2 \equiv (1 + \eta_{Sp} - \eta_{Wp})/\eta_{Sp}\eta_{Rp}$. It is assumed that $0 > \mu_1 > -1$ and $\mu_2 > 1$, and the long-run equilibrium is a saddle-point. To represent this in a phase diagram, we use the following system (where $\Phi \equiv \eta_{S\rho}\eta_{Rp}$):

$$\begin{bmatrix} \hat{p}_{t+1} - \hat{p}_t \\ \hat{k}_{t+1} - \hat{k}_t \end{bmatrix} = \begin{bmatrix} \{(1 + \eta_{S\rho}(1 - \eta_{Rp}) - \eta_{Wp})\}/\Phi & \{\eta_{Ik}/\Phi\} \\ 0 & \eta_{Ik} - 1 \end{bmatrix}$$

$$\times \begin{bmatrix} \hat{p}_t \\ \hat{k}_t \end{bmatrix} + \begin{bmatrix} 0 \\ -\hat{N} \end{bmatrix} \tag{3.21}$$

The dynamics is shown in Fig. 3.1. In the $\hat{k} - \hat{p}$ space, the KK line denotes a constant capital sock — it is vertical because of our assumption of Leontief technology. The PP line denotes a constant price of investment good and is downward sloping with the vertical arrows pointing away from it. If the production technologies were not Leontief, then $\eta_{Ip} > 0$, and the KK would be upward sloping but if this effect was very strong, then the PP could also be upward sloping.

The dynamics in Eq. (3.21) bears a family resemblance to Calvo (1978) but is different in one crucial way — namely in the assumption $\mu_2 > 1$. To see this, note that $(1 + \eta_{S\rho}(1 - \eta_{Rp}) - \eta_{Wp})/\eta_{S\rho}\eta_{Rp}$ can be positive or negative. In Calvo (1978), the short-run dynamics is assumed to be Walrasian (the term above is negative) and the long-run equilibrium is a sink. Here, we assume that the short-run dynamics is Marshallian and hence get a saddle-point steady-state equilibrium.

To elaborate on this: savings constitutes demand for the investment goods and the supply of investment goods depends only on the capital stock via our Leontief assumption. In the steady state, if $(1 + \eta_{S\rho}(1 - \eta_{Rp}) - \eta_{Wp})$ is positive, then an increase in p causes excess supply of the investment good. We then have Walrasian

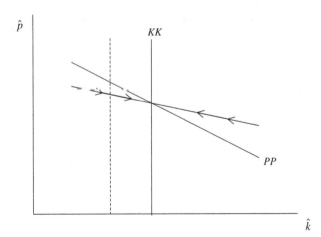

Fig. 3.1.   Phase-diagram of capital stock and price of investment goods.

short-run dynamics. *Per contra*, if this term is negative, then an increase in p causes an excess demand (by raising wages more) — here we have Marshallian dynamics.

Before turning to the effects of an increase in the population growth rate, let us note that GDP per worker (y) is given by (GDP per capita is $y \cdot (n + 1)/(n + 2)$).

$$y \equiv C + p \cdot I \tag{3.22}$$

Hence, by the envelope theorem, $dy = I \cdot dp$. Therefore, y and p move together. Below, we shall see that given dynamic efficiency, so does welfare.

3.3. Population Growth

We are interested in the long-run effects of a sustained increase in population. This was achieved by a more liberal immigration policy in the countries whose experience is summarized in Table 3.1. What are the effects of this output and welfare per head? Let us assume that immigrants have the same utility function as the original residents. In a model such as ours, in a steady state, all variables (in levels) grow at a rate n and all ratios are constant. Therefore, the new steady-state growth rate of all variables is higher.

The effect of a change in $N(\equiv(1 + n))$ on the steady-state values of p and k are obtained from Eqs. (3.19) and (3.20).

$$\hat{k}/\hat{N} = (\eta_{Ik} - 1)^{-1} < 0 \tag{3.23}$$

$$\hat{p}/\hat{N} = -\eta_{Ik}/[(\eta_{s\rho}(1 - .\eta_{Rp}) - \eta_{Wp}](\eta_{Ik} - 1) > 0 \tag{3.24}$$

This, in turn, implies from Eqs. (3.14) and (3.15) $\hat{W}/\hat{N} > 0$, $\hat{R}/\hat{N} < 0$ and (from Eq. (3.22)), $\hat{y}/\hat{N} > 0$.

For determining the changes in welfare the steady state we have, the indirect utility function[6] is $V(W, \rho)$.

Following the derivations in the Appendix,

$$dV/\hat{N} = -V_W pk(\rho - N)\hat{R}./\hat{N} > 0 \quad \text{(if, initially, } \rho > N) \tag{3.25}$$

where V_W is the marginal utility of income.

The intuition for the result is as follows: an increase in the rate of immigration increases the output of the investment good but lowers the capital per worker in the new steady state. This is true of all (exogenous) growth models. But in a two-sector set-up with the consumption good being capital-intensive and "Marshallian adjustment," a rise in p causes the wage rate to rise accompanied by a decline in the rental rate. A higher wage rate implies higher savings per worker (although the lower interest rate tends to lower it). And, the steady-state welfare increases, if

---

[6]The original residents and immigrants are assumed to have identical utility functions.

initially the interest factor was above the population growth factor. Note that steady-state utility is declining in K *does not mean* — borrowing from a one-sector model where there is overaccumulation of capital — that throwing away capital cannot be Pareto-improving. The consumption good is capital-intensive and throwing away capital will reduce its supply.

3.4. Conclusions

The historical data in immigration-receiving countries in the 19th century points to a positive association between population growth and output (and welfare). The prediction of one-sector (and other) growth models is at variance with this. An increase in population growth in a two-sector overlapping generations model (under our assumptions about capital intensities and short-run adjustment) increases the long-run growth rate (as in any exogenous growth model), but, in addition, it increases output and welfare. As mentioned in Sec. 3.1, a two-sector model allows one of the sectors to contract, while allowing the other sector to expand with a given capital-labor ratio. Thus, it allows relocation across sectors in addition to capital accumulation to determine factor prices, and hence welfare. It is easy to extend the analysis to look at the dynamic adjustment path. This is not done here because the dynamic process could depend on a number of factors that we abstract from. We had started off to explain long-run output and welfare, and to emphasize that the results obtained are in stark contrast to the existing models.

Appendix

$V(W, \rho)$ from $U(C_1, C_2) = U(W - S, \rho S)$ where S is chosen optimally

$$dV = V_W dW + V_\rho d\rho \quad \text{Note } V_W = U_1 > 0, \quad V_\rho = SU_2$$
$$dV = V_W(dW + S\rho^{-1}d\rho) \quad \text{because } U_1 = \rho U_2$$
$$- V_W(Idp - kdR + S\rho^{-1}d\rho)$$

(from $W + Rk = C + p \cdot I$ and the envelope theorem
implies $dW + kdR = I \cdot dp$)

$$= V_W(Nkdp - kdR + S\rho^{-1}(dR - \rho)\hat{p})$$
$$= V_W(Nkdp - S\hat{p} + S\hat{R} - kdR)$$
$$= V_W \cdot pk \cdot (N - \rho)\hat{R} \quad \text{(This is Eq. (17) in the text.)}$$

(because the first two terms in the previous line cancel out (i.e., $(1 + n) \cdot k = I = S/p$)).

References

Broome, J (1996). The welfare economics of population. *Oxford Economic Papers*, 48, 177–193.

Buiter, WH (1981). Time preference and international lending and borrowing in an overlapping generations model. *Journal of Political Economy*, 89, 769–797.

Calvo, G (1978). On the indeterminacy of interest rates and wages with perfect foresight. *Journal of Economic Theory*, 19, 321–337.

Djajic, S (1986). International migration remittances and welfare in a developing economy. *Journal of Development Economics*, 21, 229–234.

Ehrlich, I and F Lui (1997). The problem of population and growth: a review of the literature from Malthus to contemporary models of endogenous population and endogenous growth. *Journal of Economic Dynamics and Control*, 21, 205–242.

Galor, O (1986). Time preference and international migration. *Journal of Economic Theory*, 38, 1–20.

Galor, O and O Stark (1990). Migrants' savings, the probability of return migration and migrants' performance. *International Economic Review*, 31, 197–215.

Karayalcin, C (1994). Temporary and permanent migration with and without an immobile factor. *Journal of Development Economics*, 43, 197–215.

Kemp, MC and H Kondo (1989). An analysis of international migration: the unilateral case. In *Economic Theory of Optimal Population*, KF Zimmerman (ed.), Berlin: Springer-Verlag., pp. 153–165.

Kuznets, S (1971). *Economic Growth of Nations: Total Output and Production Structure*. Cambridge, Massachusetts: Harvard University Press.

Ng, Y-K (2002). The welfare economics of encouraging more births. In *Economic Theory and International Trade: Essays in Honour of Murray C. Kemp*, AD Woodland (ed.), Cheltenham, UK: Edward Elgar, pp. 57–67.

Quibria, MG (1989). International migration and real wages: is there any neoclassical ambiguity? *Journal of Development Economics*, 28, 177–183.

Razin, A and C-W Yuen (1999). Understanding the "Problem of Development": The Role of Factor Mobility and International Taxation, National Bureau of Economic Research Working Paper No. 7115.

Rivera-Batiz, FL (1989). The impact of international migration on real wages. *Journal of Development Economics*, 31, 185–192.

Sen, P (2006). Population growth and steady state welfare in an overlapping generations. *Model Economics Letters*, 91, 325–329.

PART 2

LABOR MARKET AND ECONOMIC POLICY

CHAPTER 4

INTER-GOVERNMENTAL MONETARY COOPERATION AND INTERNATIONAL MIGRATION OF LABOR

Akira Shimada

Nagasaki University, Japan

4.1. Introduction

This paper deals with monetary policy games in a two-country economy characterized by international migration of labor and efficiency wages. We compare the
two regimes, i.e., inter-government monetary cooperation between the two independent monetary authorities and centralization of the monetary policies by a single
monetary authority under a monetary union, and attempt to show that forming a
monetary union and centralizing the monetary policies may prove to be advantageous if a two-country economy is subject to shocks. On the other hand, in the
absence of shocks, even if the two countries do not form a monetary union, inter-
government monetary cooperation gives the monetary authority and the workers
the same utilities as those attainable under a monetary union.

Currently, it is impossible for many monetary authorities to ignore policy interdependence among countries. This is because countries have become increasingly
interrelated not only on account of the growing volume of international trade of
goods and flow of financial capital but also on account of the growing mobility of
labor across borders.

Therefore, monetary policies are often decided upon cooperatively among
countries without affecting the independence of the monetary authority of each
country. In some cases, however, countries form a monetary union and centralize
their monetary policies.

Needless to say, the question with regard to the optimal monetary regime in
interdependent economies is not new. Studies pertaining to this question have
produced a vast amount of literatures. Hamada (1976), Oudiz and Sachs (1984),

Canzoneri and Henderson (1988, 1991), and Lewis (1989) are a few of the early contributors. Some argue that cooperation is preferable to non-cooperation, whereas others, such as Rogoff (1985), argue that non-cooperation is preferable to cooperation. Cooley and Quadrini (2003) studied the optimal monetary policies in a two-country economy under two regimes — multiple currencies controlled by independent monetary authorities and common currencies controlled by a centralized monetary authority. Pappa (2004) compared the three regimes, i.e., cooperation, non-cooperation, and monetary union in order to investigate the implications for macro-economic stability and its welfare properties by assuming a two-country economy with monopolistic competition. Since the conclusions with regard to the optimal monetary regime depend on the type of economy that we aim to analyze, they are not uniform.

Although previous studies on the optimal monetary regimes assumed various types of open economies, they did not pay sufficient attention to the mobility of labor. Many of the open macro-economic models used for the analyses of monetary policy games in interdependent economies overlook the possibility of international migration.

In contrast with the previous analyses, Agiomirgianakis (1998) assumed a symmetric two-country economy where the workers are assumed to migrate between the two countries due to the differences in real-consumption wages (nominal wages divided by the consumer price index (CPI)).

He showed that under the possibility of international migration of labor, inter-government monetary cooperation may prove to be advantageous. In particular, he revealed the fact that the utility of the monetary authority is likely to be higher when there is inter-government monetary cooperation rather than non-cooperation, whereas the utility of the workers does not differ across regimes.

In order to obtain this result, Agiomirgianakis modeled labor markets by assuming labor unions and determined nominal wages and employment in the same manner as that assumed in the monopoly union model. He also modeled a symmetric two-country economy that is not subject to any shocks.

His result suggests that under the possibility of international migration of labor, it would be preferable for the monetary authorities of the two countries to cooperate with each other. We may infer the following from his result: the monetary authority and the workers may be able to attain even higher utilities by centralizing the monetary policies under a monetary union since policy centralization under a monetary union is a more direct manner of cooperation.

However, we cannot immediately deduce the above implication from his result. This is because, in his model, the monetary authority of each country does not lose its independence even under inter-government monetary cooperation and each country has its own currency and money market. Agiomirgianakis did not deal with the case where the two countries form a monetary union and one common monetary authority centralizes the monetary policies of the two countries.

Therefore, assuming a two-country economy with labor migration, this paper compares inter-government monetary cooperation between the two independent monetary authorities and centralization of the monetary policies by a single monetary authority under a monetary union, and attempts to ascertain which of the two regimes is advantageous to both the monetary authority and the workers. Doing this will enable us to reveal the monetary regime that gives higher utilities to the monetary authority and the workers.

For this purpose, we assume efficiency wages, i.e., the non-shirk model, rather than labor unions, in order to model labor markets, since in reality, labor unions are not always influential in the determination of nominal wages and employment and are exogenous factors. We also assume that a two-country economy may be affected by supply or demand shocks. Shocks are included in our model not only because actual economies are often subject to shocks but also because their existence is likely to change the ranking of alternative regimes.

We demonstrate that if a two-country economy is not subjected to any shocks, the utilities of the monetary authority and the workers are the same under both inter-government monetary cooperation and a monetary union. This can be explained as follows: in the absence of any shocks, the money market equilibrium conditions are virtually the same in the two regimes, since the economic structures of the two countries are symmetric in both regimes. This suggests that the structural equations are virtually the same in the two regimes. Moreover, even if the two countries do not form a monetary union, under the possibility of international migration of labor, they can eliminate the negative effects arising from macro-economic interdependence through migration flows by cooperating with each other. Therefore, if the two countries are not affected by shocks, cooperation between the two independent monetary authorities enables the monetary authority to attain the same utility as that under a monetary union. Moreover, the workers' utility does not differ across regimes, since their utility is dependent on the expectation of the CPI, which is the same under the two regimes.

We also demonstrate that if a two-country economy is subjected to supply or demand shocks, centralization of the monetary policies by a single monetary authority under a monetary union may prove to be advantageous. This is can be explained as follows: even if two countries are affected by shocks, cooperation between the two independent monetary authorities increases the utilities of both the monetary authority and the workers. However, if two countries are subjected to shocks, the economic structures of the two regimes will be different. If two countries are affected by supply shocks, unemployment is more variable (has a larger variance) under a monetary union, whereas the CPI is more variable under inter-government monetary cooperation. If they are affected by demand shocks, both unemployment and the CPI are more variable under inter-government monetary cooperation. Therefore, under supply or demand shocks, if the monetary authority gives sufficient importance to the stability of the CPI, it can attain a higher utility by forming a monetary union and centralizing the monetary policies. Moreover, the utility of the workers does not differ across regimes, since the expectation of the CPI is the same in both the regimes.

Our analysis has the following implications: if the two countries are not subjected to any shocks and labor migrates between them, there is no need for them to form a monetary union. On the other hand, if they are affected by shocks and international migration of labor is possible, it would be preferable for both the countries to form a monetary union and centralize the monetary policies. Therefore, the question of whether the monetary authority of each country should retain its independence or whether the two countries should form a monetary union depends on the existence or non-existence of shocks.

The remainder of this paper is organized as follows: Section 4.2 presents a two-country macro-economic model with labor migration and efficiency wages. The manner in which the workers migrate between the two countries will be assumed. Since a firm in each country cannot perfectly detect shirking by the workers, it sets nominal wages in a manner that would prevent shirking. Section 4.3 deals with a two-country economy under certainty, and we compare the utilities of the monetary authority and the workers under inter-government monetary cooperation between the two independent monetary authorities with those under a monetary union with a single monetary authority. How a two-country economy is affected by supply shocks is discussed in Section 4.4 and demand shocks in Section 4.5, and the utilities of the monetary authority and the workers in the two regimes are compared. Section 4.6 presents the concluding comments.

4.2. The Model

We assume a two-country economy. The home and foreign countries are interdependent on account of international trade of goods and international migration of labor.

We assume two cases: in one case, each country has an independent monetary authority and both the countries have different currencies; in this case, each country has a money market and the monetary authority of each country can manipulate the stock of currency in each country. In another case, the two countries form a monetary union and they have a common monetary authority and a common currency. In this case, the two countries have a common money market and the common monetary authority manipulates the stock of the common currency.

In either case, there are workers and a firm in each country. The workers are not organized into labor unions and are assumed to migrate between the two countries.

Each country's firm demands labor for producing a single type of product. Since the firm cannot perfectly detect shirking by workers, it sets nominal wages in a manner that would prevent shirking, treating the workers' effort and the money stock as given.

The home (foreign) country's product is not only demanded in the home (foreign) country but also in the foreign (home) country, where it is exported. The products produced in the two countries are imperfect substitutes, and there are no financial capital movements between the two countries.

The structure of a two-country economy is summarized via Eqs. (4.1)–(4.7). These are similar to those employed by Jensen (1993), Zervoyianni (1997), Agiomirgianakis (1998), and Shimada (2004, 2005). However, they did not deal with a case where the two countries form a monetary union. In contrast to these previous studies, this study utilizes these equations to describe the two-abovementioned cases. Moreover, in this study, we discuss whether a two-country economy may be affected by supply or demand shocks. Variables are expressed in logs, unless specified otherwise. Variables without the asterisk represent the home country and those with the asterisk represent the foreign country.

$$y = al + u, \quad y^* = al^* + u^*, \quad 0 < a < 1 \tag{4.1}$$

$$l = -\frac{1}{1-a}(w-p) + \frac{1}{1-a}\ln a + \frac{1}{1-a}u,$$

$$l^* = -\frac{1}{1-a}(w^*-p^*) + \frac{1}{1-a}\ln a + u^* \tag{4.2}$$

$$z \equiv ex + p^* - p \tag{4.3}$$

$$y - y^* = bz, \quad b > 0 \tag{4.4}$$

$$q \equiv p + cz, \quad q^* \equiv p^* - cz, \quad 0 < c < 1/2 \tag{4.5}$$

$$w_c \equiv w - q, \quad w_c^* \equiv w^* - q^* \tag{4.6}$$

$$m^d = p + y + v, \quad m^{*d} = p^* + y^* + v^* \tag{4.7}$$

Equation (4.1) presents the production functions, where y represents output, l represents the employment level, and a is a constant not expressed in the log. Production may be subject to supply shocks, which are represented by random variables u and u^* with zero mean and variance σ_u^2. They are assumed to be independent of each other. All agents in a two-country economy have to make decisions with regard to migration, labor supply, labor demand, and the money stocks, prior to the realization of these shocks. This is because of the fact that they know only the means of these variables when they make their decisions.

Equation (4.2) presents the labor demand functions, where w represents nominal wages and p represents the product price. They are derived from profit maximization of each country's firm.

Equation (4.3) defines the real exchange rate z. In a case where each country has an independent monetary authority and its own currency, the nominal exchange rate, i.e., the home currency price of the foreign currency, ex changes in response to the changes in the trade balance. In another case, where the two countries form a monetary union and have a common currency, exchange rate changes are ruled out by definition, i.e., $ex = 0$. In such a case, z can be interpreted as a relative price of the foreign country's product to the home country's product.

Equation (4.4) presents the equilibrium condition of the trade balances, where b is a constant not expressed in the log. The changes in the real exchange rates are assumed to have stronger effects on the trade balance than the changes in the difference between the two countries' national products, such that $b > 1$. In a case where the two countries form a monetary union and have a common currency, Eq. (4.4) can be considered as the demand functions for each country's product, according to which, the demand for the home (foreign) country's product increases with increases in the foreign (home) country's national product and the relative price of the foreign (home) country's product to the home (foreign) country's product.

Equation (4.5) defines the CPI q, where c is a constant not expressed in the log. In the case of two independent monetary authorities, the home (foreign) country's CPI is a weighted average of the price of the home (foreign) country's product and the home (foreign) currency price of the foreign (home) country's product. In the case of a monetary union, it is a weighted average of the prices of the two countries' products.

Real-consumption wages w_c are given by Eq. (4.6).

Equation (4.7) presents the money demand functions. Money demand may be subject to demand shocks, which are represented by random variables v and v^* with zero mean and variance σ_v^2. They are assumed to be independent of each other and also to be independent from u and u^*. All agents in a two-country economy know only the means of v and v^* when they make decisions about migration, labor supply, labor demand, and the money stocks.

Equation (4.7) enables us to define the money market equilibrium conditions as follows: in the case of two independent monetary authorities, the money markets are in equilibrium if each country's money demand is equal to the stock of each country's currency. On the other hand, in the case of a monetary union, the money market is in equilibrium if the sum of two countries' money demand is equal to the stock of a common currency.

We assume that the workers migrate between the two countries due to the expected real-consumption wage differentials. Under uncertainty, real-consumption wages are affected by supply or demand shocks. In such a case, as mentioned before, the workers have to make their decisions with regard to migration prior to the realization of these shocks. For this reason, their decisions with regard to whether or not to migrate do not depend on the real-consumption wage differentials, but on their expectation with regards to the wages.

This assumption leads to the following definitions of the effective labor forces l^f:

$$l^f \equiv \bar{l} + d(Ew_c - Ew_c^*) \tag{4.8}$$

$$l^{*f} \equiv \bar{l}^* + d(Ew_c^* - Ew_c), \quad \bar{l} = \bar{l}^* \tag{4.9}$$

where $\bar{l}$, which is a positive constant, denotes the domestic labor force in the absence of migration, i.e., the initial labor endowment, E denotes the expectation, and d, which is a positive constant not expressed in the log, measures the sensitivity of migration flows to changes in the expected real-consumption wage differentials. Equations (4.8) and (4.9) say that, for example, if the expected real-consumption wages in the home country are higher than those in the foreign country, then the native workers of the foreign country migrate to the home country by $d(Ew_c - Ew_c^*)$, and thereby the home country's effective labor force increases in comparison with its initial labor endowment.

The firm in each country sets nominal wages in a manner that would prevent shirking by the employed workers since, as mentioned before, each country's firm cannot perfectly detect whether or not the workers are shirking (Shapiro and Stiglitz, 1984).

If a representative employed worker in each country does not shirk, his instantaneous utility can be measured by the expected real-consumption wages minus effort. On the other hand, if he does shirk, his instantaneous utility is measured by the expected real-consumption wages. However, in such a case, he is detected and fired at the probability ρ, where $0 < \rho < 1$. This probability is assumed to be the same between the two countries. In addition, some of the employed workers in each country may separate from their jobs, even if they are not fired on the grounds of shirking. This separation rate, which is defined as the ratio of separations due to reasons other than shirking to the number of employed workers, is given by β, where $0 \leq \beta < 1$. The separation rate is assumed to be the same between the two countries.

The expected lifetime utility of a representative employed shirker in the home country V_E^S is,

$$rV_E^S = Ew_c + (\beta + \rho)(V_U - V_E^S) \tag{4.10}$$

where r is the discount rate, which is assumed to be the same between the two countries, and V_U is the expected lifetime utility of a representative unemployed worker in the home country. Equation (4.10) can be rewritten as,

$$V_E^S = \frac{Ew_c + (\beta + \rho)V_U}{r + \beta + \rho} \tag{4.10'}$$

On the other hand, the expected lifetime utility of a representative employed non-shirker in the home country V_E^N is,

$$rV_E^N = Ew_c - \ln e + \beta(V_U - V_E^N) \qquad (4.11)$$

where $e > 1$, and e, which is not expressed in the log, is the effort exerted by a representative employed non-shirker in the home country. In this study, the level of effort is given exogenously and does not change throughout the analysis. The level of effort exerted by a representative employed non-shirker is assumed to be the same between the two countries, i.e., $e = e^*$. Equation (4.11) can be rewritten as,

$$V_E^N = \frac{Ew_c - \ln e + \beta V_U}{r + \beta} \qquad (4.11')$$

The employed workers in the home country may or may not shirk based on a comparison of V_E^N and V_E^S. In order to prevent them from shirking, the firm in the home country has to set nominal wages that are sufficiently high to ensure that $V_E^N \geq V_E^S$. However, because there is no reason for the firm in the home country to pay more than what is essential to eliminate shirking, it will set nominal wages such that $V_E^N = V_E^S (\equiv V_E)$. The following is obtained by substituting Eqs. (4.10') and (4.11') into this condition:

$$Ew_c = rV_U + (r + \beta + \rho)\frac{\ln e}{\rho} \qquad (4.12)$$

In turn, V_U is given by,

$$rV_U = E\ln\left(\frac{\bar{W}}{Q}\right) + \alpha(V_E - V_U), \qquad (4.13)$$

where $\bar{W}$ is the unemployment benefit in the home country, which is a constant not expressed in the log, $Q \equiv \exp q$, and α, where $0 \leq \alpha < 1$, is the accession rate, which is defined as the ratio of new hires in the home country to the number of workers unemployed in the home country. The accession rate is assumed to be the same between the two countries.

In order to simplify the analysis, we assume that there are no separations or accessions, i.e., $\beta = \alpha = 0$ and that $\bar{W} = \bar{W}^* = 1$. Substituting these assumptions into Eqs. (4.12) and (4.13), nominal wages in the home country are derived as follows:

$$w = \left(1 + \frac{r}{\rho}\right)\ln e \qquad (4.14)$$

Equation (4.14) suggests that nominal wages in the home country increase with increases in the efforts of the employed workers in the home country and decrease with increases in the detection probability.

The expected lifetime utility of a representative employed worker in the home country under the non-shirk condition takes the form of,

$$V_E = -\frac{Eq}{r} + \frac{\ln e}{\rho} \tag{4.15}$$

Equation (4.15) implies that under the non-shirk condition, the expected lifetime utility of a representative employed worker in the home country decreases with increases in the home country's expected CPI.

By a similar argument, nominal wages and the expected lifetime utility of a representative employed worker in the foreign country are obtained as follows:

$$w^* = \left(1 + \frac{r}{\rho}\right)\ln e^*, \tag{4.16}$$

$$V_E^* = -\frac{Eq^*}{r} + \frac{\ln e^*}{\rho} \tag{4.17}$$

According to Eqs. (4.14), (4.16), (4.15), and (4.17), the nominal wages of the home and foreign countries are the same and the expected lifetime utility of a representative employed worker is symmetric between the two countries.

We assume that each country wants to attain full employment and the CPI target. Accordingly, if the monetary authorities of the two countries are independent, they have the following utility functions:

$$V_{PA} = -E\{(l - l^f)^2\} - hE(q^2), \quad h > 0, \tag{4.18}$$

$$V_{PA}^* = -E\{(l^* - l^{*f})^2\} - hE(q^{*2}), \tag{4.19}$$

where h, which is a constant not expressed in the log, reflects the relative weight assigned by the monetary authorities to the CPI as against employment. Equations (4.18) and (4.19) imply that monetary authorities dislike deviations of the actual levels of employment from the effective labor forces, i.e., unemployment, and changes in the consumer price index. The above-mentioned equations can be rewritten as the functions of means and variances of both unemployment and the CPI.

$$V_{PA} = -\{E(l - l^f)\}^2 - h(Eq)^2 - \mathrm{Var}(l - l^f) - h\,\mathrm{Var}(q) \tag{4.18'}$$

$$V_{PA}^* = -\{E(l^* - l^{*f})\}^2 - h(Eq^*)^2 - \mathrm{Var}(l^* - l^{*f}) - h\,\mathrm{Var}(q^*) \tag{4.19'}$$

In the case of two independent monetary authorities, we focus our analysis on the inter-government monetary cooperation regime, where the monetary authorities of the home and foreign countries manipulate the stock of the two countries' currencies in such a manner that the sum of their utilities is maximized.

On the other hand, if the two countries form a monetary union and have a single monetary authority, the monetary authority's utility function is $V_{PA} + V_{PA}^*$ and the monetary authority attempts to maximize it by controlling the stock of a common currency.

4.3. The Economy Under Certainty

In this section, we assume a two-country economy without any shocks, i.e., u, u^*, v, and v^* are zero, and we compare the utilities of the monetary authority and the workers under inter-government monetary cooperation and a monetary union.

Since the two-country economy is not subjected to any shocks, the utility functions of the monetary authorities (Eqs. (4.18) and (4.19)) under inter-government monetary cooperation can be rewritten as,

$$V_{PA} = -(l - l^f)^2 - hq^2,$$
$$V_{PA}^* = -(l^* - l^{*f})^2 - hq^{*2}.$$

Under inter-government monetary cooperation, as mentioned before, since each country has a money market, the money markets in the home and foreign countries without demand shocks are in equilibrium if the following conditions are satisfied:

$$m = p + y, \quad m^* = p^* + y^*, \tag{4.20}$$

where m and m^* denote the home and foreign countries' money stocks under the two independent monetary authorities.

Structural equations under inter-government monetary cooperation, i.e., Eqs. (4.1)–(4.6) and (4.20), where $u, u^*, v, v^* = 0$, can be solved for l, l^*, y, y^*, p, p^*, z, q, q^*, w_c, and w_c^* as functions of w, m, and m^*.

$$l = m - w + \ln a \tag{4.21}$$

$$l^* = m^* - w + \ln a \tag{4.22}$$

$$y = a(m - w) + a \ln a \tag{4.23}$$

$$y^* = a(m^* - w) + a \ln a \tag{4.24}$$

$$p = (1 - a)m + aw - a \ln a \tag{4.25}$$

$$p^* = (1 - a)m^* + aw - a \ln a \tag{4.26}$$

$$z = \frac{a}{b}(m - m^*) \tag{4.27}$$

$$q = \left(1 - a + \frac{ac}{b}\right)m - \frac{ac}{b}m^* + aw - a \ln a \tag{4.28}$$

$$q^* = \left(1 - a + \frac{ac}{b}\right)m^* - \frac{ac}{b}m + aw - a\ln a \qquad (4.29)$$

$$w_c = -\left(1 - a + \frac{ac}{b}\right)m + \frac{ac}{b}m^* + (1-a)w + a\ln a \qquad (4.30)$$

$$w_c^* = -\left(1 - a + \frac{ac}{b}\right)m^* + \frac{ac}{b}m + (1-a)w + a\ln a \qquad (4.31)$$

Since the monetary authorities in the two countries cooperate with each other, they will set their money stocks such that the sum of their utilities is maximized, i.e., they will solve, $\max_{m,m^*} V_{PA} + V_{PA}^*$ subject to Eqs. (4.21), (4.8), (4.30), (4.31), (4.28), (4.22), (4.9), and (4.29).

The first order conditions imply that $m = m^*$. This gives us the following relation between the CPI and unemployment:

$$q = -\frac{1}{h(1-a)}(l - l^f) \qquad (4.32)$$

Utilizing Eq. (4.32), the money stocks under inter-government monetary cooperation without any shocks are derived as follows:

$$m = m^* = \frac{\{1 - ah(1-a)\}(1 + r/\rho)\ln e + h(1-a)a\ln a}{1 + h(1-a)^2}$$

$$(\equiv m^{IGC}\big|_{u,u^*,v,v^*=0}) \qquad (4.33)$$

Equation (4.33) shows that the money stocks do not depend on the sensitivity of migration flows to changes in the expected real-consumption wage differentials. This is because the monetary authorities are aware of the fact that the influence of a domestic monetary expansion for reducing unemployment through the induced fall in the effective labor force will be offset by an equal expansion abroad. Accordingly, the monetary authorities do not utilize monetary expansions to induce migration flows and thereby to reduce unemployment. Therefore, as suggested by Agiomirgianakis (1998), macro-economic interdependence through migration flows is not operative.

Unemployment and the CPI are given as follows:

$$l - l^f = l^* - l^{*f}$$

$$= \frac{h(1-a)\{-(1 + r/\rho)\ln e + a\ln a\}}{1 + h(1-a)^2}(\equiv [l - l^f]^{IGC}\big|_{u,u^*,v,v^*=0}), \quad (4.34)$$

$$q = q^* = -\frac{-(1 + r/\rho)\ln e + a\ln a}{1 + h(1-a)^2}(\equiv q^{IGC}\big|_{u,u^*,v,v^*=0}). \qquad (4.35)$$

The utilities of the monetary authority and the employed workers under inter-government monetary cooperation without any shocks can be calculated by substituting Eqs. (4.34) and (4.35) into Eqs. (4.15), (4.17), (4.18), and (4.19).

Under a monetary union, as mentioned before, since the two countries have a common money market, the money market without demand shocks is in equilibrium if the following condition is satisfied:

$$m^{MU} = p + y + p^* + y^* \qquad (4.36)$$

where m^{MU} denotes the money stock under a monetary union.

Through appropriate substitutions, the model of Eqs. (4.1)–(4.6) and (4.36), where $ex = 0$ and u, u^*, v, $v^* = 0$, can be solved for l, l^*, y, y^*, p, p^*, z, q, q^*, w_c, and w_c^* as functions of w and m^{MU}.

$$l = l^* = \frac{m^{MU}}{2} - w + \ln a \qquad (4.37)$$

$$y = y^* = \frac{a}{2} m^{MU} - aw + a \ln a \qquad (4.38)$$

$$p = p^* = q = q^* = \frac{1-a}{2} m^{MU} + aw - a \ln a \qquad (4.39)$$

$$z = 0 \qquad (4.40)$$

$$w_c = w_c^* = -\frac{1-a}{2} m^{MU} + (1-a)w + a \ln a \qquad (4.41)$$

If the two-country economy is not affected by any shocks, the difference in the two countries' national products depends only on the difference in the two countries' product prices, as suggested by Eqs. (4.1) and (4.2), since nominal wages are the same in the two countries. This implies that even under a monetary union, the product prices and thereby the national products are the same in the two countries, since, in Eq. (4.4) with $ex = 0$, both the difference in the two countries' national products (the left-hand side) and the real exchange rate (the right-hand side) depend only on the difference in the two countries' product prices. Consequently, the two countries have the same money demand, suggesting that the right-hand side of Eq. (4.36) can be rewritten as $2(p + y)$. In addition, the money stock under a monetary union m^{MU} is equivalent to the sum of the two countries' money stocks under inter-government monetary cooperation, i.e., $m + m^*(= 2m)$. As a result, the money market equilibrium condition under a monetary union can be rewritten as $2m = 2(p + y)$. This implies that the money market equilibrium condition under a monetary union is virtually the same as the one under inter-government monetary cooperation. Therefore, under certainty, we have virtually the same structural equations and thereby the same reduced form equations in the two regimes.

The monetary authority, i.e., the common monetary authority of the two countries, manipulates the money stock in such a way as to maximize $V_{PA} + V_{PA}^*$, i.e., the countries will solve, $\max_{m^{MU}} V_{PA} + V_{PA}^*$ subject to Eqs. (4.8), (4.9), (4.37), (4.39), and (4.41).

The first order condition gives us the following relation between the CPI and unemployment:

$$q = -\frac{1}{h(1-a)}(l - l^f) \tag{4.42}$$

Equations (4.32) and (4.42) suggest that the CPI and unemployment are in the same relation under both inter-government monetary cooperation and a monetary union. This is because, as explained before, the structural equations and the utility function under a monetary union are virtually the same as those under two independent monetary authorities.

Utilizing Eq. (4.42), the money stock under a monetary union without any shocks is derived as follows:

$$m^{MU} = \frac{2[\{1 - ah(1-a)\}(1 + r/\rho)\ln e + h(1-a)a\ln a]}{1 + h(1-a)^2}(\equiv m^{MU}|_{u,u^*,v,v^*=0}) \tag{4.43}$$

Equation (4.43) suggests that the money stock does not depend on d. This is because the monetary authority does not utilize monetary policies to induce migration flows and thereby to reduce unemployment. Therefore, macro-economic interdependence through migration flows is not operative under a monetary union.

Unemployment and the CPI are given as follows:

$$\begin{aligned} l - l^f &= l^* - l^{*f} \\ &= \frac{h(1-a)\{-(1 + r/\rho)\ln e + a\ln a\}}{1 + h(1-a)^2}(\equiv [l - l^f]^{MU}|_{u,u^*,v,v^*=0}), \quad (4.44) \end{aligned}$$

$$q = q^* = -\frac{-(1 + r/\rho)\ln e + a\ln a}{1 + h(1-a)^2}(\equiv q^{MU}|_{u,u^*,v,v^*=0}). \tag{4.45}$$

Equations (4.34), (4.35), (4.44), and (4.45) suggest that, without any shocks, there is no difference between inter-government monetary cooperation and a monetary union with respect to unemployment and the CPI.

This implies that,

$$V_{PA}^{IGC}|_{u,u^*,v,v^*=0} = V_{PA}^{*IGC}|_{u,u^*,v,v^*=0} = V_{PA}^{MU}|_{u,u^*,v,v^*=0} = V_{PA}^{*MU}|_{u,u^*,v,v^*=0},$$

$$V_{E}^{IGC}|_{u,u^*,v,v^*=0} = V_{E}^{*IGC}|_{u,u^*,v,v^*=0} = V_{E}^{MU}|_{u,u^*,v,v^*=0} = V_{E}^{*MU}|_{u,u^*,v,v^*=0}.$$

Therefore, $V_{PA} + V_{PA}^*$ and the utilities of the employed and unemployed workers do not differ under inter-government monetary cooperation and a monetary union. In other words, under certainty, the monetary authorities and all the workers can attain the same utility in either regime.

This result can be explained as follows: since the economic structures of the two countries are symmetric in either regime, they have virtually the same economic structure in the two regimes under certainty, regardless of whether each country has a money market or the two countries have a common money market. Moreover, even if each country has an independent monetary authority, by cooperating with each other, the two countries can eliminate the negative effects on the utilities of the monetary authority and the workers arising from macro-economic interdependence through migration flows, i.e., the higher CPI due to the monetary expansion to induce migration flows and thereby to reduce unemployment. This enables the monetary authority and the workers under inter-government monetary cooperation to achieve the same utilities as those achieved under a monetary union.

4.4. The Economy Under Supply Shocks

In this section, the two-country economy is assumed to be subject to supply shocks, i.e., $u, u^* \neq 0$, $v, v^* = 0$, and we compare the utilities of the monetary authority and the workers under inter-government monetary cooperation and a monetary union.

Structural equations in the inter-government monetary cooperation regime under supply shocks, i.e., Eqs. (4.1)–(4.6) and (4.20), where $u, u^* \neq 0$ and $v, v^* = 0$, can be solved for $l, l^*, y, y^*, p, p^*, z, q, q^*, w_c$, and w_c^* as functions of w, m, and m^*.

$$l = m - w + \ln a \tag{4.46}$$

$$l^* = m^* - w + \ln a \tag{4.47}$$

$$y = a(m - w) + a \ln a + u \tag{4.48}$$

$$y^* = a(m^* - w) + a \ln a + u^* \tag{4.49}$$

$$p = (1 - a)m + aw - a \ln a - u \tag{4.50}$$

$$p^* = (1 - a)m^* + aw - a \ln a - u^* \tag{4.51}$$

$$z = \frac{a}{b}(m - m^*) + \frac{1}{b}(u - u^*) \tag{4.52}$$

$$q = \left(1 - a + \frac{ac}{b}\right)m - \frac{ac}{b}m^* + aw - a \ln a + \left(-1 + \frac{c}{b}\right)u - \frac{c}{b}u^* \tag{4.53}$$

$$q^* = \left(1 - a + \frac{ac}{b}\right)m^* - \frac{ac}{b}m + aw - a \ln a + \left(-1 + \frac{c}{b}\right)u^* - \frac{c}{b}u \tag{4.54}$$

$$w_c = -\left(1 - a + \frac{ac}{b}\right)m + \frac{ac}{b}m^* + (1-a)w + a\ln a - \left(-1 + \frac{c}{b}\right)u + \frac{c}{b}u^*$$
(4.55)

$$w_c^* = -\left(1 - a + \frac{ac}{b}\right)m^* + \frac{ac}{b}m + (1-a)w + a\ln a - \left(-1 + \frac{c}{b}\right)u^* + \frac{c}{b}u$$
(4.56)

Equations (4.46), (4.47), (4.55), and (4.56) as well as (4.21), (4.22), (4.30), and (4.31) suggest that the expectation of unemployment under supply shocks is equal to that of unemployment under certainty. Similarly, Eqs. (4.53) and (4.54) as well as (4.28) and (4.29) suggest that the expectation of the CPI under supply shocks is equal to that of the CPI under certainty. Moreover, the variances of unemployment and the CPI are independent of the money stocks. Therefore, Eqs. (4.18′) and (4.19′) suggest that utility maximization in the inter-government monetary cooperation regime under supply shocks gives us the same money stocks as those under certainty (Eq. 4.33).

This implies that,

$$[-\{E(l - l^f)\}^2]^{IGC}\Big|_{u,u^* \neq 0, v, v^* = 0} - [h(Eq)^2]^{IGC}\Big|_{u,u^* \neq 0, v, v^* = 0}$$

$$= V_{PA}^{IGC}\Big|_{u,u^*, v, v^* = 0},$$
(4.57)

$$[-\{E(l^* - l^{*f})\}^2]^{IGC}\Big|_{u,u^* \neq 0, v, v^* = 0} - [h(Eq^*)^2]^{IGC}\Big|_{u,u^* \neq 0, v, v^* = 0}$$

$$= V_{PA}^{*IGC}\Big|_{u,u^*, v, v^* = 0}.$$
(4.58)

On the other hand, the variances of unemployment and the CPI under supply shocks are as follows:

$$\mathrm{Var}(l - l^f)^{IGC}\Big|_{u,u^* \neq 0, v, v^* = 0} = \mathrm{Var}(l^* - l^{*f})^{IGC}\Big|_{u,u^* \neq 0, v, v^* = 0} = 0, \quad (4.59)$$

$$\mathrm{Var}(q)^{IGC}\Big|_{u,u^* \neq 0, v, v^* = 0} = \mathrm{Var}(q^*)^{IGC}\Big|_{u,u^* \neq 0, v, v^* = 0} = \left\{\left(-1 + \frac{c}{b}\right)^2 + \left(\frac{c}{b}\right)^2\right\}\sigma_u^2.$$
(4.60)

The utility of the monetary authority can be calculated by substituting Eqs. (4.57), (4.58), (4.59), and (4.60) into Eqs. (4.18′) and (4.19′); the utility of the employed workers can be calculated by substituting Eqs. (4.53) and (4.54) into Eqs. (4.15) and (4.17).

Structural equations under a monetary union, i.e., Eqs. (4.1)–(4.6) and (4.36), where $ex = 0$, $u, u^* \neq 0$ and $v, v^* = 0$, can be solved for $l, l^*, y, y^*, p, p^*, z, q, q^*, w_c$, and w_c^* as functions of w, m, and m^*.

$$l = \frac{m^{MU}}{2} - w + \ln a + \frac{1}{2(1-a)}\left\{1 - \frac{1}{a + b(1-a)}\right\}(u - u^*) \quad (4.61)$$

$$l^* = \frac{m^{MU}}{2} - w + \ln a + \frac{1}{2(1-a)}\left\{1 - \frac{1}{a+b(1-a)}\right\}(u^* - u) \quad (4.62)$$

$$y = \frac{a}{2}m^{MU} - aw + a\ln a + \left\{-\frac{a}{2(1-a)}\frac{1}{a+b(1-a)} + \frac{1-1/a}{1-a}\right\}u$$
$$-\frac{a}{2(1-a)}\left\{1 - \frac{1}{a+b(1-a)}\right\}u^* \quad (4.63)$$

$$y^* = \frac{a}{2}m^{MU} - aw + a\ln a + \left\{-\frac{a}{2(1-a)}\frac{1}{a+b(1-a)} + \frac{1-1/a}{1-a}\right\}u^*$$
$$-\frac{a}{2(1-a)}\left\{1 - \frac{1}{a+b(1-a)}\right\}u \quad (4.64)$$

$$p = \frac{1-a}{2}m^{MU} + aw - a\ln a - \frac{1}{2}\left\{\frac{1}{a+b(1-a)} + 1\right\}u$$
$$-\frac{1}{2}\left\{-\frac{1}{a+b(1-a)} + 1\right\}u^* \quad (4.65)$$

$$p^* = \frac{1-a}{2}m^{MU} + aw - a\ln a - \frac{1}{2}\left\{\frac{1}{a+b(1-a)} + 1\right\}u^*$$
$$-\frac{1}{2}\left\{-\frac{1}{a+b(1-a)} + 1\right\}u \quad (4.66)$$

$$z = \frac{1}{a+b(1-a)}(u - u^*) \quad (4.67)$$

$$q = \frac{1-a}{2}m^{MU} + aw - a\ln a - \frac{1}{2}\left\{\frac{1-2c}{a+b(1-a)} + 1\right\}u$$
$$-\frac{1}{2}\left\{-\frac{1-2c}{a+b(1-a)} + 1\right\}u^* \quad (4.68)$$

$$q^* = \frac{1-a}{2}m^{MU} + aw - a\ln a - \frac{1}{2}\left\{\frac{1-2c}{a+b(1-a)} + 1\right\}u^*$$
$$-\frac{1}{2}\left\{-\frac{1-2c}{a+b(1-a)} + 1\right\}u \quad (4.69)$$

$$w_c = -\frac{1-a}{2}m^{MU} + (1-a)w + a\ln a + \frac{1}{2}\left\{\frac{1-2c}{a+b(1-a)} + 1\right\}u$$
$$+\frac{1}{2}\left\{-\frac{1-2c}{a+b(1-a)} + 1\right\}u^* \quad (4.70)$$

$$w_c^* = -\frac{1-a}{2}m^{MU} + (1-a)w + a\ln a + \frac{1}{2}\left\{\frac{1-2c}{a+b(1-a)}+1\right\}u^*$$

$$+\frac{1}{2}\left\{-\frac{1-2c}{a+b(1-a)}+1\right\}u \qquad (4.71)$$

If a two-country economy is affected by supply shocks, reduced form equations under a monetary union are different from those under inter-government monetary cooperation. This is because the money market equilibrium conditions are not affected by supply shocks under inter-government monetary cooperation (Eqs. (4.48) and (4.50)), whereas the money market equilibrium condition is affected by supply shocks under a monetary union (Eqs. (4.63) and (4.65)). This implies that the money market equilibrium condition under a monetary union is different from the one under inter-government monetary cooperation, making the economic structures different in the two regimes.

However, Eqs. (4.61), (4.62), (4.68), (4.69), (4.70), and (4.71) imply that the expectations of unemployment and the CPI under supply shocks are equal to those of unemployment and the CPI under certainty. In addition, variances of unemployment and the CPI do not depend on the money stock. Accordingly, Eqs. (4.18′) and (4.19′) suggest that utility maximization by the monetary authority gives us the same money stock as that under certainty (Eq. 4.43). Therefore, the sum of the first and second terms of Eqs. (4.18′) and (4.19′) under supply shocks is equal to $V_{PA}^{MU}\big|_{u,u^*,v,v^*=0}$ ($V_{PA}^{*MU}\big|_{u,u^*,v,v^*=0}$).

On the other hand, the variances of unemployment and the CPI under supply shocks are as follows:

$$\text{Var}(l-l^f)^{MU}\big|_{u,u^*\neq 0,v,v^*=0} = \text{Var}(l^*-l^{*f})^{MU}\big|_{u,u^*\neq 0,v,v^*=0}$$

$$= \frac{(1-b)^2}{2\{a+b(1-a)\}^2}\sigma_u^2, \qquad (4.72)$$

$$\text{Var}(q)^{MU}\big|_{u,u^*\neq 0,v,v^*=0} = \text{Var}(q^*)^{MU}\big|_{u,u^*\neq 0,v,v^*=0}$$

$$= \frac{1}{2}\left[\left\{\frac{1-2c}{a+b(1-a)}\right\}^2+1\right]\sigma_u^2. \qquad (4.73)$$

The utility of the monetary authority can be calculated by utilizing $V_{PA}^{MU}\big|_{u,u^*,v,v^*=0}$, $V_{PA}^{*MU}\big|_{u,u^*,v,v^*=0}$, Eqs. (4.72) and (4.73); the utility of the employed workers can be calculated by substituting Eqs. (4.68) and (4.69) into Eqs. (4.15) and (4.17).

According to Eqs. (4.59) and (4.72),

$$\text{Var}(l-l^f)^{IGC}\big|_{u,u^*\neq 0,v,v^*=0} = \text{Var}(l^*-l^{*f})^{IGC}\big|_{u,u^*\neq 0,v,v^*=0}$$

$$< \text{Var}(l-l^f)^{MU}\big|_{u,u^*\neq 0,v,v^*=0} = \text{Var}(l^*-l^{*f})^{MU}\big|_{u,u^*\neq 0,v,v^*=0}.$$

We can explain this as follows: in either regime, the effective labor forces are not stochastic. Under inter-government monetary cooperation, the direct effects of supply shocks on labor demand and the indirect effects of the supply shocks on labor demand — which take place through the product price — offset each other, thereby making employment non-stochastic, as shown by Eqs. (4.46) and (4.47). On the other hand, under a monetary union, the domestic supply shocks directly affect the domestic labor demand. Moreover, as Eqs. (4.65) and (4.66) show, not only the domestic but also the foreign supply shocks indirectly affect the domestic labor demand through the product price. This is because the two countries have a common money market. The direct and indirect effects of the supply shocks on the labor demand do not offset each other, thereby making employment stochastic under a monetary union (Eqs. (4.61) and (4.62)).

According to Eqs. (4.60) and (4.73),

$$\text{Var}(q)^{IGC}\big|_{u,u^* \neq 0, v, v^*=0} = \text{Var}(q^*)^{IGC}\big|_{u,u^* \neq 0, v, v^*=0}$$

$$> \text{Var}(q)^{MU}\big|_{u,u^* \neq 0, v, v^*=0} = \text{Var}(q^*)^{MU}\big|_{u,u^* \neq 0, v, v^*=0}.$$

The above equations can be explained as follows: supply shocks affect the consumer price index through the product price and the real exchange rate. Equations (4.50) and (4.51) as well as Eqs. (4.65) and (4.66) show that the effects of supply shocks on the product price under inter-government monetary cooperation are stronger than those under a monetary union. On the other hand, Eqs. (4.52) and (4.67) show that the effects of supply shocks on the real exchange rate under a monetary union are stronger than those under inter-government monetary cooperation. Since the effects of the supply shocks on the CPI through the product price are stronger than those through the real exchange rate, the CPI has a larger variance under inter-government monetary cooperation than under a monetary union.

Therefore, if h is large and the effects of the larger variance of the CPI under inter-government monetary cooperation dominate, $V_{PA} + V_{PA}^*$ may be larger under a monetary union than under inter-government monetary cooperation. However, if h is small and the effects of the larger variance of unemployment under a monetary union dominate, $V_{PA} + V_{PA}^*$ may be larger under inter-government monetary cooperation than under a monetary union.

In other words, under supply shocks, a monetary union may prove to be advantageous to the monetary authority if it gives greater importance to the stability of the CPI, whereas inter-government monetary cooperation may prove to be advantageous to the monetary authority if it gives greater importance to the reduction of unemployment.

This result can be explained as follows: even in the presence of supply shocks, cooperation between the two independent monetary authorities makes it possible for them to eliminate the negative effects arising from the possibility of labor migration between the two countries and macro-economic interdependence.

However, if the two countries are affected by supply shocks and greater importance is given to the stability of the CPI, negative effects on the inter-government monetary cooperation regime due to supply shocks will outweigh the positive effects due to cooperation. This will lead to a lower utility of the monetary authority under inter-government monetary cooperation.

Since the expectations of the CPI under supply shocks do not differ across regimes, the utilities of the employed and unemployed workers take the same values under both inter-government monetary cooperation and a monetary union.

These results have the following implications: in the presence of supply shocks, whether the two countries should form a monetary union or should remain independent and cooperate in the conduct of the monetary policy depends on how much importance is given to the stability of the CPI. If the two countries give substantial importance to the stability of the CPI, it would be preferable for them to form a monetary union.

4.5. The Economy Under Demand Shocks

In this section, the two-country economy is assumed to be subject to demand shocks, i.e., $u, u^* = 0$, $v, v^* \neq 0$, and we compare the utilities of the monetary authority and the workers under inter-government monetary cooperation and a monetary union.

Structural equations in the inter-government monetary cooperation regime under demand shocks, i.e., Eqs. (4.1)–(4.6), and the money market equilibrium conditions $m = p + y + v$ and $m^* = p^* + y^* + v^*$, where $u, u^* = 0$ and $v, v^* \neq 0$, can be solved for $l, l^*, y, y^*, p, p^*, z, q, q^*, w_c$, and w_c^* as functions of w, m, and m^*.

$$l = m - w + \ln a - v \tag{4.74}$$

$$l^* = m^* - w + \ln a - v^* \tag{4.75}$$

$$y = a(m - w) + a \ln a - av \tag{4.76}$$

$$y^* = a(m^* - w) + a \ln a - av^* \tag{4.77}$$

$$p = (1 - a)m + aw - a \ln a - (1 - a)v \tag{4.78}$$

$$p^* = (1 - a)m^* + aw - a \ln a - (1 - a)v^* \tag{4.79}$$

$$z = \frac{a}{b}(m - m^*) - \frac{a}{b}(v - v^*) \tag{4.80}$$

$$q = \left(1 - a + \frac{ac}{b}\right)m - \frac{ac}{b}m^* + aw$$
$$- a \ln a - \left(1 - a + \frac{c}{b}\right)v + \frac{ac}{b}v^* \tag{4.81}$$

$$q^* = \left(1 - a + \frac{ac}{b}\right) m^* - \frac{ac}{b} m + aw$$

$$- a \ln a - \left(1 - a + \frac{c}{b}\right) v^* + \frac{ac}{b} v \qquad (4.82)$$

$$w_c = - \left(1 - a + \frac{ac}{b}\right) m + \frac{ac}{b} m^* + (1 - a)w$$

$$+ a \ln a + \left(1 - a + \frac{c}{b}\right) v - \frac{ac}{b} v^* \qquad (4.83)$$

$$w_c^* = - \left(1 - a + \frac{ac}{b}\right) m^* + \frac{ac}{b} m + (1 - a)w$$

$$+ a \ln a + \left(1 - a + \frac{c}{b}\right) v^* - \frac{ac}{b} v \qquad (4.84)$$

According to Eqs. (4.74), (4.75), (4.83), and (4.84) as well as Eqs. (4.21), (4.22), (4.30), and (4.31), the expectation of unemployment under demand shocks is equal to that of unemployment under certainty. Similarly, according to Eqs. (4.81) and (4.82) as well as (4.28) and (4.29), the expectation of the CPI under demand shocks is equal to that of the CPI under certainty. Moreover, the variances of unemployment and the CPI are independent of the money stocks. Therefore, as under supply shocks, Eqs. (4.18′) and (4.19′) suggest that utility maximization in the inter-government monetary cooperation regime under demand shocks gives us the same money stocks as those under certainty (Eq. 4.33).

This implies that,

$$[-\{E(l - l^f)\}^2]^{IGC}\Big|_{u,u^*=0,v,v^*\neq0} - [h(Eq)^2]^{IGC}\Big|_{u,u^*=0,v,v^*\neq0}$$

$$= V_{PA}^{IGC}\Big|_{u,u^*,v,v^*=0}, \qquad (4.85)$$

$$[-\{E(l^* - l^{*f})\}^2]^{IGC}\Big|_{u,u^*=0,v,v^*\neq0} - [h(Eq^*)^2]^{IGC}\Big|_{u,u^*=0,v,v^*\neq0}$$

$$= V_{PA}^{*IGC}\Big|_{u,u^*,v,v^*=0}. \qquad (4.86)$$

On the other hand, the variances of unemployment and the CPI under demand shocks are as follows:

$$\text{Var}(l - l^f)^{IGC}\Big|_{u,u^*=0,v,v^*\neq0} = \text{Var}(l^* - l^{*f})^{IGC}\Big|_{u,u^*=0,v,v^*\neq0} = \sigma_v^2, \quad (4.87)$$

$$\text{Var}(q)^{IGC}\Big|_{u,u^*=0,v,v^*\neq0} = \text{Var}(q^*)^{IGC}\Big|_{u,u^*=0,v,v^*\neq0}$$

$$= \left\{\left(1 - a + \frac{ac}{b}\right)^2 + \left(\frac{ac}{b}\right)^2\right\} \sigma_v^2. \qquad (4.88)$$

The utility of the monetary authority can be calculated by substituting Eqs. (4.85), (4.86), (4.87), and (4.88) into Eqs. (4.18′) and (4.19′); the utility of the employed workers can be calculated by substituting Eqs. (4.81) and (4.82) into Eqs. (4.15) and (4.17).

Structural equations under a monetary union, i.e., (4.1)–(4.6), and the money market equilibrium condition $m^{MU} = p + y + v + p^* + y^* + v^*$, where $ex = 0$, $u, u^* = 0$ and $v, v^* \neq 0$, can be solved for $l, l^*, y, y^*, p, p^*, z, q, q^*, w_c$, and w_c^* as functions of w, m, and m^*.

$$l = l^* = \frac{m^{MU}}{2} - w + \ln a - \frac{v + v^*}{2} \qquad (4.89)$$

$$y = y^* = \frac{a}{2} m^{MU} - aw + a \ln a - \frac{a}{2}(v + v^*) \qquad (4.90)$$

$$p = p^* = q = q^* = \frac{1-a}{2} m^{MU} + aw - a \ln a - \frac{1-a}{2}(v + v^*) \qquad (4.91)$$

$$z = 0 \qquad (4.92)$$

$$w_c = w_c^* = -\frac{1-a}{2} m^{MU} + (1-a)w + a \ln a + \frac{1-a}{2}(v + v^*) \qquad (4.93)$$

If the two-country economy is affected by demand shocks, the reduced form equations under a monetary union are different from those under inter-government monetary cooperation. This is because the product prices and the national products in the two countries are the same under a monetary union (Eqs. (4.91) and (4.92)), whereas they are different in the two countries under inter-government monetary cooperation (Eqs. (4.78), (4.79), (4.76), and (4.77)). As a result, the money market equilibrium conditions are different in the two regimes, making the structural equations and thereby the reduced form equations different under the two regimes.

However, Eqs. (4.89), (4.91), and (4.93) imply that the expectations of unemployment and the CPI under supply shocks are equal to those of unemployment and the CPI under certainty. In addition, the variances of unemployment and the CPI do not depend on the money stock. Accordingly, as under supply shocks, Eqs. (4.18′) and (4.19′) suggest that utility maximization by the monetary authority gives us the same money stock as that under certainty (Eq. 4.43). Therefore, the sum of the first and second terms of Eqs. (4.18′) and (4.19′) under demand shocks equals $V_{PA}^{MU}|_{u,u^*,v,v^*=0}$ ($V_{PA}^{*MU}|_{u,u^*,v,v^*=0}$).

On the other hand, the variances of unemployment and the CPI under demand shocks are as follows:

$$\mathrm{Var}(l - l^f)^{MU}\Big|_{u,u^*=0,v,v^* \neq 0} = \mathrm{Var}(l^* - l^{*f})^{MU}\Big|_{u,u^*=0,v,v^* \neq 0} = \frac{\sigma_v^2}{2}, \qquad (4.94)$$

$$\mathrm{Var}(q)^{MU}\Big|_{u,u^*=0,v,v^* \neq 0} = \mathrm{Var}(q^*)^{MU}\Big|_{u,u^*=0,v,v^* \neq 0} = \frac{(1-a)^2}{2}\sigma_v^2. \qquad (4.95)$$

According to Eqs. (4.87) and (4.94),

$$\text{Var}(l - l^f)^{IGC}\big|_{u,u^*=0,v,v^*\neq0} = \text{Var}(l^* - l^{*f})^{IGC}\big|_{u,u^*=0,v,v^*\neq0}$$
$$> \text{Var}(l - l^f)^{MU}\big|_{u,u^*=0,v,v^*\neq0} = \text{Var}(l^* - l^{*f})^{MU}\big|_{u,u^*=0,v,v^*\neq0}.$$

We can explain this as follows: under inter-government monetary cooperation, since each country has its own money market and demand shocks affect employment indirectly through the product price, only domestic demand shocks affect the product price and thereby employment. On the other hand, under a monetary union, since the two countries have a common money market, not only domestic but also foreign demand shocks affect the product price, making employment subject to domestic and foreign demand shocks. However, the effects of demand shocks on employment are weaker under a monetary union than under inter-government monetary cooperation. Moreover, as mentioned before, the effective labor forces are not stochastic in either regime. This implies that the variance of unemployment is larger under inter-government monetary cooperation than under a monetary union.

According to Eqs. (4.88) and (4.95),

$$\text{Var}(q)^{IGC}\big|_{u,u^*=0,v,v^*\neq0} = \text{Var}(q^*)^{IGC}\big|_{u,u^*=0,v,v^*\neq0}$$
$$> \text{Var}(q)^{MU}\big|_{u,u^*=0,v,v^*\neq0} = \text{Var}(q^*)^{MU}\big|_{u,u^*=0,v,v^*\neq0}.$$

The above equations can be explained as follows: under inter-government monetary cooperation, demand shocks affect the CPI through the product price and the real exchange rate, as can be seen by Eqs. (4.78), (4.79), and (4.80). On the other hand, as Eqs. (4.91) and (4.92) show, under a monetary union, demand shocks affect the CPI only through the product price. Since the effects of demand shocks on the CPI are stronger under inter-government monetary cooperation, the variance of the CPI is larger under this regime.

Therefore, $V_{PA} + V_{PA}^*$ is larger under a monetary union than under inter-government monetary cooperation. In other words, when the two-country economy is subject to demand shocks, a monetary union is always advantageous to the monetary authority.

This can be explained as follows: as explained in the cases of certainty and supply shocks, even if the monetary authorities are independent, cooperation between them increases their utilities. However, under demand shocks, these positive effects are always smaller than the negative effects arising from demand shocks, i.e., the larger variances of unemployment and the CPI. This implies that a monetary union is advantageous to the monetary authority.

Since the expectations of the CPI under the demand shocks are the same in both the regimes, despite being affected by demand shocks, the utilities of the employed and unemployed workers are the same under both inter-government monetary cooperation and a monetary union.

The result in this section suggests that it would be preferable for the two countries to form a monetary union if they are affected by demand shocks.

4.6. Conclusions

Using a two-country macro-economic model with international migration of labor and efficiency wages, we compared the utilities of the monetary authority and the workers under the regimes of inter-government monetary cooperation and a monetary union, assuming that the two countries may be affected by supply or demand shocks.

We showed that under certainty, there is no difference in the utility of the monetary authority between both regimes; whereas, under supply or demand shocks, centralization of the monetary policies by a single monetary authority under a monetary union may prove to be advantageous to the monetary authority. We also showed that the utility of the workers is the same in both the regimes not only under certainty but also under supply or demand shocks.

Our results imply that the question of whether or not countries should form a monetary union is dependent on the existence or non-existence of shocks, and that if the countries are subject to supply or demand shocks, which is very likely in actual economies, it would be preferable for them to form a monetary union and centralize their monetary policies.

References

Agiomirgianakis, GM (1998). Monetary policy games and international migration of labor in interdependent economies. *Journal of Macroeconomics*, 20, 243–266.

Agiomirgianakis, GM and A Zervoyianni (2001a). Macroeconomic equilibrium with illegal immigration. *Economic Modelling*, 18, 181–202.

Agiomirgianakis, GM and A Zervoyianni (2001b). Economic growth, international labour mobility, and unanticipated non-monetary shocks. *Journal of Policy Modeling*, 23, 1–16.

Canzoneri, MB and DW Henderson (1988). Is sovereign policymaking bad? *Carnegie-Rochester Conference Series on Public Policy*, 28, 93–140.

Canzoneri, MB and DW Henderson (1991). *Monetary Policy in Interdependent Economies: A Game-Theoretic Approach*, Cambridge: MIT Press.

Cooley, TF and V Quadrini (2003). Common currencies vs. monetary independence. *Review of Economic Studies*, 70, 785–806.

Hamada, K (1976). A strategic analysis of monetary interdependence. *Journal of Political Economy*, 84, 677–700.

Jensen, H (1993). International monetary policy cooperation in economies with centralized wage setting. *Open Economies Review*, 4, 269–285.

Lewis, KK (1989). On occasional monetary policy coordinations that fix the exchange rate. *Journal of International Economics*, 26, 139–155.

Oudiz, G and J Sachs (1984). Macroeconomic policy coordination among the industrial economies. *Brookings Papers on Economic Activity*, 1, 1–64.

Pappa, E (2004). Do the ECB and the fed really need to cooperate? Optimal monetary policy in a two-country world. *Journal of Monetary Economics*, 51, 753–779.

Rogoff, K (1985). Can international monetary cooperation be counterproductive? *Journal of International Economics*, 18, 199–217.

Shapiro, C and JE Stiglitz (1984). Equilibrium unemployment as a worker discipline device. *American Economic Review*, 74, 433–444.

Shimada, A (2004). Reducing the inflow of unskilled foreign workers. *South-Eastern Europe Journal of Economics*, 2, 85–96.

Shimada, A (2005). Foreign worker participation in labor markets and the economy's welfare. *Journal of Policy Modeling*, 27, 355–362.

Zervoyianni, A (1997). Monetary policy games and coalitions in a two-country model with unionised wage setting. *Oxford Economic Papers*, 49, 57–76.

CHAPTER 5

GETTING TOUGH WITH WORKERS: MORE ON THE STRATEGIC ROLE OF DEBT

Gerald Garvey* and Noel Gaston[†]

*Barklays global Investors, USA
† Bond University, Australia

5.1. Introduction

This paper contributes to the growing literature on the interaction between corporate financial and employment policies. A fundamental finding is due to Abowd (1989) and DeAngelo and DeAngelo (1991), who document the costs that unionized workers can impose on shareholders through collective bargaining power. Bronars and Deere (1991) and Perotti and Spier (1993) show that firms can use debt policy to reduce these costs. More specifically, the use of higher levels of debt financing effectively commit a firm's rents to third parties (i.e., the creditors) and thereby serves to protect shareholders from opportunistic rent-seeking behavior by workers. However, this work implicitly assumes that specific investments in *physical* capital are the only source of firm rents or quasi-rents, so that wage concessions are at best purely redistributive. Hence, if investments in specific *human* capital are important, wage concessions can affect the creation as well as the distribution of wealth.

Existing models predict that firms choose to carry more debt when workers can exercise bargaining power at lower cost. Since debt is an imperfect and costly way to blunt worker bargaining power, the high-debt firms will also be observed to pay higher wages. We extend these models to allow the importance of specific human capital investments, as well as bargaining power, to vary across firms. Holding bargaining power constant, firms that rely more heavily on specific human capital investments are shown to choose lower debt-equity ratios and to pay higher wages.

The choice of lower debt levels by firms encourage workers' productive investments by lowering the possibility of bankruptcy. From the workers' perspective, lower debt increases the likelihood that a firm will be able to fulfill its contractual promises.

Our model reproduces the Bronars and Deere (1991) and Perotti and Spier (1993) result that financing with senior debt commits the firm to a "tougher" bargaining position and reduces workers' negotiated wages. The basic idea is outlined by Myers (1990) who argues that employee claims on the firm are akin to subordinated debt. While it is true that issuing senior debt and paying some of the proceeds to shareholders reduces the value of a subordinated debt claim, this does not imply that firms in which such claims are large should systematically favor the use of senior debt. Rational investors will pay less for subordinated debt if they anticipate dilution by senior debt, so there is no clear overall benefit to shareholders.

The implicit assumption is that employees' claims are *not* like subordinated debt in the sense that employees do not pay for their claim or, more generally, that shareholders receive little benefit when employees have a claim on the firm's cash-flows. The extensive labor economics literature on "efficiency wages" stresses that shareholders can benefit from apparently "surplus" employee compensation when there are important non-contractible features of workers' behavior on the job (e.g., Krueger and Summers, 1988). We introduce a strategic role of debt into an efficiency wage model by relaxing this literature's implicit assumption that the firm can choose workers' lifetime wage path at the time they join the firm. Rather, all parties know that wages will inevitably be the subject of negotiation. We show that firms in which specific human capital investments are more important to profits will choose lower debt-equity ratios, thereby commiting themselves to a relatively "soft" ex post bargaining position, in order to encourage productive actions by workers.

We then present evidence on the relationship between corporate financial structure and compensation policies. Combining firm-level data from Standard and Poor's *Compustat*, with data from the Bureau of Labor Statistics and from Hirsch and Macpherson (1993), we confirm Bronars and Deere's (1991) finding that firms in more unionized industries use more debt. However, holding constant unionization and other well-known determinants of the capital structure choice, we find a *negative* relationship between debt and employee compensation. This suggests that specific human capital or incentive considerations are important to financial as well as employment policies.

The next section presents a model that brings together wage bargaining and specific human capital considerations. Section 5.2 presents the data and the empirical model we use to estimate the relationship between financial and compensation policies. Section 5.3 presents concluding observations.

5.2. The Model

5.2.1. *Permanent Assumptions*

To simplify the exposition, and to highlight the salient features of worker bargaining power and incentives, we present two stylized models of the determination of wage and financial policies. We begin with the case where there is no bargaining power in that the firm can directly choose wages at the time the worker joins the firm. We then consider the polar case where workers have all the bargaining power ex post and the firm can only affect future wage outcomes through its debt policy. Since actual worker bargaining power is a matter of degree, real-world firms will fall between these two extremes.

Both of the models we present, use the following labor contracting problem adapted from Lazear (1981). First, if the firm does not hire a representative worker, it produces nothing. If a worker is hired, the firm's expected revenues equal V. After joining the firm, the worker chooses whether or not to invest in firm-specific human capital, at the private opportunity cost of θ dollars. If the worker fails to make the investment, the firm bears a cost S in which case the worker is detected with probability one and is dismissed. Hence S parameterizes the importance of worker incentives.

To analyze both the distributional and the efficiency effects of wage policy, we restrict the workers' ability to post bonds. In particular, we make the standard assumption that the worker receives a single wage payment after investing in specific human capital and is unable to make any up-front payment to the employer at the hiring stage. This approach ensures that bargaining power is relevant and also preserves an efficiency role for outside finance, i.e., workers cannot raise enough money on their own account to fund all the firm's activities. Employees' claim on the firm is not identical to a subordinated debt claim because they do not pay the full market price for such a claim. Shareholders benefit only indirectly through an induced change in employee behavior.

Finally, debt policy is relevant because we assume that default is costly. Specifically, we assume that workers lose any wage premium in the event of financial distress. This assumption is plausible despite the fact that wages are generally senior in the event of liquidation. As Lazear (1981) stresses, worker incentives are based on *prospective* earnings, including pension benefits based on future earnings growth, which are not contractually protected. Indeed, the prospect of financial distress often motivates firms to reduce deferred employee compensation (see Ippolito and James (1992), for a summary). Our remaining notation and order of moves are as follows:

(i) The firm issues debt of face value D for a market-determined price D_0, and leaves A of the proceeds as the firm's asset base. The amount $D_0 - A$ is paid as a dividend, so an increase in D represents an increase in the firm's debt-to-assets ratio. All parties are risk-neutral, have a zero-discount rate, and agree that final cash-flows are subject to an additive shock denoted γ which has mean zero and distribution function G that satisfies the standard hazard rate condition that $g(\gamma)/(1 - G(\gamma))$ increases in γ;

(ii) A worker, with the next-best opportunity normalized at zero, is hired. Strictly speaking, the theory refers to premia above the market rate for the worker. In our empirical work, we allow the outside opportunity to vary across firms so as to isolate actual wage premia rather than simply worker scarcity. At the time the worker is hired, all parties agree that θ is distributed according to the c.d.f. $F(\theta^*) = \Pr(\theta \leq \theta^*)$ with density $f(\theta^*)$;

(iii) The worker observes θ and decides whether or not to make the human capital investment;

(iv) The worker is dismissed if the investment is not made;

(v) If not dismissed, the worker receives a wage. In the case where wages are chosen unilaterally by the firm, the wage is w_e. In the case where workers exert bargaining power, the negotiated wage is denoted w_u and

(vi) γ is realized. If the firm is solvent, bondholders receive D and the worker receives either w_e or w_u. If the firm is insolvent, bondholders receive title to the firm and neither shareholders nor the worker receive anything. The key assumption is that there are deadweight costs of bankruptcy, some of which are borne by workers (see Dasgupta and Sengupta (1993), and Perotti and Spier (1993), for alternative formulations sharing this property). To simplify this exposition, we assume that all costs are borne by workers. In the empirical section, we take account of the standard determinants of bankruptcy costs and capital structure (see Harris and Raviv (1991) for a review).

5.2.2. *Firms Unilaterally Set Wages*

We begin with the case where the firm unilaterally sets a wage w_e at stage (i) of the game when the worker joins the firm. There is no re-negotiation at stage (v). We solve the model by backward induction. At stage (vi), there are two possibilities depending on whether or not the worker made the investment in specific capital. If the investment was made, the worker receives w_e and the firm is solvent so long as γ exceeds γ_1^*, where γ_1^* solves:

$$V - w_e + A + \gamma_1^* = D \tag{5.1}$$

If the worker fails to invest, no wage is paid but the firm's revenues fall by S. Hence the firm is solvent so long as γ exceeds γ_2^* where

$$V - S + A + \gamma_2^* = D \tag{5.2}$$

Two points should be noted at this stage. First, if $S \leq w$, the firm would prefer that the worker not make the human capital investment at all since it could save on the wage payment at a cost of only S. We, therefore, assume that $S > w$ so that it is profitable for the firm to hire a worker in the first place. Second, γ_1^* is the critical value below which the firm cannot pay D, the fixed claim due at stage (vi) of the game. In the present model, wage payments to workers who make the specific human capital investment are only at risk if there are fixed senior claims to the firm's terminal cash-flows. If there are no such claims, then $G(\gamma_1^*) = 0$.

We now turn to the worker's decision of whether to invest in specific human capital at stage (iii). If the investment is made, the worker receives w_e with the probability $(1 - G(\gamma_1^*))$. If no investment is made, the worker receives a zero wage but gains θ. Hence the worker invests unless:

$$\theta > \theta_e = w_e(1 - G(\gamma_1^*)). \tag{5.3}$$

It follows from Eq. (5.3) that an increase in leverage reduces employee compensation but also disrupts the firm's labor contracting process. The two remaining inputs to the initial choice of financial structure are the worker's and the bondholders' participation constraints. Since the worker receives strictly more than zero in expected value (θ if the investment is not made and $w_e(1 - G)$ otherwise), the participation constraint does not bind. The bondholders' participation (or, equivalently, rational pricing) constraint implies that

$$D_0 = F(\theta_e) \left[D(1 - G(\gamma_1^*)) + \int_{\underline{\gamma}}^{\gamma_1^*} (V - w_e + A + \gamma) dG(\gamma) \right]$$

$$+ (1 - F(\theta_e)) \left[D(1 - G(\gamma_2^*)) + \int_{\underline{\gamma}}^{\gamma_2^*} (V - S + A + \gamma) dG(\gamma) \right] \tag{5.4}$$

Since the shareholders receive $D_0 - A$ as an up-front dividend, their objective is to choose D to maximize

$$D_0 - A + F(\theta_e) \int_{\gamma_1^*}^{\bar{\gamma}} (V - w_e + A - D + \gamma) dG(\gamma)$$

$$+ [1 - F(\theta_e)] \int_{\gamma_2^*}^{\bar{\gamma}} (V - S + A - D + \gamma) dG(\gamma) \tag{5.5}$$

Substituting Eq. (5.4) into Eq. (5.5) allows us to simplify the shareholders' objective to

$$F(\theta_e)(V - w_e) + (1 - F(\theta_e))(V - S) = V - S + F(\theta_e)(S - w_e). \tag{5.6}$$

The first-order condition for w_e is

$$(S - w_e) f(\theta_e) \frac{\partial \theta_e}{\partial w_e} - F(\theta_e) = (S - w_e) f(\theta_e) \left(1 - G(\gamma_1^*) \right) - F(\theta_e) = 0. \tag{5.7}$$

Since neither V, S, nor w_e are affected by the choice of debt, the first-order condition is

$$(S - w_e)\frac{\partial \theta_e}{\partial D} f(\theta_e) = -(S - w_e)w_e g(\gamma_1^*) f(\theta_e) \tag{5.8}$$

Since $(S - w_e) > 0$ by Eq. (5.7), the optimal D is zero. Hence, the firm is always solvent so that $G(\gamma_1^*) = 0$. Hence, Eq. (5.7) can be re-arranged to yield

$$w_e = S - \frac{F(w_e)}{f(w_e)} \tag{5.9}$$

Equation (5.9) is analogous to the standard optimal choice of an efficiency wage, since S is effectively the marginal product of effort and the remaining term reflects the marginal cost of higher wages. The key findings of this section are that wages increase in the importance of human capital investments and that debt is avoided altogether. The extreme result for debt policy is based on the assumption that workers have no bargaining power. We now turn to the other extreme case in which workers can make a take-it-or-leave-it wage demand on their employers.

5.2.3. *The Case of Negotiated Wages*

In this section, we allow the wage to be the outcome of a stylized bargaining procedure in which workers make a take-it-or-leave-it demand of w_u dollars on their employer at stage (v) of the game. While this is an extreme way to depict worker bargaining power, the results that guide our empirical work would be obtained under any Nash or Rubinstein (1982) bargaining approach. What matters is that the firm can alter the worker's effective bargaining power by its choice of capital structure.

The outcomes in stage (vi) of the game are the same as in the previous case where workers had no bargaining power. At stage (v), the workers now make a demand knowing that they will receive their negotiated wage so long as $\gamma > \gamma_1^*$. Hence, the optimal demand, w_u, maximizes expected payments $w(1 - G(\gamma_1^*))$ and satisfies the first-order condition

$$1 - G(\gamma_1^*) - w_u g(\gamma_1^*) = 0 \tag{5.10}$$

The hazard rate condition on G ensures that Eq. (5.10) yields a unique optimal w_u. The key feature from the firm's perspective is that the wage demand falls as leverage is increased. Such an increase can be implemented by increasing D while holding A fixed, that is, by paying out all the increased proceeds from the debt as a dividend. Formally, we have

$$\frac{\partial w_u}{\partial D} = -\frac{g(\gamma_1^*) + w_u g'(\gamma_1^*)}{2g(\gamma_1^*) + w_u g'(\gamma_1^*)} < 0 \tag{5.11}$$

Note that Eq. (5.11) is strictly between negative one and zero. The worker's decision of whether or not to invest in specific human capital is undertaken at stage (iii).

If the investment is made, the worker receives the negotiated wage w_u with the probability $(1 - G(\gamma_1^*))$. If the worker chooses not to invest, he receives no wage but gains θ. Hence, the worker invests unless

$$\theta > \theta_u = w_u(1 - G(\gamma_1^*)) \tag{5.12}$$

The pricing of debt and equity are the same as in the case where wages are predetermined. Hence, the shareholders' objective at the time they choose financial policy is the same as in Eq. (5.6), except that w_u is determined by Eq. (5.10) and the critical cost is θ_u rather than θ_e. The first-order condition for debt is, therefore,

$$(S - w_n)\frac{\partial \theta_u}{\partial D}f(\theta_u) - F(\theta_u)\frac{\partial W_u}{\partial D} = 0 \tag{5.13}$$

Differentiating Eq. (5.12) with respect to D we obtain

$$\frac{\partial \theta_u}{\partial D} = (1 - G(\gamma_1^*))\frac{\partial w_u}{\partial D} - w_u g(\gamma_1^*)\frac{\partial \gamma_1^*}{\partial D}$$
$$= -w_u g(\gamma_1^*) = -(1 - G(\gamma_1^*)) < 0, \tag{5.14}$$

using $\partial \gamma_1^*/\partial D = (1 + \partial w_u/\partial D)$ and Eq. (5.10). Equation (5.14) has the straightforward implication that workers' willingness to invest in firm-specific human capital strictly decreases in the firm's debt-equity ratio. The intuition is that while high debt levels reduce workers' ability to extract rents from shareholders, they also dilute their incentives to take productive actions.

Equation (5.13) can now be written as

$$-F(\theta_u)\frac{\partial w_u}{\partial D} - (S - w_u)f(\theta_u)(1 - G(\gamma_1^*)) = 0, \tag{5.15}$$

where the first term, which captures the re-distributional effect of debt, is strictly positive since $\partial w_u/\partial D < 0$. The second term, which captures the incentive effect of tougher wage bargaining due to increased leverage, is strictly negative.

The first important result is that for any level of debt financing, debt is more valuable in the case where wages are bargained than in the case where they are chosen by the firm. Thus, for an interior solution, debt-equity ratios are strictly higher when workers exercise bargaining power. This statement, however, holds constant the importance of workers' specific human capital investments, S. In the present case, w_u and θ_u are independent of S (see Eq. (5.10)), so Eq. (5.15) implies that debt levels strictly fall in S, i.e.,

$$\frac{\partial(\text{Eq. (15)})}{\partial S} = -f(\theta_u)(1 - G(\gamma_1^*)) < 0 \tag{5.16}$$

The intuition is that when human capital considerations are more important, it is less desirable to squeeze employees' wages by the use of debt finance. In essence, the firm voluntarily places itself in a weaker bargaining position to assure workers that they will be rewarded for making investments in firm-specific human capital.

5.2.4. *Summary*

To illustrate our two sets of results, suppose that both G and F are uniform unit interval distributions. The derivation of the following expressions for optimal debt and wages for our two cases is provided in the Appendix. In the case in which workers have bargaining power, the firm will optimally incur a net debt obligation of $1 - 4S/3$ dollars and will default with the probability $1 - 2S/3$. Since there are no bankruptcy costs, the firm will be entirely debt-financed if human capital investments are completely unimportant ($S = 0$), and optimal leverage falls as S increases. The negotiated wage when debt is optimally set, w_u, equals $2S/3$. When there is no bargaining power, Eq. (5.9) implies that $w_e = S/2$, which is less than w_u. The optimal debt level, therefore, is zero.

The empirical implications of the two cases for debt policy are as follows. First, by holding S constant, both debt-equity ratios and wages increase in worker bargaining power. Optimal debt levels in the non-bargaining case are strictly zero and are generally positive in the case where wages are bargained. Also, as we show in the Appendix, workers with bargaining power are paid strictly more even when debt is optimally chosen. On the other hand, holding constant worker bargaining power, debt strictly decreases and wages strictly increase in S. That is, if higher wages are used to encourage human capital investments, debt levels will be lower.

5.3. Empirical Evidence

Section 5.2 outlined two distinct relationships between capital structure and the wage payments that firms make. The key difference is whether wages are driven by incentive or productivity considerations, or alternatively, reflect the successful exercise of worker bargaining power. Our empirical work combines a study of the cross-sectional determinants of corporate capital structure choices with the labor economics literature on the relationship between employment and compensation policy, firm characteristics, and labor market imperfections. Related papers have focused on the relationship between employer characteristics, such as profitability or industry affiliation, and the compensation paid to employees (Bronars and Deere, 1991; Curme and Kahn, 1990; Neumark and Sharpe, 1996). Our approach is to examine the relationship between firms' capital structure choices and its wage policy, holding constant the extent of unionization and other more standard determinants of firm leverage.

5.3.1. *Data Description*

Our data on the financial characteristics of obtained firms are obtained from Standard and Poor's *Compustat*. These data were merged with industry-level wage data from the Bureau of Labor Statistics (BLS). All nominal values are deflated by the consumer price index (CPI). With some exceptions, the data are averaged across three-year subperiods in order to reduce the effects of measurement error. The variable label suffixes are: $1 = 1980-81-82$ and $2 = 1983-84-85$. The regressors denoted with a 2 suffix are contemporaneous. Those variables with a 1 indicate that they are lagged. For example, the return on assets, $ROA1$, is lagged to capture the long-term impact of profitability on financial policy (see Titman and Wessels, 1988). All other data are specific to the year 1984.

5.3.1.1. *Measures of debt policy*

The main variable is the debt-to-assets ratio, $DOAT2$. It is defined as total long-term debt, or debt obligations due in more than one year, divided by the firm's total assets. While we also consider alternative measures of debt policy in the sensitivity analysis, there are good reasons to focus on long-term debt and total assets. First, debt affects wages because shareholders and employees bargain over wages in the belief that creditors will *not* re-negotiate their claim on the firm once γ is revealed (see Perotti and Spier, 1993). Short-term debt is more likely to be held by banks and other large creditors who are in fact often able to coordinate renegotiation (see Gilson *et al.*, 1990). As stressed in analyses such as Gertner and Scharfstein (1991), the costs of re-negotiating long-term debt are likely to be substantially greater, because it is more likely to be held publicly and negotiations are more likely to be anonymous and one-shot.

For our purposes, it is also more appropriate to use total assets as opposed to the market value of equity in the denominator. The market value of equity reflects expected discounted dividend payments to shareholders over the firm's entire lifespan. In our model, however, if dividends are paid out before wage negotiations take place then they represent an increase in the firm's "toughness". In terms of our model in Section 5.2, a dividend paid out at any time before stage (v) of the game would have the same effect as an increase in leverage chosen by the founder. Total tangible assets are thus a more direct measure of the expected amount of assets that the firm will have to cover its senior debt obligations.

5.3.1.2. *Measures of employee compensation*

For each firm in our sample, we measure wages as labor and related expenses divided by the number of employees. The firm's labor expenses are defined as salaries, wages, pension costs, profit sharing and incentive compensation, payroll taxes, and other employee benefits. The wage is deflated and expressed in dollars per week. The minimum hourly wage mandated under the Fair Labor Standards Act was $3.35 in 1981. Observations with nominal wages less than $134 ($3.35 × 40) in 1981 were assumed to be misreported and dropped from the sample. The mean and standard deviation of the firm-level wage are roughly comparable to those for an alternative wage measure from the BLS at the 4-digit SIC industry level (with the correlation between the two wage measures being 0.64).

Our primary wage measure is lagged real wages, $RW1$, because we are concerned about the possible simultaneity of contemporaneous wages and capital structure. Our model states that whether high-wage firms have higher or lower debt, depends on whether high-wage payments reflect the return to specific human capital investments or rents captured by employees. An alternative, which is not considered in our model, is that high current wages simply reflect suboptimally low debt levels. Hence, a regression of debt levels on contemporaneous wages may be contaminated by a spurious negative correlation. Debt affects contemporaneous, and possibly future wage payments, so historical or lagged wages are not subject to this criticism. We also use alternative wage measures to examine our basic hypotheses.

In addition to $RW1$, we also use interindustry wage premia as a direct measure of above-market wages. A wage premium is that portion of an individual's wage that cannot be explained by their individual characteristics such as human capital, demographics, or occupation, but is explained by their industry of affiliation. The mean of 0.16 implies that the firms in our sample are from relatively high-wage industries (on average, those industries with wages about 16% more than the economy-wide average wage). By construction, the premia data are unrelated to observable characteristics. Krueger and Summers (1988) have also shown that these premia are not explained by union bargaining strength but are likely to reflect either efficiency wage concerns or unobserved worker quality.

5.3.1.3. Other variables

The growth measure $ESALEGRO$ is the percentage rate of sales growth during the period 1984–1988. Another measure, VOL is the standard deviation of the percentage change in pre-tax income. It is calculated using all the nine years in the sample in order to obtain an efficient measure as possible (see Titman and Wessels, 1988). For each firm, the capital-labor ratio, $RKL1$, is measured as the real value of property, plant, and equipment divided by the number of employees. The union coverage measure, $COV2$, is the average union coverage of workers in each 3-digit industry.

The sample size is 369 observations after listwise deletion of missing values. Descriptive statistics and data sources are listed in Table 5.1. In Table 5.2, we split the sample into "union" and "non-union" subsamples (union coverage above and below the mean union coverage, respectively). The split is extremely informative. Firms in relatively unionized industries have higher debt and higher wages. They also tend to be larger, more capital intensive, and display slower growth. This suggests, consistent with the re-distributive version of our model, that firms where employees have more bargaining power have higher debt and pay higher wages.

Table 5.1. Descriptive statistics.

Variable	Label	Mean	SD	Source
Measures of Debt Policy				
Long-term debt to assets	*DOAT2*	18.11	15.02	a
Total debt to assets	*TDAT2*	24.47	14.07	a
Measures of Real Wages				
Average weekly earnings	*RW1*	529.33	155.46	a*
Average weekly earnings (4-digit)	*RBLSW*	472.41	124.03	b*
Industry wage premiums	*PREMIA*	0.16	0.12	c
Firm-Level Variables				
Real sales	*RS1*	2617.28	8050.27	a*
Sales growth 1984–1988	*ESALEGRO*	4.47	11.59	a
Return on assets	*ROA1*	4.60	4.55	a
Volatility 1980–1988	*VOL*	0.16	0.75	a
Real capital to labor ratio	*RKL1*	0.16	0.23	a
Industry-Level Variables				
Machine-producing industry	*MACHINES*	0.09	0.29	a[†]
Regulated industry	*REGULATE*	0.53	0.50	a[‡]
Workers covered by union contracts	*COV2*	28.53	21.66	d

Sources:
a. *Compustat.*
b. *Employment and Wages, Annual Averages 1984*, (1985).
c. Krueger and Summers (1988), Table A1.
d. Hirsch and Macpherson (1993).
e. CPI data, used to deflate all nominal values, are from the *Economic Report of the President*, 1994.
Notes: Observations = 369.
[*] Variable is logged in the empirical work (distinguished by '*L*' prefix in the following tables).
[†] SIC industries 3400–4000.
[‡] SIC industries 4600–4699, 4900–4999, and 6000–6499.

It also underscores the importance of controlling for union coverage when examining the relationship between financial and compensation policy. We now examine the hypotheses derived from the wage bargaining and the specific human capital approaches in a regression setting.

Table 5.2. Means (SD) for non-union and union firms.

Variable	Non-union	Union	t-test[a]
DOAT2	7.74	27.77	17.21**
	(10.69)	(11.66)	
RW1	451.86	601.53	10.48**
	(146.91)	(125.84)	
RS1	1756.25	3419.71	2.05*
	(3705.39)	(10554.06)	
ESALEGRO	7.54	1.61	5.04**
	(12.34)	(10.06)	
ROA1	4.57	4.63	0.11
	(5.63)	(3.23)	
VOL	0.20	0.13	0.86
	(0.99)	(0.42)	
RKL1	0.03	0.28	12.81**
	(0.06)	(0.26)	
COV2	8.49	47.21	38.75**
	(7.87)	(11.15)	
MACHINES	0.12	0.07	1.64
	(0.32)	(0.25)	
REGULATE	0.57	0.49	1.55
	(0.50)	(0.50)	

Notes: The non-union sample ($COV2 \leq 28.53$) has 178 observations. The union sample ($COV2 > 28.53$) has 191 observations.
[a]t-test for the hypothesis that the means of the two groups are equal.
*denotes (5%) level of statistical significance.
**denotes (1%) level of statistical significance.

5.3.2. The Empirical Model and Results

In this section, we examine the effect of employee bargaining and incentive considerations on firm capital structure choice, controlling for other determinants documented in the literature. Our empirical specification takes the following form:

$$D_{ij}^* = \alpha + \beta_w W_{ij} + \beta_x' X_{ij} + \delta' I_j + \varepsilon_{ij}$$

where

$$D_{ij} = \begin{cases} 0 & \text{if } D_{ij}^* \leq 0 \\ D_{ij}^* & \text{if } D_{ij}^* > 0 \end{cases}, \tag{5.17}$$

and $D_{ij} = DOAT2$ is the debt–equity ratio and $W_{ij} = LRW1$ is the natural log of the real wage paid to employees by firm i in industry j. Additionally, α, β_w, β_x, and δ denote unknown coefficient vectors and ε_{ij} is a normally distributed random disturbance.

The vector $X_{ij} = (RKL1, LRS1, ESALEGRO, ROA1, VOL, COV2)$ contains variables that are known to influence firm-level debt policies — the capital-intensity of production, firm size as measured by sales, expected growth, profits, and income volatility, respectively (see Titman and Wessels (1988) and the review by Harris and Raviv (1991)). In addition, as discussed above, we include $COV2$, which measures the percentage of workers covered by union contracts in the firm's industry. It controls for the direct effect of unionization on employee bargaining power and firms' capital structure choices.

As capital structure is also known to vary systematically along industry lines, we include a vector of industry dummies, I_j. *REGULATE* is a dummy for regulated industries — banking, insurance, and public utilities. Compared to their unregulated counterparts, Smith and Watts (1992) find that regulated industries tend to finance new projects with debt rather than equity. *MACHINES* is a dummy for industries that manufacture machines or equipment. Titman and Wessels (1988) argue that firms in these industries, rely heavily on specialised inputs, which increases the costs of liquidation.

Equation (5.17) is a Tobit specification (nine firms in our sample report $DOAT2 = 0$). Our main interest is in β_w, the coefficient for W_{ij}. If β_w were zero, we would conclude that wage effects are unimportant for debt policy. A finding that $\beta_w > 0$ would imply that the debt–wage relationship is driven by worker bargaining power considerations, which are not captured by our union coverage variable. Finally, a finding that $\beta_w < 0$ would support the specific human capital interpretation.

The estimates of Eq. (5.17) appear in Table 5.3. As expected, based on the results in Table 5.2 and the findings of Bronars and Deere (1991), the estimates in column (1) indicate that firms in more heavily unionized industries are significantly more leveraged. The results indicate that firms carry more debt when they are more capital-intensive, are not in a machine-producing industry, are less profitable, and when their returns are more variable. Titman and Wessels (1988) have for similar findings (see also Harris and Raviv (1991) for a survey of existing cross-sectional evidence).

In column (2), we report estimates for a specification that includes wages, but not union coverage. The estimate of β_w is statistically insignificant. To us, this indicates the presence of both the specific human capital and re-distribution forces at work. To isolate the specific human capital effect, it is therefore important to control for worker bargaining power. This specification appears in column (3). Of greatest interest is the fact that the coefficient on wages is now negative, large, and highly significant. This supports the specific human capital model. Column (4)

Table 5.3. Tobit estimates of Eq. (5.17) (dependent variable = DOAT2).

Variable	(1)	(2)	(3)	Elasticities (4)
Intercept	5.606*	10.024	30.048*	.
	(2.499)	(12.415)	(11.308)	
LRW1		0.470	−4.176*	−0.224
		(2.033)	(1.885)	
LRS1	0.045	0.627	0.186	0.010
	(0.301)	(0.339)	(0.306)	
ESALEGRO	0.016	−0.017	0.009	0.002
	(0.046)	(0.015)	(0.046)	
ROA1	−0.329*	−0.554*	−0.329*	−0.081
	(0.140)	(0.154)	(0.141)	
VOL	1.568*	1.147	1.725*	0.015
	(0.693)	(0.773)	(0.693)	
RKL1	29.358*	48.615*	30.587*	0.258
	(3.295)	(3.073)	(3.327)	
MACHINES	−4.068*	−5.134*	−4.141*	−0.020
	(1.893)	(2.106)	(1.883)	
REGULATE	0.430	−7.191*	0.201	0.006
	(1.553)	(1.503)	(1.550)	
COV2	0.308*	.	0.328*	0.501
	(0.033)		(0.034)	
Scale parameter	9.730	10.835	9.676	
	(0.364)	(0.406)	(0.362)	
Log likelihood	−1340.12	−1378.66	−1337.68	

Notes: 369 observations.
Asymptotic standard errors in parentheses.
* Statistically significant at the 5% level.

presents normalized elasticity coefficients and indicates that the effect of wages on debt has an effect that is equivalent in size to that of capital intensity.

Overall, the results are supportive of the specific human capital and incentives explanation for wages and their impact on capital structure. After controlling for the firm's collective bargaining environment, debt is lower in firms in which the value of specific human capital investments is greater. In the unconditional sense, of course, both the re-distribution and incentive stories are at work, which has the commonsense interpretation that observed wages reflect both negotiated rents and incentive payments.

5.3.3. Further Results on the Measurement of Wages and Capital Structure

5.3.3.1. *Alternative measures of debt*

In column 1 of Table 5.4, we examine the effects of using *TDAT*2, the ratio of total debt to total assets, as the measure of the firm's leverage. Since short-term

Table 5.4. Sensitivity of the wage coefficient to different model specifications.

Variable	TDAT2 (1)	PREMIA (2)	WDIF (3)
Intercept	5.495	11.343*	5.689*
	(12.507)	(3.977)	(2.477)
Wage	1.443	−6.246	−5.862*
	(2.084)	(9.084)	(2.081)
*LRS*1	0.270	0.644	0.214
	(0.339)	(0.489)	(0.304)
ESALEGRO	0.053	0.159	0.010
	(0.051)	(0.122)	(0.046)
*ROA*1	−0.656*	−0.808*	−0.352*
	(0.157)	(0.213)	(0.139)
VOL	1.463	0.551	1.634*
	(0.769)	(0.725)	(0.687)
*RKL*1	20.527*	38.723*	29.519*
	(3.688)	(12.365)	(3.265)
MACHINES	−5.090*	−3.212	−4.754*
	(2.088)	(2.348)	(1.890)
REGULATE	5.082*	−0.645*	0.508
	(1.718)	(3.219)	(1.539)
*COV*2	0.184*	0.111	0.304*
	(0.038)	(0.069)	(0.033)
Scale parameter	10.734	9.135	9.632
	(0.400)	(0.666)	(0.361)
Log likelihood	−1383.134	−347.921	−1336.187
Observations	369	98	369

Notes: Asymptotic standard errors in parentheses.
*Statistically significant at the 5% level.
Column (1): *Wage* = *LRW*1, dependent = *TDAT*2.
Column (2): *Wage* = *PREMIA*, dependent = *DOAT*2.
Column (3): *Wage* = *WDIF*, dependent = *DOAT*2.

debt is less likely to have an effect on employees' bargaining power, either for re-distributional or incentive reasons, we expected to find no significant relationship between wages and *TDAT*2. The results support this interpretation.

5.3.3.2.   *The endogeneity of wages*

An alternative explanation for our results is that the causality is reversed. Since firm-level wages are highly positively correlated through time, lagging wages may still not adequately eliminate the potential inconsistency of our estimate of β_w. Myers (1984) "pecking-order" theory suggests that observed debt-assets ratios are a by-product of the firm's cash inflows and expenditures rather than the deliberate, wealth-maximizing approach that we adopted. The explanation would be that more profitable firms simply carry less debt and pay higher wages. Hanka (1998) effec-tively makes the assumption that leverage is exogenous by regressing wages on debt to assets. His sample covers the entire *Compustat* file and produces a signif-icant negative relationship between debt and wages.

Our single-equation approach prevents us from directly ruling out the possi-bility that debt is exogenous. However, our coefficient estimates allow us to shed light on the plausibility of this explanation for our findings. The following calcu-lations indicate the magnitude of opportunity cost that shareholders would bear if the firm were in fact to *neglect* the optimal management of its capital structure. Suppose that the average firm in our sample had a once-off windfall increase in its cash-flows of $500 million, or approximately 10% of its total assets, and that these funds were not paid out to shareholders as a dividend. This firm would experience a fall in *DOAT*2 from 18.1% to 16.4%, and using the estimate for β_w, would expe-rience an increase in weekly earnings from $562.37 to $700.55. If this increase were to persist for only one year for a firm with average employment of nearly 20,000, over 27% of the initial cash windfall of $500 million would be paid out to employees rather than to shareholders. In our theory, of course, such a fall in leverage and increase in compensation would not come about exogenously. Rather, the reduced leverage would be a wealth-maximizing response to an increase in the importance of firm-specific human capital.

An alternative approach to the potential endogeneity problem is to consider wage measures other than *LRW*1. The variable *PREMIA* is a direct measure of industry wage premiums. Unfortunately, the latter data are only available at the 3-digit SIC level. To examine the effects of the alternative wage measures, all the data are averaged by industry. This is a solution to the possible inefficiency of estimates derived from "mixed-mode" regressions, i.e., when industry-level variables are regressed on firm-level variables (see Bronars and Deere, 1991). Since the effects of observable worker characteristics are controlled for in the calculation of *PREMIA*, we expected that the measure of wage premiums would be even "more negatively" related to debt than our firm-level wage measure. While this appears to be the case, the coefficient was not statistically significant (see column (2) of Table 5.4).

Another, rather similar, approach to endogeneity is to approximate wage premia by deviations from the industry average. Specifically, we define *WDIF* = *LRW2* − *LRBLSW* where *LRBLSW* is the logarithm of the average real wage of non-supervisory employees at the 4-digit SIC industry level. A positive *WDIF* would indicate that this particular firm has higher wages than its 4-digit industry counterparts. The idea is that collective bargaining strength and the influence of observable characteristics are likely to be captured by the industry wage level, so that *WDIF* provides a supplementary measure of premium wages. From column 3 of Table 5.4, it is clear that *WDIF* is strongly negatively related to leverage, which lends further support to the specific human capital model.

Overall, we find that the results reported in the previous section are quite robust to changes in the measurement of wages and capital structure. With appropriate controls for worker bargaining power, the "efficiency" component of wages is negatively related to firm leverage.

5.4. Conclusion

Recent research has recognized that financial structure affects a firm's labor policies as well as its choice of capital investment projects. Many of these studies have examined the role that debt can play in moderating wage demands by organized labor. One of the objectives of this paper was to show that the strategic use of debt has efficiency, as well as distributional, consequences. This was shown to be the case when firm-specific human capital investments were important.

We presented two stylized models of wage determination and showed that debt was used more intensively when bargaining power was the primary cause of high wages, but that debt was lower if high wages were chosen as a worker incentive device. More precisely, debt levels and wages both increased in worker bargaining power. However, for any given degree of worker bargaining power, debt strictly decreased and wages strictly increased in the importance of worker specific investments.

Using data from *Compustat* and a number of other sources, we also examined the relationship between debt and wages for a sample of firms that varied in the extent to which their workforce was unionized. In line with the earlier studies, we found that firms in more unionized industries carried higher levels of debt. However, holding constant the degree of unionization, we found that high-wage firms carried less debt, as predicted by our worker incentive model. We concluded that financial and employment policies were interrelated, even when the primary concern is not to blunt the bargaining power of organized labor.

Appendix

A.1. *Solutions for the Uniform Distribution Case*

First, define $\tilde{D}$ to be debt obligations in excess of expected available cash, $D - (V + A)$. When both F and G are uniform on the unit interval, $G(\gamma) = \gamma$ and $F(\theta) = \theta$ for $\gamma, \theta \leq 1$. It follows that $w_u = (1 - \tilde{D})/2$; $\gamma^* = (\tilde{D} + 1)/2$; and $\theta_u = (1 - \tilde{D})^2/4$. The shareholders' objective can now be written as:

$$V - S + \theta_u[S - w_u] = V - S + \frac{(1 - \tilde{D})^2}{4}\left(S - \frac{1 - \tilde{D}}{2}\right)$$

$$= V - S + \frac{S(1 - \tilde{D})^2}{4} - \frac{(1 - \tilde{D})^3}{8}. \qquad (A.1)$$

The first-order condition for $\tilde{D}$ is

$$-\frac{S(1 - \tilde{D})}{2} + \frac{3(1 - \tilde{D})^2}{8} = 0 \qquad (A.2)$$

Equation (A.2) has two solutions, $\tilde{D} = 1 - 4S/3$ so that $w_u = 2S/3$; and $\tilde{D} = 1$, which yields strictly lower profits for $S > 0$. Also, the optimal $\tilde{D}$ for $S > 3/4$ is zero. The second-order condition is satisfied since $\partial(A.2)/\partial\tilde{D} = -S/2 < 0$ (evaluated at the optimal $\tilde{D}$). In the case where the wage is set at stage (i), then $w_e = S - F(w_e)/f(w_e) = S/2$.

A.2. *Comparison of w_u and w_e*

We assumed that the workers' loss of w_e is a deadweight loss. Suppose that bond-holders rescind w_e in the event of a default. While Eq. (5.10) continues to char-acterise the workers' wage, w_u will be lower because debt is higher and w_u falls in D. Hence, if w_u exceeds w_e for the case where bondholders rescind wages, it certainly will do so for the case in which w_u is a deadweight loss. Specifically, the pricing of debt is no longer given by Eq. (5.4) but by

$$D_0 = F(\theta_u)\left[D(1 - G(\gamma_1^*)) + \int_\gamma^{\gamma_1^*} (V + A + \gamma)dG(\gamma)\right]$$

$$+ (1 - F(\theta_u))\left[D(1 - G(\gamma_2^*)) + \int_\gamma^{\gamma_2^*} (V - S + A + \gamma)dG(\gamma)\right] \qquad (A.3)$$

Substituting Eq. (A.3) into the expression for founder wealth yields

$$F(\theta_u)[V - w_u(1 - G(\gamma_1^*))] + (1 - F(\theta_u))(V - S)$$
$$= V - S + F(\theta_u)(S - \theta_u) \qquad (A.4)$$

The only difference from the founder's point of view is that the costs of debt are reduced by the factor $G(\gamma_1^*)w_u$. The first-order condition for D can now be written as:

$$((S - \theta_u)f(\theta_u) - F(\theta_u))\partial\theta_u/\partial D = 0 \qquad (A.5)$$

Hence, $\theta_u^* = S - F(\theta_u^*)/f(\theta_u^*)$ which by Eq. (5.9) also equals w_e. Since $w_u = \theta_u/(1 - G(\gamma_1^*))$, then $w_u > w_e$.

References

Abowd, JM (1989). The effect of wage bargains on the stock market value of the firm. *American Economic Review*, 79, 774–809.

Bronars, SG and DR Deere (1991). The threat of unionization, the use of debt, and the preservation of shareholder wealth. *Quarterly Journal of Economics*, 56, 231–254.

Curme, M and LM Kahn (1990). The impact of the threat of bankruptcy on the structure of compensation. *Journal of Labor Economics*, 8, 419–447.

Dasgupta, S and K Sengupta (1993). Sunk investment, bargaining, and the choice of capital structure. *International Economic Review*, 34, 203–220.

DeAngelo, H and L DeAngelo (1991). Union negotiations and corporate policy: a study of labor concessions in the domestic steel industry during the 1980s. *Journal of Financial Economics*, 30, 3–43.

Gertner, R and DS Scharfstein (1991). A theory of workouts and the effects of reorganization law. *Journal of Finance*, 46, 1189–1222.

Gilson, S, K John and LHP Lang (1990). Troubled debt restructurings: an empirical study of private reorganization of firms in default. *Journal of Financial Economics*, 26, 315–353.

Hanka, G (1998). Debt and the terms of employment. *Journal of Financial Economics*, 48(3), 245–282.

Harris, M and A Raviv (1992). The theory of capital structure. *Journal of Finance*, 46, 297–255.

Hirsch, BT and DA Macpherson (1993). Union membership and contract coverage files from the current population surveys: note. *Industrial and Labor Relations Review*, 46, 574–578.

Ippolito, RA and WH James (1992). LBOs, reversions, and implicit contracts. *Journal of Finance*, 47, 139–168.

Krueger, AB and LH Summers (1988). Efficiency wages and the inter-industry wage structure. *Econometrica*, 56, 259–293.

Lazear, EP (1981). Agency, earnings profiles, and hours restrictions. *American Economic Review*, 71, 606–620.

Myers, SC (1984). The capital structure puzzle. *Journal of Finance*, 39, 575–592.

Myers, SC (1990). Still searching for optimal capital structure. In *Are the Distinctions Between Equity and Debt Disappearing?* R Kopcke and E Rosengren (eds.), pp. 80–105, Boston: Federal Reserve Bank of Boston.

Neumark, D and SA Sharpe (1996). Rents and quasi-rents in the wage structure: evidence from hostile takeovers. *Industrial Relations*, 35, 145–179.

Perotti, E and K Spier (1993). Capital structure as a bargaining tool: the role of leverage in contract renegotiation. *American Economic Review*, 83, 1131–1141.

Smith, Clifford Jr and RL Watts (1992). The investment opportunity set and corporate financing, dividend, and compensation policies. *Journal of Financial Economics*, 32, 263–292.

Titman, S and R Wessels (1988). The determinants of capital structure choice. *Journal of Finance*, 43, 1–19.

PART 3

RESOURCE ALLOCATION, CONFLICTS, AND RESOLUTIONS

CHAPTER 6

EQUITABLE AND DECENTRALIZED SOLUTIONS FOR THE ALLOCATION OF INDIVISIBLE OBJECTS

Somdeb Lahiri

Institute of Petroleum Management, Ghandinagar, India

6.1. Introduction

The literature on the allocation of indivisible objects amongst a finite number of individuals, was modeled by Alkan, Demange, and Gale (1991), with money being used as an instrument of compensation. Subsequent contributions by Brams and Kilgour (2001), Brams and Taylor (1999), Brams and Fishburn (2002), Edelman and Fishburn (2001), Brams, Edelman and Fishburn (2002), Herreiner and Puppe (2002), consider a similar problem without incorporating money explicitly as an instrument of compensation. However, if the unit of money is fixed and indivisible (as it usually is for most practical purposes), then if we assume that the total amount of money to be distributed is fixed (which is also a reasonable assumption in reality), each unit of money that is available can be modeled as an indivisible object. Hence, the subsequent literature differs essentially from the initial work of Alkan, Demange, and Gale (1991), in that the latter paper models money as an infinitely divisible good, with preferences of individuals being represented by quasi-linear utility functions. This is also the framework that has been adopted in a recent paper by Haake, Raith and Su (2002).

The paper by Herreiner and Puppe (2002), mentioned above, considers the allocation of indivisible objects, where an agent may receive more than one object. This apparently is different from the treatment in Brams and Taylor (1999), where each individual receives at most one object. Herreiner and Puppe (2002), therefore assume that individual preferences are defined over subsets of objects, and they consider allocations, where no two individuals share an object. However, given that preferences are defined over subsets of objects which are then distributed among the individuals, the formal structure of the two models is not significantly different, except that the model with set allocation as proposed by Herreiner and Puppe (2002), would require some allocations (: in the sense of Brams and Taylor, 1999), to be *a priori* infeasible. For instance, since no allocation can contain two intersecting sets, feasibility would require allocations to be partitions of the set of objects and thus rule out these combinations from the power set of the set of alternatives, which contain two intersecting elements (i.e., subsets of the set of alternatives). Thus, the model of Herreiner and Puppe (2002) can be alternatively interpreted and generalized to a model, where at most one object is allocated to each individual, with no two individuals sharing one or more objects, and possibly some allocations being defined infeasible. When all allocations, where no two individuals share an object are feasible, we are once again back in the framework of Brams and Taylor (1999). In the existing literature, such problems are known as house-allocation problems. Moulin (1995) has documented an extensive discussion of the house-allocation problem, where the objects to be distributed are houses. Our formulation is very similar to the model proposed by Quint (1997) for a housing market.

Modeled this way, the procedure defined in Herreiner and Puppe (2002), called the descending demand procedure (DDP), selects feasible allocations which are Pareto efficient, and satisfy the property that the worst-off individuals are not ranked lower than the worst-off individuals at any other Pareto efficient allocation. This renders the solution both efficient and egalitarian. Such solutions are called balanced allocations. However, as discussed by Herreiner and Puppe (2002), not all balanced solutions can be obtained as an outcome of the DDP, in the general case. We propose a weaker sufficient condition than the one suggested by Herreiner and Puppe (2002) for a balanced solution to be an outcome of the DDP, for some ordering of the individuals.

A related model due to Shapley and Scarf (1974) called the housing market, considers a private ownership economy, where each individual owns exactly one object and what is sought is the existence of an allocation in the core of the economy. Roth and Postelwaite (1977) used Gale's *Top Trading Cycle Algorithm* to show that if preferences are strict, then there exists a unique competitive equilibrium allocation, which is also the unique core allocation, for such economies. An allocation in the core is the one that guarantees stability and hence conforms to the requirements of decentralized allocation of objects. Sonmez (1996, 1999) and Quint (1997) formulated more general matching problems of which the Shapley and Scarf economy was a special case. Moulin (1995) considers a generalization, where instead of one type of object being available for transaction in the market, there are two types of objects available in the market. Assuming separable preferences over the two types of objects for the agents, the main problem identified by Moulin (1995) was about the non-emptiness of the core, and the same treatise provides answers to this question for several different cases. However, as argued earlier, given the fact that preferences are defined over subsets of objects or pairs of objects, which are then distributed among the individuals, the generalization studied by Moulin (1995) can *in principle* be generalized to a model where objects of a single type are traded, allowing for the possibility that some allocations (: in the sense of Shapley and Scarf, 1974) may be *a priori* infeasible. This is precisely the model studied by Quint (1997). For instance, the model with two types of objects would require each agent being represented by two distinct copies, each owning a different kind of object. A feasible allocation would now have to restrict re-allocations among agents owning the same type of object, in the replicated economy. Thus, the model of Moulin (1995) can *in principle* be alternatively interpreted and generalized to a model, where at most one object is allocated to each individual, with no two individuals sharing one or more objects, and possibly some allocations being defined infeasible. When all allocations, where no two individuals share an object are feasible, we are once again back in the earlier framework of Shapley and Scarf (1974). However, there is no guarantee that such an allocation is egalitarian.

We show in this paper, that it is possible for an allocation in a housing market to be balanced without belonging to the core and for an allocation to belong to the core in spite of not being balanced. This perhaps reveals a conflict between the two objectives of equity and decentralization, that is inherent in such models. The reason why such a conflict between the objectives of equity and decentralization in such models is worth noting, is because in the related quasi-linear model with money being used as an instrument of compensation, the notion of fair allocations as defined in Alkan, Demange and Gale (1991) is really no different from the notion of competitive equilibrium as defined by Quinzii (1984). Fairness is a concept which is meant to convey the notion of equity, whilst competitive equilibrium is probably the most significant solution for the decentralized allocation of resources. Further, there is another reason why this conflict between equity and decentralization observed in the allocation of indivisible objects, though not entirely surprising, may yet merit emphasizing. In the traditional Arrow–Debreu economy, where the concepts of decentralization (: as for instance, competitive equilibrium or an allocation in the core) are justifiably independent of concepts of egalitarianism, the preference structure of the agents exhibit the property that "more is preferred to less". It is this characteristic of the preference structure of the agents, which is either directly, or indirectly exploited to dissociate between decentralized allocations attainable via the market mechanism, and allocations, which are supposed to be egalitarian. At the level of generality where our analysis of the housing market is carried out, there is no such hypothesis built into the preference structure of the agents. In fact, the preference structures we consider are similar to the kind of preference structure that is used in the classical theory of mathematical politics pioneered by Arrow. Thus, the notion of the core in our model of a housing market, bears a closer resemblance to the notion of political stability that political theory would associate with democracy (: for instance, when executive portfolios are assigned to, or reshuffled between cabinet ministers) than to the notion of economic stability, which the concept of the competitive market mechanism is supposed to convey. It is being only gradually realized now, that "democracy" and "equity" do not necessarily go hand in hand. Thus, the conflict between decentralization and equity that we observe in the housing market, whilst not completely unrecognized in the real world, is hardly a redundant observation to make at this juncture.

This, it is hoped, would provide further insight about the issues concerning decentralization and equity in an economy comprising indivisible objects.

6.2. The Model

Consider a non-empty finite set $N = \{1, \ldots, n\}$ of individuals indexed by $i \in N$, and a non-empty finite set of objects S. Let "s" denote the cardinality of S. Each individual "i" has preferences over $S \cup \{i\}$, represented by a bijection $rk_i : S \cup \{i\} \to \{1, 2, \ldots, s + 1\}$, such that for all $a, b \in S \cup \{i\}$ with $a \neq b : rk_i(a) > rk_i(b)$ if and only if individual "i" prefers alternative "a" to alternative "b". The function rk_i is called the ranking function for individual "i" and for $a \in S \cup \{i\}$, $rk_i(a)$ is called the rank assigned to alternative "a" by individual "i". Thus, for $x \in S$: (i) $rk_i(x) > rk_i(i)$ means that x is a desirable object for individual "i"; and (ii) $rk_i(i) > rk_i(x)$, means that x is an undesirable object for individual "i".

An allocation is a function $A: N \to S \cup N$, such that (i) for all $i \in N$, $A(i) \in S \cup \{i\}$; and (ii) for all $i, j \in N$, with $i \neq j$, $A(i) \neq A(j)$.

The interpretation of $A(i) = i$, where $i \in N$ is that, individual "i" has not been assigned any object, under the allocation A.

Given an allocation A, let $r(A) = \max\{rk_i(A(i))/i \in N\}$.

An allocation A is said to be Pareto superior to an allocation B, if for all $i \in N$, $rk_i(A(i)) \geq rk_i(B(i))$, with strict inequality for at least one $i \in N$.

Let Δ denote the set of all allocations. Any non-empty subset F of Δ, is called a feasible set (of allocations).

Given any non-empty subset X of Δ, an allocation A in X is said to be Pareto efficient in X if there does not exist any other allocation B in X, which is Pareto superior to A. The set of all Pareto efficient allocations in X is denoted Par (X).

Let F be a feasible set. A Pareto efficient allocation A in F is said to be balanced in F, if there does not exist any other Pareto efficient allocation B in F, with $r(B) < r(A)$. The set of all balanced allocations in F is denoted Bal(F).

Let $\pi: N \to N$ be a one to one function. The $(s + 1) \times n$ matrix P^π, whose (i, j)th element $P^\pi_{i,j}$ is the alternative ranked "i" by individual $\pi^{-1}(j)$, is called the preference matrix with respect to the ordering π (of the individuals). When π is the identity function on N, then instead of P^π we write P.

6.2.1. *The Descending Demand Procedure (DDP)*

Let F be a feasible set of allocations. Let π be a one to one function from N into N. Without loss of generality, we may assume that π is the identity function on N. Let P^r denote the rth row of P. If $P^1 \in F$, then the procedure stops, and P^1 is the solution. Suppose $P^1 \notin F$. For $r \geq 2$, let $P_{r,j} \uparrow = \{A \in F/A_j = P_{r,j},\ A_k \in \{P_{1,k}, \ldots, P_{r,k}\}$ for $k < j$ and $A_k \in \{P_{1,k}, \ldots, P_{r-1,k}\}$ for $k > j\}$. Let $k = \min\{r/P_{r,j} \uparrow \neq \phi,\ \text{for some } j \in N\}$ and let $i = \min\{j/P_{k,j} \uparrow \neq \phi\}$. Any allocation A in Par $(P_{k,j} \uparrow)$ is a said to be a solution of the DDP, for the given permutation π. Since $F \neq \phi$, the procedure must terminate at some element.

Essentially, the DDP requires that we move from left to right along the preference matrix, starting with the first row, going down one row at a time, and stop as soon as we obtain a feasible allocation, from among the alternatives that we have already traversed. Then, from among all such feasible alternatives, we choose one, which is not Pareto dominated by any other feasible alternative of the same type.

The proof of Propositions 1 and 2 are identical to that of similar ones in Herreiner and Puppe (2002).

Proposition 6.1. *Any solution of the DDP for a given permutation π is an element of Bal(F). Thus, Bal(F) $\neq \phi$.*

Proposition 6.2. *Let $N = \{1, 2\}$. Then any element of Bal(F) can be obtained as a solution of the DDP for some permutation π.*

Note: For $N = \{1, 2\}$, Bal(F) consists of at most two allocations. However, if $F \subset\subset \Delta$, then for $n \geq 3$, the above proposition does not hold.

Example 6.1. $N = \{1, 2, 3\}$, $S = \{a,\ b,\ c,\ d,\ e,\ f,\ g,\ h\}$. Let $F = \{(a,\ c,\ h), (b,\ c,\ g), (c,\ a,\ h)\}$.

The preferences of the individuals are summarized in the following preference matrix $P = $

a	e	e
b	d	f
c	a	g
d	c	h
e	b	a
f	f	b
g	g	c
h	h	d
1	2	3

Now, Bal(F) $= F$. However, $(a,\ c,\ h)$ can never be a solution of the DDP. For, suppose, π is a permutation on N, such that $\pi(2) < \pi(3)$. Then the outcome of the DDP is $(b,\ c,\ g)$. On the other hand, if $\pi(3) < \pi(2)$, then the outcome is $(c,\ a,\ h)$.

However, $\text{Bal}(\Delta) = \{(a, \ e, \ f \ ), (a, \ d, \ e)\}$. Further, if $F = \Delta$, then for any permutation π, with $\pi(3) = 1$, $(a, \ e, \ f \ )$ is the solution of the DDP and for any permutation π, with $\pi(2) = 1$, $(a, \ d, \ e)$ is the solution of the DDP.

Given $A \in \Delta$, let $J_A = \{j \in N/rk_j(A(j)) = r(A)\}$. Given $A \in \text{Bal}(F)$, let $\Omega^*(A, F) = \{B \in \text{Bal}(F)/J_B \subset J_A\}$.

Proposition 6.3. *Let* $A \in Bal(F)$. *Then* A *is a solution of the DDP if* $\bigcap_{B\in\Omega*(A,F)} J_B \neq g\phi$.

Proof. Let $A \in Bal(F)$ and suppose $\bigcap_{B\in\Omega*(A,F)} J_B \neq \phi$. Let $m \in \bigcap_{B\in\Omega*(A,F)} J_B$. Without loss of generality, suppose that $A = \{1, \ldots, m + p\}$ for some positive integer "m" and some non-negative integer p and for some $B \in \Omega^*(A, F)$, $B = \{1, \ldots, m\}$. Let π be the permutation on N, such that (i) $\pi(j) = j$, if $j < m$; (ii) $\pi(m) = m - p$; (iii) $\pi(j) = j$, if $j < m$; (iv) $\pi(j) = j-1$, if $j \in \{m + 1, \ldots, m + p\}$ (: provided the set is non-empty). Then the DDP of π terminates, only when it reaches the element in row $r(A)$ and column $m + p$ of P^π. Thus, the DDP terminates only when it has traversed all the columns corresponding to J_A in row $r(A)$ of P^π. Thus, A is a solution of the DDP for π. ☐

In the example cited earlier, the condition stated in Proposition 6.3 is violated for A.

6.2.2. *The Housing Market*

To define a housing market, we consider a non-empty finite set $N = \{1, \ldots, n\}$ of individuals indexed by $i \in N$, and a non-empty finite set of "n" objects which for convenience is also denoted by N. Each individual "i" has preferences over N, represented by a bijection $rk_i\colon N \to \{1, 2, \ldots, n\}$, such that for all $j, k \in N$ with $j \neq k\colon rk_i(j) > rk_i(k)$ if and only if individual "i" prefers alternative "j" to alternative "k". The function rk_i is called the ranking function for individual "i" and for $j \in N, rk_i(j)$ is called the rank assigned to alternative "j" by individual "i". An ownership function is a bijection $e\colon N \to N$. Without loss of generality, we assume that $e(i) = i$ for all $i \in N$, i.e., individual "i" initially owns object (or house) "i".

An allocation is a function $A\colon N \to N$, such that (i) for all $i, j \in N$, with $i \neq j$, $A(i) \neq A(j)$; (ii) for all $i \in N\colon rk_i(A(i)) \geq rk_i(i)$.

Given an allocation A, let $r(A) = \max\{rk_i(A(i))/i \in N\}$.

An allocation A is said to be Pareto superior to an allocation B, if for all $i \in N$, $rk_i(A(i)) \geq rk_i(B(i))$, with strict inequality for at least one $i \in N$.

Let Δ denote the set of all allocations. Any non-empty subset F of Δ, is called a feasible set (of allocations). An ordered triple $E = \langle N, F, (rk_i)_{i\in N} \rangle$ is called a housing market.

Given a housing market $E = \langle N, F, (rk_i)_{i \in N} \rangle$ and an $A \in F$, let $\Pi(A) = \{S \in [N]/\{A(i)/i \in S\}\} = S\}$. Clearly, $N \in \Pi(A)$ for all $A \in F\}$. Let $\Pi^0(A) = \{S \in \Pi(A)/[T \in \Pi(A), T \subset S]$ implies $[T = S]\}$.

Special cases of the housing market are the room-mate problems of Gale and Shapley (1962), where $F = \{A \in \Delta/[S \in \Pi^0(A)]$ implies $[\#S \in \{1, 3\}]\}$ and a variant of the marriage problem of Gale and Shapley (1962), where $F = \{A \in \Delta/[S \in \Pi^0(A)]$ implies $[\#S \in \{1, 2\}]\}$.

Given a housing market E and any non-empty subset X of Δ, an allocation A in X is said to be Pareto efficient in X if there does not exist any other allocation B in X, which is Pareto superior to A. The set of all Pareto efficient allocations in X is denoted Par (X). A Pareto efficient allocation A in F is said to be balanced in F, if there does not exist any other Pareto efficient allocation B in F, with $r(B) < r(A)$. The set of all balanced allocations for a housing market E is denoted Bal(E).

An allocation A is said to be Pareto superior to an allocation B, if for all $i \in N$, $rk_i(A(i)) \geq rk_i(B(i))$, with strict inequality for at least one $i \in N$.

Given a housing market E, an allocation A is said to be blocked by a coalition $T \subset N$, if there exists an allocation $B \in F$: (i) $\{B(i)/i \in T\} = T$; (ii) $rk_i(B(i)) > rk_i(A(i))$ for all $i \in T$. An allocation $A \in F$ is said to belong to the core of a housing market, if it is not blocked by any coalition. Let Core(E) denote the set of all allocations in the core of the housing market E.

Proposition 6.4. *There exists a housing market in which a balanced allocation does not belong to the core and a core allocation that is not balanced.*

Proof.   The example we provide consists of three agents and three objects. Thus, $n = 3$. Let $F = \Delta$. We will denote by $>$ the fact that an agent prefers one object to another.

The following are the preferences of the agents:

Agent 1: $2 > 3 > 1$
Agent 2: $3 > 1 > 2$
Agent 3: $2 > 3 > 1$

Consider the allocation A defined thus:
$A(1) = 2$, $A(2) = 1$, $A(3) = 3$. A does not belong to the core, since agent "2" prefers 3 over $A(2)$ and agent "3" prefers 2 over $A(3)$ and can thus block A. However, allocation A is balanced. The only allocation that belongs to the core is the allocation, where individual 1 gets "1", individual two gets "3" and individual three gets "2". This allocation is, however, not balanced.   □

A price rule is a function $p: N \to \Re_+$.

Given a housing market E, a pair (p, A) where p is a price rule and A is an allocation is said to be a competitive equilibrium for E, if:

(i) $A \in F$;
(ii) for all $i, j \in N$: $rk_i(A(j)) > rk_i(A(i))$ implies $p(A(j)) > p(i) \geq p(A(i))$.

If (p, A) is a competitive equilibrium for E, then A is called a competitive equilibrium allocation.

Note that if (p, A) is a competitive equilibrium, then $p(A(i)) = p(i)$ for all $i \in N$. To see this, let $i \in N$. If $A(i) = i$, then there is nothing to prove. Hence suppose, that $A(i) \neq i$. Clearly, there exists a smallest positive integer $k > 1$, such that $A^k(i) = i$, where $A^1(i) = A(i)$, $A^2(i) = A(A(i))$, and in general $A^h(i) = A(A^{h-1}(i))$ for any positive integer $h > 1$. Since (p, A) is a competitive equilibrium, the following string of inequalities hold: $p(i) \geq p(A(i)) \geq p(A^2(i)) \geq \cdots \geq p(A^{k-1}(i)) \geq p(A^k(i)) = p(i)$. Thus, $p(i) = p(A(i))$.

Let $C(E)$ denote the set of all competitive equilibrium allocations, for the housing market E. Clearly, $C(\langle N, F, (rk_i)_{i \in N} \rangle) \subset C(\langle N, X, (rk_i)_{i \in N} \rangle)$. Roth and Postelwaite (1977) show that $C(\langle N, X, (rk_i)_{i \in N} \rangle)$ is a singleton. Thus, if for some feasible set F, $C(\langle N, F, (rk_i)_{i \in N} \rangle)$ is non-empty, then $C(\langle N, F, (rk_i)_{i \in N} \rangle)$ must also be a singleton. Further, $C(\langle N, F, (rk_i)_{i \in N} \rangle)$ can be non-empty if and only if the unique element of $C(\langle N, X, (rk_i)_{i \in N} \rangle)$ belongs to F.

Thus, $C(\langle N, F, (rk_i)_{i \in N} \rangle)$ is non-empty if and only if $C(\langle N, F, (rk_i)_{i \in N} \rangle) = C(\langle N, X, (rk_i)_{i \in N} \rangle)$ (: or equivalently the unique element of $C(\langle N, X, (rk_i)_{i \in N} \rangle)$ belongs to F.)

A feasible allocation A is said to be weakly blocked by a coalition $T \subset N$, if there exists another feasible allocation B (different from A), such that $\{B(i)/i \in T\} = T$, $rk_i(B(i)) \geq rk_i(A(i))$ for all $i \in T$ with strict inequality for at least one $i \in T$. A feasible allocation is said to belong to the strict core, if it is not weakly blocked by any coalition. The set of all strict core allocations for a housing market E, is denoted $SCore(E)$. Clearly, the strict core is included in the core.

Theorem 6.1. *Let (p, A) be a competitive equilibrium for some housing market E. Then A belongs to the $SCore(E)$.*

Proof. Towards a contradiction, suppose (p, A) is a competitive equilibrium for some housing market E and yet A does not belong to the strict core. Clearly, $p(i) = p(A(i))$ for all $i \in N$. Then, there exists a coalition $S \subset N$ and a feasible allocation B (different from A), such that $\{B(i)/i \in S\} = S$ $rk_i(B(i)) \geq rk_i(A(i))$ for all $i \in S$, with strict inequality for at least one $i \in S$. Let $T = \{i \in S/rk_i(B(i)) > rk_i(A(i))\}$. Since S weakly blocks A via B, it must be the case that $T \neq \phi$. Further, since the ranking function of each agent is a one to one, it must be the case that $B(i) = A(i)$ for all $i \in S \backslash T$. Since (p, A) is a competitive equilibrium, this implies that $p(B(i)) > p(i)$ for all $i \in T$ and $p(B(i)) = p(A(i)) = p(i)$ for all $i \in S \backslash T$.

Thus, $\sum_{i \in S} p(i) = \sum_{i \in S} p(B(i)) > \sum_{i \in S} p(i)$, since $\{B(i)/i \in S\} = S$, which is not possible. Thus, A must belong to the strict core. □

Corollary of Theorem 6.1. Let (p, A) be a competitive equilibrium for some housing market E. Then, A belongs to the Core(E).

Example 6.2. Let $N = \{1, 2\}$ and suppose $rk_1(2) > rk_1(1)$, $rk_2(1) > rk_2(2)$. Let $F = \{(1, 2)\}$. Then, there is no competitive equilibrium in this economy. Suppose $(1, 2)$ is a competitive equilibrium allocation. If $p(1) \geq p(2)$, then agent 1 prefers object "2" to object "1" and further object "2" is affordable to agent "1". This contradicts that $(1, 2)$ is a competitive equilibrium. On the other hand, if $p(2) > p(1)$, then agent 2 prefers object "1" to object "2" and further object "1" is affordable to agent "2". This contradicts that $(1, 2)$ is a competitive equilibrium allocation. However, the core is clearly non-empty.

Example 6.3. Let $N = \{1, 2\}$ and suppose $rk_1(2) > rk_1(1)$, $rk_2(1) > rk_2(2)$. Let $(2, 1) \in F$. Since by Theorem 6.1, a competitive equilibrium allocation belongs to the core, $(1, 2)$ cannot be a competitive equilibrium allocation. However, (p, A) is a competitive equilibrium, with $p(1) = p(2) = 1$, $A(1) = 2$, $A(2) = 1$. Since $p(A(i)) = p(i) = 1$ for all $i \in N$, by Example 6.2, $(2, 1)$ belongs to the strict core, which it indeed does.

Example 6.4. Let $N = \{1, 2, 3, 4\}$ and $F = \{(4, 2, 3, 1), (1, 3, 2, 4)\}$. Suppose the preferences of the agents are as follows:

Agent 1: $2 > 4 > 1 > 3$
Agent 2: $3 > 1 > 2 > 4$
Agent 3: $4 > 2 > 3 > 1$
Agent 4: $1 > 3 > 4 > 2$

where, $i > j$ indicates that the concerned agent prefers "i" to "j".

Here $(4, 2, 3, 1)$ is blocked by $\{2, 3\}$ via $(1, 3, 2, 4)$ and $(1, 3, 2, 4)$ is blocked by $\{1, 4\}$ via $(4, 3, 2, 1)$. Hence the core is empty.

Acknowledgments

An earlier version of this paper has benefited immensely from the comments that I received from Steve Brams, for which I would like to thank him. I would also like to thank Herve Moulin and Tayfun Sonmez for their invaluable comments on this paper, which ultimately lead to desirable amendments.

References

Alkan, A, G Demange and D Gale (1991). Fair allocation of indivisible goods and criteria of justice. *Econometrica*, 59, 1023–1039.

Brams, SJ and PC Fishburn (2002). Fair division of indivisible items between two people with identical preferences: envy-freeness, Pareto-optimality, and equity. *Social Choice and Welfare*, 17, 247–267.

Brams, SJ and DM Kilgour (2001). Fallback bargaining. *Group Decision and Negotiation*, 10, 287–316.

Brams, SJ and AD Taylor (1999). *The Win-Win Solution: Guaranteeing Fair Shares to Everybody*, New York: W.W. Norton.

Brams, SJ, PH Edelman and PC Fishburn (2002). Paradoxes of fair divisions. *Journal of Philosophy*, 98, 300–314.

Edelman, P and PC Fishburn (2001). Fair division of indivisible items among people with similar preferences. *Mathematical Social Sciences*, 41, 327–347.

Gale, D and L Shapley (1962). College admissions and the stability of marriage. *American Mathematical Monthly*, 69, 9–15.

Hakke, C-J, MG Raith and FE Su (2002). Bidding for envy-freeness: a procedural approach to n-player fair-division problems. *Social Choice and Welfare*, 19, 723–749.

Herreiner, D and C Puppe (2002). A simple procedure for finding equitable allocations of indivisible goods. *Social Choice and Welfare*, 19, 415–430.

Moulin, H (1995). *Cooperative Microeconomics: A Game Theoretic Introduction*, Princeton: Princeton University Press.

Quint, T (1997). Restricted houseswapping games. *Journal of Mathematical Economics*, 27, 451–470.

Quinzii, M (1984). Core and competitive equilibria with indivisibilities. *International Journal of Game Theory*, 13, 41–60.

Roth, AE and A Postelwaite (1977). Weak versus strong domination in a market with indivisible goods. *Journal of Mathematical Economics*, 4, 131–137.

Shapley, L and H Scarf (1974). On cores and indivisibility. *Journal of Mathematical Economics*, 1, 23–28.

Sonmez, T (1996). Implementation in generalized matching problems. *Journal of Mathematical Economics*, 26, 429–439.

Sonmez, T (1999). Strategy-proofness and essentially single-valued cores. *Econometrica*, 67, 677–689.

CHAPTER 7

PLANNING, COMPETITION, AND COOPERATION: THE
SCOPE FOR NEGOTIATED SETTLEMENTS

Stephen Littlechild

University of Cambridge and University of Birmingham, England

7.1. Introduction

In this article, I want to explore how these inter-related themes have characterized —
or could characterize — regulatory approaches to the utilities sector. Hitherto, the
main choice has been between planning and competition. I want to suggest that a
particular cooperative approach, known as negotiated settlements, has an important
contribution to make.

7.2. Planning and Competition

During the 1960s and 1970s, public policy towards the UK utilities sector —
the nationalized industries — was based on marginal cost pricing and associated
investment programs. Several White Papers championed this. The energy sector
was perhaps in the forefront. Economists at Electricité de France had shown the
way (Nelson, 1964). The National Board for Prices and Incomes explored and
encouraged the implications of optimal pricing and investment for other nationalized industries (Turvey, 1968; 1971). Some of us devoted considerable effort to
the construction of an integrated model of the whole UK energy sector (Littlechild
et al., 1982). It would focus on decision-making and optimization rather than
forecasting and simulation.

Yet limitations became apparent. The industries themselves never fully wel-
comed or adopted the majority of these ideas. Planning models did not always

identify the most relevant options. (Our 50-year energy model, based on all the technologies under consideration by the energy industries themselves, failed to identify combined cycle gas turbines, which now account for over one third of the British electricity capacity and output.) There was an increasing doubt whether nationalized industries had sufficient incentives to efficient investment and operation. Nor were they particularly innovative or responsive to change.

During the 1980s and 1990s, privatization and competition provided the needed impetus to efficiency and innovation. Nationalized monopolies were typically restructured to provide conditions more conducive to competition. For example, whereas the Central Electricity Generating Board was previously responsible for almost 100% of generation in England and Wales, now there are over 12 generating companies, none of them accounting for more than one fifth of the market. Where competition was not yet feasible, or unlikely to be so, incentive price cap regulation — the so-called RPI-X regulation — was put in place.

The impact has been very considerable. Efficiency has increased more than anyone could have imagined. A greater electricity output is now provided with less than one third of the previous workforce. Investment and quality of service have increased too. There has been innovation in technology, products, and services. A similar record has been achieved by the other privatized utility sectors (National Audit Office, 2001–2002).

7.3. Limitations of Present Regulation

Competition is now extensive in the utility sector, but there remain areas of monopoly. Generation and retail supply, which are competitive, account for nearly three quarters of the average electricity bill, but the transmission and distribution networks, which are not competitive, account for nearly one quarter of the total cost. Similar proportions apply in gas. In some sectors, like water, there is relatively little competition as yet. Even in the competitive telecommunications sector, smaller competitors are often dependent on British Telecom for access to "the last mile."

Some form of price control remains in all the privatized utility sectors. In some respects, regulation has increased, with bigger staffs and budgets. Yet, regulation is subject to similar limitations as national planning. Hitherto, these limitations have been outweighed by the scope for cost cutting, efficiency improvement, and resultant price cutting. However, as the "surplus fat" is removed, it will be increasingly necessary to give careful thought to what form regulation should take, and how to overcome its intrinsic limitations.

My own experience in setting price controls suggests several difficulties for a regulator. How to know what levels of quality of service, and what quality/price tradeoffs, the customers would prefer? In consequence, it is difficult to identify the most appropriate investment programs and their timing. Insofar as regulators make the key decisions, the outcomes reflect their preferences rather than those of the customers.

This sets up a different dynamic in the industry. Utilities look to serve regulators rather than seek to discover and meet the wishes of customers. Interest groups are encouraged to lobby the regulator for subsidized favors rather than to discuss with companies the services they judge worth paying for. Company–customer relationships suffer.

Moreover, regulation means "one size fits all." It is too difficult to identify, explore, and justify different treatments for different companies and customers. Consequently, there is less variety, less innovation, and less scope for learning from experience.

These problems are not specific to the UK energy sector. They are common to all regulated sectors, and indeed to all countries. They suggest the need to find an alternative or complementary method of regulation that provides a greater role for market participants, and a less intrusive role for the regulatory body, even in parts of these sectors that are characterized by monopoly rather than competition.

7.4. Negotiated Settlements

Alternative approaches are indeed available. In some countries, market participants, customers, and utility companies negotiate mutually beneficial settlements of issues that are determined by a regulatory body in the UK and elsewhere (Doucet and Littlechild, 2006). Regulation remains as a standby in case negotiation fails, and thereby provides protection against monopoly power. But regulation facilitates the market process; it does not replace it.

The US Federal Power Commission in the 1960s used negotiated settlements to cope with an enormous backlog. The Federal Energy Regulatory Commission (FERC) still uses them. From 1994 to 2000, 39 out of 41 gas pipeline rate cases were settled by negotiation between the companies and their customers. The parties got a better outcome than they would have done with regulation. Most settlements embodied innovative rate moratorium provisions that FERC could approve but could not impose (Wang, 2004).

Florida Public Services Commission has encouraged settlements with telephone and electric utilities. Typically, these involve the Public Counsel on behalf of customers plus numerous other parties. In the last quarter of this century, such settlements were used in 31% of earnings reviews and accounted for three quarters of utility rate reductions — worth nearly $4 billion in the electricity sector alone (Littlechild, 2003; 2006; 2007). The utilities benefited from the introduction of incentive regulation and customers got lower prices sooner.

7.5. Experience in Canada

Until the mid-1990s, almost all the major Canadian oil and gas pipelines had to endure repeated regulatory hearings, often annually. These were often lengthy, sometimes lasting 40 days or more. Since 1997, however, almost all the major pipelines have settled all their rate cases with their users (producers, shippers, major industrial consumers, and local distribution companies) (Doucet and Littlechild, 2006). The only exception, for only four years, was one pipeline that was in dispute with the National Energy Board itself.

These Canadian settlements have introduced many features going beyond previous regulations. These include, for example, multi-year incentive arrangements that have increased efficiency and benefited companies and users; innovative provisions to improve quality of service; agreed terms for pipeline expansions; agreements on the provision of information and arrangements for monitoring; and agreed remedial actions in a few instances where performance has been inadequate. In short, negotiated settlements have done all that regulation does, and more. But they have done it by agreement, and by focusing on the issues and outcomes that the parties themselves find most important. Some pipelines are now on their third five-year settlement.

This change of approach required no new statute in Canada. There were two key factors. First, the Board encouraged settlements and set out guidelines. It refrained from "cherrypicking" only those aspects of settlements that it liked. It explained that if the negotiating process was sound — if all the interested parties were able to participate in negotiations and if there was a broad agreement — the Board would consider that the public interest had been satisfied.

Second, the Board established a method for determining the generic cost of capital that would apply to each pipeline in the event of litigation. Each year it announces this value. This removes a major area of dispute and enables participants to focus on what added value can be offered to warrant a higher return. Settlements either incorporate the generic cost of capital or agree alternative provisions.

7.6. Application in the UK and Elsewhere

This approach could be applied in other countries also. In the UK, for example, it would require no change of law, simply encouragement by the regulatory body. The Civil Aviation Authority (CAA) has, in fact, instituted a process called "constructive engagement" between airports and airlines, which is developing well at Heathrow and Gatwick. Similarly, users' representatives could negotiate with electricity, gas, water, and telephone companies, to establish the expansions and allowed revenues for the monopoly networks.

Who would these representatives be? Major users often represent themselves, and there are established representative groups for smaller industrial and commercial users. Independent consumer organizations including energywatch and the Water Consumer Counsel already represent domestic consumers before the regulatory bodies.

The regulatory bodies could ensure that such representative groups have adequate information and resources. A regulatory cost of capital formula would provide a counterweight to the market power of the utilities. Would the user groups participate? International experience is that they do. If not, the case would go to the regulator as at present.

The processes would be similar to present regulation but less confrontational, with more emphasis on trying to find a common ground. The outcomes might be similar in some respects but more varied, more innovative, and more attuned to the actual needs of customers and companies. Smaller parties need not suffer from this process since all those with a legitimate interest could participate in the negotiations and could appeal to the regulator if unsatisfied.

Would utility regulation still be needed? Yes, but it would facilitate the market process rather than replace it. Negotiated settlements could thus enable further deregulation that has so far eluded regulators and governments alike. It would also add an important element of cooperation to the present mix of planning and competition.

References

Doucet, J and SC Littlechild (2006a). Negotiated settlements and the national energy board in Canada. Electricity Policy Research Group Working Papers, No. EPRG 06/29, Cambridge: University of Cambridge. http://www.electricitypolicy.org.uk/pubs/index.html.

Doucet, J and SC Littlechild (2006b). Negotiated settlements: the development of legal and economic thinking. *Utilities Policy*, 14(4), 266–277.

Littlechild, SC (2003). Consumer participation in regulation: stipulated settlements, the consumer advocate and utility regulation in Florida. In *Proc. of Market Design 2003 Conference*, pp. 77–84. Stockholm, www.elforsk-marketdesign.net.

Littlechild, SC (2006). Stipulations, the consumer advocate and utility regulation in Florida. Electricity Policy Research Group Working Papers, No. EPRG 06/15, Cambridge: University of Cambridge. http://www.electricitypolicy.org.uk/pubs/index.html.

Littlechild, SC (2007). The bird in hand: stipulated settlements and electricity regulation in Florida. Electricity Policy Research Group Working Papers, No. EPRG 0705, Cambridge: University of Cambridge. http://www.electricitypolicy.org.uk/pubs/index.html.

Littlechild, SC, KG Vaidya, M Carey, PG Soldatos, *et al.* (1982). *Energy Strategies for the UK*, London: George Allen & Unwin.

National Audit Office, *Pipes and Wires*, HC 723 Session 2001–2002, London: HMSO [10 April 2002].

Nelson, JR (ed.) (1964). *Marginal Pricing in Practice*, Englewood Cliffs: Prentice-Hall.

Turvey, R (1968). *Optimal Pricing and Investment in Electricity Supply*, London: George Allen & Unwin.

Turvey, R (1971). *Economic Analysis and Public Enterprises*. London: George Allen & Unwin.

Wang, Z (2004). Settling utility rate cases: an alternative ratemaking procedure. *Journal of Regulatory Economics*, 26(2), 141–164.

CHAPTER 8

THE ROLE OF RELATIONSHIP BANKING ON THE PERFORMANCE OF FIRMS IN BANGLADESH

Shigeru Uchida* and Sarwar Uddin Ahmed[†]

*Nagasaki University, Japan
†Independent University, Bangladesh

8.1. Introduction

Bank-based financial system of corporate financing and governance is regarded as one of the best suited alternatives for the Asian economies. This is due to the absence of strong financial market and regulatory bodies to supply funds and support their corporate firms in times of financial distress. Accordingly, the American model of corporate governance, where banks are prohibited by legislation to exercise close monitoring on client firm's decisions, is difficult to replicate in Asian economies. Among the Asian economies, Japan is the role model for bank-based corporate governance system. The corporate governance, which the Japanese banks exercise by establishing a long-term relationship with the corporate firms, attracted lot of attention and became an area of great interest for the Asian economies. On this background, this paper discusses relationship banking: concept, merits, and demerits; contemporary status of relationship banking in Japan and Bangladesh, and also its effect on the performance and profitability of the corporate borrowers in both the countries.

8.2. Relationship Banking

8.2.1. *Definition*

The term relationship banking is still vague and not clearly defined in various literatures. Berger (1999) defined the existence of relationship banking where the following three conditions are met:

1. the intermediary gathers information beyond readily available public information;
2. information gathering takes place over time through multiple interactions with the borrower, often through the provision of multiple financial services and
3. the information remains confidential.

Boot (2000) also defined relationship banking somewhat in the same direction, as the provision of financial services by a financial intermediary that invests in obtaining customer-specific information, often proprietary in nature; and evaluates the profitability of theses investments through interactions with the same customer over time and/or across products.

The relationship banking esteemed from the Japanese main bank system is often defined as the relationship of the bank having the largest loan share with the firm is not true as largest loan share often changes in times of sudden long-term borrowing from long-term credit or trust banks (Hirota and Horiuchi, 2001).

Thus, from the above discussion, the term relationship banking can be defined as a long-term relationship between the financial intermediary and the corporate firm developed by repeated interactions transpired from diversified transactions, accumulation of specific information, and major loan concentration. This overlapping aspects which give birth to relationship banking are described by the Venn Diagram shown in Fig. 8.1.

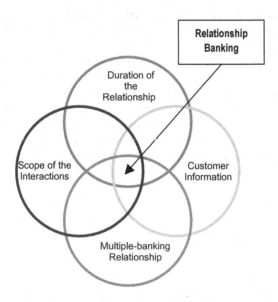

Fig. 8.1. Concept of relationship banking.

8.2.2. *Merits and Demerits of Relationship Banking*

There are various merits and demerits of relationship banking. These are summarized in Table 8.1 with reference to the relevant literatures.

8.3. Contemporary Status of Banking Sector and Relationship Banking in Japan

8.3.1. *Present State of Banking Sector in Japan*

Japanese firms depend more on debt than on issuing stocks. Banks play the most dominant role in the financial markets of Japan (see Fig. 8.2 showing the category and number of financial institutions operating in Japan). The share of banks is approximately 60% in both raising and lending of funds among all the financial institutions (see Fig. 8.3). This indicates the active role of banking sector in financial markets. Even after financial liberalizations and burst of the bubble economy in 1991, this dominance of the banking system is still prevalent. Table 8.2 summarizes the various measures taken to reform and stabilize the banking sector throughout the last 10 years.

8.3.2. *Relationship Banking in Japan*

In Japan, where the size of the banking sector to GNP is the largest, we can find the most typical and conventional nature of relationship banking. This typical kind of relationship is also interchangeably referred to as *main-bank relationship*. According to Aoki, Patrick and Sheard (1995), there are five main aspects of relationship banking in Japan, such as, bank loans; bond-issue related services; shareholding; payment settlement account and supply of management and information resources.

As shown in Fig. 8.4, financing aspects refer to bank loans and bond-issue related services, of which bank loan has been traditionally the key one, while settlement accounts, stockholding, and supply of management resources are the monitoring and governance aspects of the relationship. In Japan, this second dimension of the bank-firm relationship is ensured by the activities that are discussed below.

8.3.2.1. *Stockholding of firms*

In Japan, banks maintain a substantial stockholding in the firms to which they act as the main bank. According to the *The Japanese Anti-Monopoly Law*, banks can hold up to 5% of a firm's stock (prior to 1987 up to 10%) on their own account. But in 2001, the Financial Council report suggested a proposal to restrict the total

Table 8.1.   Merits and demerits of relationship banking.

Merits	
Overcoming asymmetry of information	Due to relationship banking, a borrowing firm might disclose specific information to its bank which would never been disclosed to the financial markets (Bhattacharya and Chiesa, 1995). The firm would be willing to do so as the bank is the financier and needs to worry about information leakage to competitors (Boot, 2000).
Flexibility of contract	Relationship banking provides less rigid nature of relationship compared to capital market funding, as rearrangement of the contract can be done easily and can improve welfare (Boot, Greenbum and Thakor, 1993).
Detailed covenants	Inclusion of covenants in relationship lending might provide a chance for better control of potential conflicts of interest and reduce agency costs (Boot, 2000). As lending contracts are easy to renegotiate compared to other bond issues or public capital market funding instruments, strict and detailed covenants can be included (Berlin and Mester, 1992).
Accommodation and monitoring of collateral	Bank lending contract can include collateral which is proved to be effective in mitigating moral hazard and adverse selection problems in loan contracting (Chan and Thakor, 1987). Monitoring of collateral is possible with closeness and proprietary information obtained from relationship banking.
Lending at lower profit	Relationship banking allows the bank to provide loans which are not profitable in the short-term, as it can compensate the former with higher rents from the borrower in the long-term. This is known as intertemporal transfers in loan pricing (Berlin and Mester, 1992; Boot, 2000).
Demerits	
Lower investment efficiency	Relationship banking might lower investment efficiency due to soft-budget constraints (Bolton and Scharfstein, 1996). This is due to the flexibility in loan negotiations that would provide less incentive in making efficient investment of borrowed funds.
Hold up problem	In relationship banking, the bank might charge higher lending rate as it has information monopoly and the borrower cannot turn to other lenders (Nam, 2004).
Avoid risky investment	Firms having relationship banking might take too few risky investments as the bank will discourage projects with high risk and high return (Nam, 2004).

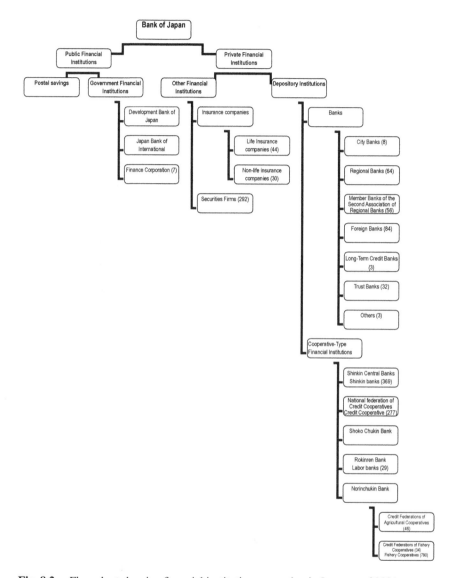

Fig. 8.2. Flow chart showing financial institutions operating in Japan as of 2001.
Source: Compiled from Bank of Japan, 2005 and Japanese Bankers Association, 2005.

shareholding by banks exceeding their own capital from 2004 as soon as possible. The main bank usually is in the top five shareholders of the client firm and is normally the top shareholder among banks. This enables the main bank to protect a customer firm from hostile take-over.

Raising of funds

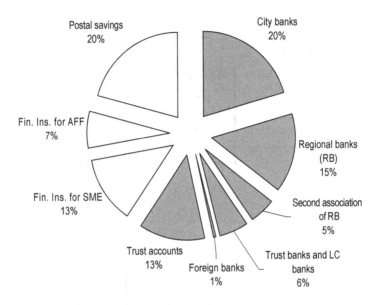

Lending of funds

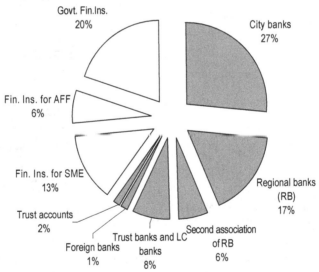

Fig. 8.3. Raising and lending of funds by the financial institutions in Japan at the end of 2000 (The gray pieces of the pies represent the share of the banking sector).

Table 8.2. Measures taken to stabilize the banking sector after the burst of bubble economy.

1. Dealing with bad loans
   a) Classification and disclosure of bad loans
   To tackle bad loans, the banking law instructed that banks classify their assets into four categories and disclose:

   I. Loans to borrowers in legal bankruptcy;
   II. Past due loans in arrears by 6 months or more;
   III. Past due loans in arrears by 3 months or more; and
   IV. Restructured loans.

   b) Writing-off of bad loans from balance sheets
   The emergency economic package revealed on April 2001, instructed writing-off of bad loans from the bank's balance sheet within 2 years for existing bad loans.

2. Limitation on bank shareholdings
   According to the Japanese Anti-Monopoly Law, banks can hold up to 5% of a firm's stock (prior to 1987 up to 10%) on their own account. In 2001, the Financial Council report suggested a proposal to restrict the total shareholding by banks exceeding their own capital from 2004.

3. Establishing the banks shareholdings purchase cooperation
   Bank's Shareholding Purchase Corporation was established in January 30, 2002 to absorb the excess supply of shares due to the implementation of limited shareholding law.

4. Removal of full deposit insurance
   The full deposit protection provided under the Deposit Insurance Law of 1996 was revised in April 2002. Accordingly, deposit insurance will protect deposits up to 10 million yen plus interest per depositor.

Source: Stabilizing the financial system, Japanese Bankers Association, 2005.

8.3.2.2. *Supply of management resources*

In Japan, banks often send their managers as directors or auditors to the board of client firms. In 1992, about one quarter (24.4%) of the 40,045 directors of listed Japanese firms were from outside the firm (Aoki, Patrick and Sheard, 1995). Of these, about one fifth (21.7%, or just over 5% of all directors) were from banks. The shifts of managers from the main bank to its customer firms promote close management relationship and enable the transfer of management know-how. On the other hand, banks can also prevent the board of directors of the firm from making an illegal or seriously unjust decision.

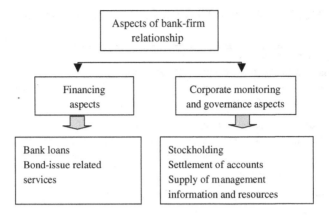

Fig. 8.4.   Aspects of bank-firm relationship.

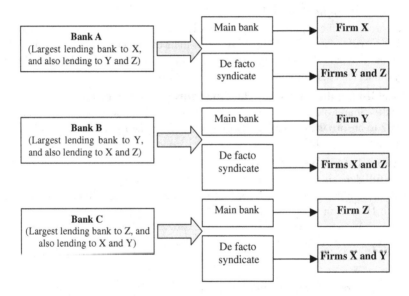

Fig. 8.5.   Loan syndication procedure under Japanese banking system.

8.3.2.3. *Loan syndication*

Another unique nature of bank–firm relationship in Japan is the *reciprocal delegated monitoring* in the form of loan syndication. For example, banks A, B, and C lends to firms X, Y, and Z. Then, A will serve as main bank to X, B as the main bank to Y, and C to Z (see Fig. 8.5). The main bank is expected to play the leading role in case of corporate distress and organizes financial rescue, restructuring and bear a disproportionate share of the costs of financial assistance in terms of interest exemptions or deferrals, loan rescheduling, loan losses and new funds supply relative to the syndicate as a whole (Aoki, Patrick and Sheard, 1995). In Japan, all these above corporate monitoring and governance have been made possible by the main bank because it is the stockholder, management representatives, and also major settler of payment accounts for borrowing firms.

8.4. Literature Review on the Effect of Relationship Banking in Japan

Now, let us examine the effect of relationship banking practices in Japan by gathering examples from various theoretical and empirical literatures.

8.4.1. *Availability of Credit*

The first question regarding the impact of relationship banking is whether it made it easy for the firms in accessing to credit. Many studies concluded that Japanese firms with relationship bank enjoy easier access to credit and did not fall into liquidity constraints (Fukuda and Hirota, 1996; Mori, 1994). Also, there are studies drawing opposite conclusions too. For example, Hayashi (2000) finds no evidence that relationship banking esteemed from main banking did not help the firm in meeting liquidity crisis.

8.4.2. *Rescuing in Financial Distress*

It is widely argued that relationship banking is very much effective in rescuing firms in times of financial distress. Based on the information obtained as result of relationship banking, banks tend to respond quickly to the distress by mitigating liquidity shortfalls, debt restructuring, and operational restructuring of borrower firms (Nam, 2004). Japanese firms with a strong main bank relationship seem to have better protection than those without such relationship (Hoshi, Kashyap, and Scharfstein, 1990; Okazaki and Horiuchi, 1992).

8.4.3. *Reduction of Risk*

Relationship banking can contribute in reducing the risk of corporate borrowers by assisting the firms in times of financial distress and reducing corporate fluctuations. Considerable amount of loans supplied to a firm send positive signal to the market participants concerning the quality of the borrower, its profitability, and its riskiness. Firms with bank borrowing pay lower interest rate premium in times of financial distress as observed through 1964 to 1993 (Kawai, Hashimoto and Izumida, 1996).

8.4.4. Performance of Borrowing Firms

Relationship banking is believed to solve the problem information asymmetry, liquidity constraints, and agency problem. But this does not mean that this improves the performance of the corporate firms. According to Hosono (1997), the lending interest rate spread was significantly negatively affected by the main bank loan ratio in total debt during the period 1982–1995 for the exchange-listed Japanese firms. However, Japanese main banks extracted higher rents through higher than average lending rates before financial market liberalization in the 1980s (Weinstein and Yafeh, 1998).

8.5. Contemporary Status of Banking Sector and Relationship Banking in Bangladesh

8.5.1. Present State of Banking Sector in Bangladesh

The banking sector of Bangladesh is characterized by problems of non-performing loans, capital inadequacy, provisioning shortfall etc., although it accounts for about 97% of the market in terms of assets, and in turn making the entire financial sector vulnerable to economic crisis. Even the different banking sector reform programs are not giving any significant results. The banking sector ailing with different problems is, in turn, hindering the industrial development of the country as the majority of the industrial firms rely on indirect financing from banks as a source of finance, as shown in Fig. 8.6 for the conceptual process. A most frequently

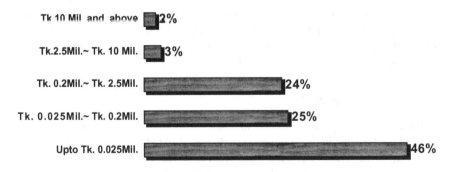

Fig. 8.6. Number of credit account holders in different amounts of credit (2002).

cited reason for these problems is the widespread practice of multiple borrowing in the banking sector. Although numerous studies on theoretical aspects have been conducted to examine the effect of multiple borrowing, a few empirical studies can be found to check the effect of multiple borrowing relationships on the financial status of the borrowing firms. In one of our previous studies, we have found that there is enough evidence of widespread practice of multiple borrowing among the corporate borrowers in Bangladesh and the results of the empirical analysis revealed that, although such practice enables firms to borrow at comparatively lower interest expense, but suffer from limited access to credit.

8.5.1.1. *Banking problems in Bangladesh*

In a country like Bangladesh where capital market is underdeveloped, industries rely heavily on the banking sector's indirect finance for meeting their funds need. But for ensuring this continuous flow of funds, the banking sector need to be sound and well managed. Unfortunately, this is not happening in the case of Bangladesh as the banking sector is beset with different core managerial problems in addition to the more common problems. At this juncture, we are going to summarize these unique problems supported with relevant literatures and not the common problems such as *loan default, capital inadequacy*, and *financing concentration* that are also seen in the banking sector of other countries.

8.5.1.1.1. Absence of close bank–firm relationship

The bank–firm relationship in Bangladesh takes in a conventional form, where bank loan is the main link between the bank and the firm. The monitoring and governance aspect of the relationship, such as stockholding and dispatch of management personnel are not seen. Banks give advice to firms as outsiders and remained away from firms facing financial difficulties. Thus, financing aspect of the bank–firm relationship is the most common feature present in the banking system of Bangladesh. Ahmed (1997), who is one of the few researchers comparing the Japanese and Bangladeshi financial systems, commented that under the present practice in Bangladesh, the banks give advice to customers as outsiders rather than insiders and have tended to keep away from firms facing financial constraints. Banks even may compel a firm for premature liquidation to protect its own interest. The commercial banks are reluctant to go for long-term investments, such as loan. And an examination of the statements of the individual banks reveals very small-holding of shares. Although Bangladeshi firms are highly levered, the bank–firm relationship is not so close. If the bank–firm relationship is promoted to be closer, it may have its likely positive impact on the prevailing "default culture" of the borrowing firms.

8.5.1.1.2. Concentration on retail nature of transactions

If we review the nature of accounts in which banks are providing loans, then
we can see that they are concentrating more on retail than wholesale transactions. Figure 8.6 shows that as of 31st December 1998, 89.07% of the accounts of
advances of NCBs are for loan amount up to Tk. 25,000 (about US\$ 420)[1]; 8.27%
of the advance accounts are for loan amounts from Tk. 25,001 to Tk. 200,000. And
only 2.66% of the total number of advance accounts are for loan amounts more
than Tk. 200,001 (about US\$ 3704) and above. This indicates heavy concentration
of banks on small amount of retail transactions. These retail transactions are small
in amount and are normally short-term in nature. Hence, from this data, we can
also conclude that about 90% of all the lending of the banks is of retail in nature
and wholesale lending accounts for only a very small fraction of the total loan portfolio. This indicates that although banking sector is the main source of funds for
the industrial firms, they are not actually carrying out this responsibility by going
mainly for retail transactions, which are comparatively less risky and requires less
analytical expertise.

8.5.1.1.3. Presence of extensive credit rationing

Credit rationing takes place when lenders limit the amount that individuals can
borrow, even though the borrowers are willing to pay the going interest rate on
their loans (Dornbusch and Fischer, 1998). If credit is rationed, borrowers might
be unable to obtain the credit necessary to carry out an investment project even
when the project passes the test of profitability. Credit rationing arises principally
in two cases: first, when governments put ceilings on interest rates that keep them
below market equilibrium, and second, when lenders cannot accurately assess the
risks of lending to particular borrowers (Sachs and Larrain, 1993).

Now, let us examine the case of Bangladesh. In Bangladesh, deposits as a
source of funds have increased from 42.7% in 1975–1976 to 54% in 1993–1994.
While advances by banks, as a use of funds, increased only to 37.1% from 33.9%
in the same period. Also, as shown in Figure 8.6, among the total deposit of banks,
time deposits are about 82%. As we come to the recent period, time deposits have
increased more rapidly than have demand deposits … the structural shift even in
the face of falling interest rates in recent years may reflect, inter alia, the growing
confidence of savers in the banking system (Ahmed, 1997). But on the other hand,
banks failed to channel this fund into credit. Then the question arises: where did
this growth in time deposits go? The answer is: to other retail financing sectors.
Again, why are banks doing so?

Firstly, credit rationing is present in Bangladesh not because of the first reason
of government imposed interest-rate ceilings but because of the second reason

---

[1]Taking 1 US\$ = Tk. 68.95 rate quoted as of August 18, 2007.

cited above, i.e., inability of the banks to accurately assess the risks of lending to particular borrowers.[2]

In practice, access to borrower's internal information becomes really critical particularly in developing countries like Bangladesh, where true and accurate information about borrowers are hard to get. But, if banks have a close and long-term relationship with a particular borrower, they feel easier to provide credit, depending on the smoothness of the previous relationship. Hence, in the absence of government ceiling on interest rates, banks will loosen credit rationing when there is a close and long-term nature of relationship between the bank and the borrowing customer. But, in Bangladesh, this type of close bank–firm relationship is absent. Hence, it can be concluded that, credit rationing is occurring because of inability on the part of the banks to assess credit risk accurately resulting in unwillingness to provide credit.

8.5.1.1.4. Higher interest margin

In the banking sector in Bangladesh, the spread between the deposit and lending interest rate is very high. In a competitive market, relationship between the lending interest rate and deposit interest rate can be derived as follows (Wahba and Mohieldin, 1998).

$$i_l = \frac{1}{1-k} i_d$$

where, k = required reserve ratio (20% of deposits), i_d = deposit interest rate and i_l = lending interest rate.

Accordingly, the nominal interest rate spread is calculated as follows:

$$i_l - i_d = \frac{k}{1-k} i_d$$

We calculated desirable spread between lending interest rate and deposit interest and plotted in Fig. 8.8. The figure shows that the actual spread is as high as 7%, where the desirable spread is around 2%. This implies serious operational and managerial inefficiency in reducing the spread. But, the main inherent reason behind this big gap is the high-risk premium that banks are charging inside lending interest rates. Banks charge higher risk premium because they do not have adequate information about the borrower and also there is lack of consistent long-term relationship between them to ensure credit worthiness of the prospective borrower.

---

[2]Effective April 1, 1992, Bangladesh Bank removed all ceilings on deposit rates and all floors and ceilings on all lending rates with the exception of the rates applicable to the export, agriculture, and small cottage industries sectors. But, later ceilings on interest rates to agriculture and small and cottage industries were also lifted in July 1999; loan rate ceilings are only in effect for export loans (IMF, 1998).

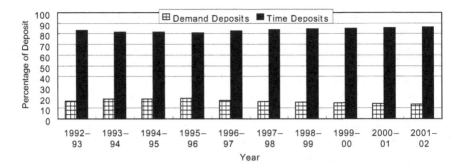

Fig. 8.7.   Proportion of bank deposits.

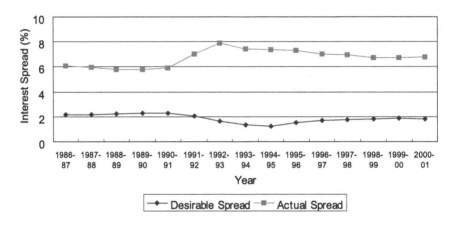

Fig. 8.8.   Actual vs. desirable interest spread.

8.5.1.1.5. High transaction cost and delay in loan decisions

Also, in Bangladesh, the transaction cost of getting loans is very high, which is
again accentuated by the delay in decision making. According to a study conducted
by the Bangladesh Institute of Bank Management (BIBM), it was revealed that the
average loan-related expenses of the 800 borrowers taken as sample, were from
Tk. 20 to Tk. 36 for each borrower and the number of days lost in getting the
loan varies from 5 to 12 days, depending upon the amount of loan received (see
Table 8.3). These loan-related expenses and days lost in getting the loans, which are
more literally known as transaction cost, may arise if banks are having inadequate
information base about borrowers. Also, inter-bank exchange of information is not
so popular. Hence, when a new loan application is made, it takes a considerable
amount of time for a bank to process the application to judge the loan competency

Table 8.3. Average costs of loan to the borrowers.

Loan amount	Number of borrowers	Average days lost	Average loan-related expenditure
Up to Tk. 1000	56	5	Tk. 20
Tk. 1000–2000	142	7	Tk. 24
Tk. 2000–3000	176	8	Tk. 26
Tk. 3000–5000	327	10	Tk. 32
Tk. 5000 and above	99	12	Tk. 36
Total	800		

of the borrower. Accordingly, the banking problem in Bangladesh is summarized in Fig. 8.9.

8.5.1.2. *Comparative characteristics of the banking system of Bangladesh with that of Japan*

Holding of Stakes.   Bangladeshi banks hold large stakes in some sectors but their role in disciplining management and monitoring performance does not seem to be as important as it is in Japan.

Capital Market.   The Bangladeshi capital market is very much underdeveloped than the Japanese markets. And it is very difficult for firms to raise funds through the issue of bonds and shares. As a result, bank loans are their major source of external finance.

Ownership Structure.   The ownership structure of the Bangladeshi firms is somewhat similar to the structure found in many Japanese firms, in the sense that the separation of ownership and management is not as radical as in the US.

Agency Problem.   The ownership of Bangladeshi firms is very concentrated and the control group can exercise a close vigilance over the management behavior and mitigate the agency problem. Thus, in the case of Bangladesh, we should not be concerned about the implication of a separation between ownership and control resulting from limited shareholding concentration, but on the implications for efficiency of the nature of the control group, in our case, the banks.

Accordingly, we can conclude that, the role of monitoring and control by banks is also important for Bangladesh as it is in Japan for similarities in the areas of — dominance of the banking sector as a source of fund, greater stake of the banking sector, concentrated ownership structure etc. On the other hand, for the

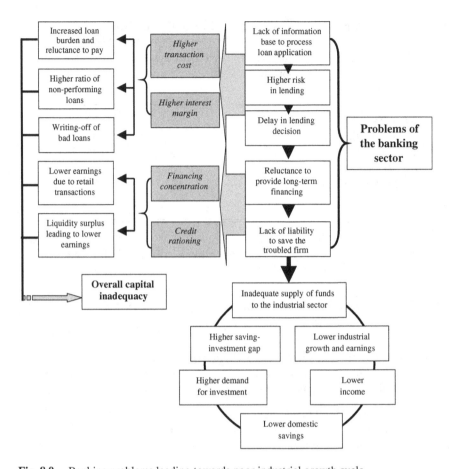

Fig. 8.9.   Banking problems leading towards poor industrial growth cycle.
Source: Compiled and reconstructed by the authors with reference to Alam (1994) (Alam *et al.*, 1999) and Choudhury and Moral (1999).

US, monitoring by banks is less important because of separation of ownership and control, easy access to capital market and above all for restrictions imposed by regulatory barriers (Glass-Steagall Banking Act). Thus, for the purpose of comparison, Bangladesh stands closer to Japan than any other countries.

8.5.2. *Relationship Banking in Bangladesh*

In recent days, multiple borrowing propensity of corporate firms in Bangladesh are in increasing trend, although not completely unknown elsewhere in the world. As a result of this, banks are giving advice to firms as outsiders rather than insiders and have tended to keep away from firms facing financial constraints. Banks even may compel a firm for premature liquidation to protect its own interest (Ahmed, 1997). Out of the 155 joint stock companies listed in the Dhaka Stock Exchange, 73 were found to be maintaining borrowing relationship with a single bank and the rest 82 were having borrowing relationship with multiple banks (two or more banks). And some companies even maintain borrowing relationship with as high as 11 banks. Thus, the propensity of corporate borrowers in Bangladesh to maintain multiple banking relationships is also very high.

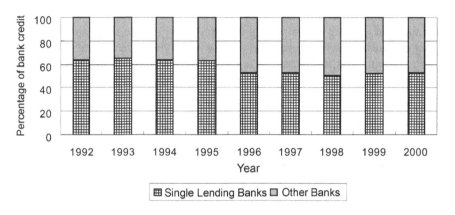

Fig. 8.10.   Share of bank credits: single lending bank vs. other banks.

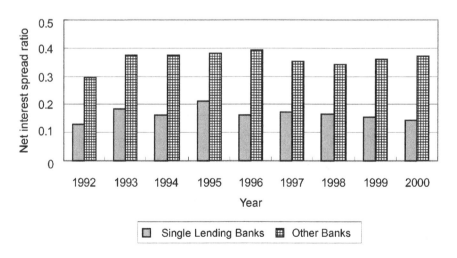

Fig. 8.11.   Comparative interest spread: single lending bank vs. other banks.

Majority Share of the Banks Lending As Single Lender: As shown in Fig. 8.7, in Bangladesh, among the banks, only Sonali, Agrani, Janata, NBL and IFIC Bank are identified as the banks, which are mainly lending to the sample firms as their sole or single bank.[3] These banks are lending approximately 55–65% of the total advances of all banks. Thus, banks which are serving more as the single lender to firms are also providing most of the loans in Bangladesh.

Interest Rate Spread: In the banking sector of Bangladesh, the spread between the deposit and lending interest rate is very high. As shown in Fig. 8.8, the actual spread is as high as 7%, where the desirable spread is around 2%.

However, if we compare the status of the firms under study, then we can find that the banks having single lending relationship with these firms are having a lower net interest spread as compared to those which are not having any such kind of relationship. Thus, it is interesting to verify from the following analysis whether firms borrowing from these single lender banks can borrow at lower interest rates too (see Figs. 8.9, 8.10, and 8.11).

8.6. Empirical Analysis on the Impact of Relationship Banking

Among the Asian economies including Bangladesh, Japan is the role model for relationship banking-based corporate governance system. Accordingly, in our previous papers, e.g., Ahmed and Uchida (2003) and Uchida and Ahmed (2004), we have conducted empirical analysis to perceive the impact of relationship both in Japan and in Bangladesh. The most commonly observed impacts of relationship banking on corporate firms of an economy are summarized in Table 8.4. On this background, the objective of this paper is to summarize the findings of the empirical

Table 8.4. Possible impact of relationship banking.

Impacts
Increased availability of credit
Rescuing in financial distress
Reduction of risk for client firms
Higher rates charged on client firms
Corporate growth and profits

---

[3]The term *single lender banks* is used to refer to banks, which are providing loans to firms as the only lending bank.

analysis papers regarding the impact of relationship banking on the performance of corporate firms conducted by using data of Japan and Bangladesh.

8.6.1. *Impact of Relationship Banking on Corporate Firms of Bangladesh*

Ahmed and Uchida (2003) have conducted an empirical analysis to see the impact of relationship banking on the corporate firms of Bangladesh. The balance sheet data of 174 joint stock companies listed in the Dhaka Stock Exchange in the year 2001 are used. The results of the analysis can be summarized as follows:

8.6.1.1. *Findings of t-tests*

t-tests of the differences between two means to find the significance of difference on two financial ratios, viz., *debt-equity ratio (DER)* and *interest expense to loans ratio (IELO)* were calculated for all the sample companies. A total of 155 joint stock companies listed in the Dhaka Stock Exchange are included in the analysis. Out of these, 73 were found to be maintaining borrowing relationship with a single bank and the rest 82 were having borrowing relationship with multiple banks (two or more banks). Next, we conducted applied *t*-tests to see whether there is any significant difference in DER and IELO between the companies having a single lending bank vis-à-vis companies having relationship with multiple banks.[4]

As shown in Table 8.5, the average debt-equity ratio of the companies having borrowing relationship with single banks is higher as compared to that of the companies borrowing from multiple banks. This indicates that, multiple banking makes access to credit difficult. On the other hand, the average interest expense to loans outstanding ratio of the companies having borrowing relationship with single banks is higher as compared to that of the companies borrowing from multiple banks. This indicates that by exploiting competition between banks, firms borrowing from multiple banks can borrow at lower cost.

Thus, from the results of the analysis, we can conclude that relationship-banking practices in Bangladesh result into higher access to credit at comparatively higher cost.

8.6.1.2. *Findings of multivariate analysis*

The balance sheet data of 174 joint stock companies listed in the Dhaka Stock Exchange in the year 2001 are used to construct multivariate models for identifying the most influential factors deciding the profitability of the corporate firms.

---

[4]Debt-equity ratio (DER) $= \dfrac{\text{Total fixed liabilities}}{\text{Total shareholders' equity}}$

Interest expense to loans outstanding (IELO) $= \dfrac{\text{Total interest expense}}{\text{Total loans outstanding}}$

Table 8.5.   *t*-test result for the ratio analysis.

	Single bank (Mean)	Multiple banks (Mean)	Results of the *t*-tests
Debt-equity ratio	0.40	−0.14	There is difference in mean value
Interest expense to loans outstanding ratio	0.57	0.33	There is no significant difference in mean value

In doing so, logistic regression analysis has been conducted. A hypothetical multivariate model is constructed to determine the factors, which influences the performance of the firms (profitability) as follows:

$$PRF = f(TAS, TCA, SAL, EQT, LOA, REX, SHA, NBK) \qquad (8.1)$$

The explanation of the variables, expected and revealed relationship sign derived from the multivariate analysis are presented in Table 8.6. Accordingly, the findings of the study can be summed up as follows:

(1) Interest expense, share of the financial institutions and number of banks did not show any significant relationship with the profitability of firms. Thus, the effect of having multiple borrowing relationships on the corporate profitability cannot be confirmed through this empirical model analysis.

(2) Whereas, equity exhibited positive and loan showed negative relationship with profitability, which indicates that firms having higher financial leverage are prone to be a losing concern in terms of profitability. Thus, firms, which are taking bank loans more, are having comparatively more financial difficulties. Conversely, firms relying more on equity capital are comparatively more profitable.

8.6.2. *Impact of Relationship Banking on Corporate Firms of Japan*

Uchida and Ahmed (2004) and Ahmed and Uchida (2005a,b), constructed a hypothetical multivariate model based on conceptual relationship to determine the factors, which influence the performance of the corporate firms (profitability). The objective was to observe how relationship banking is affecting the performance of the corporate firms. As a data source, three yearly time series balance sheet data (March 2002–March 2004) of 98 exchange listed SMEs in Japan were used. As a parameter to represent profitability, time series mean of return on assets (ROAs) of the companies are used. The model consists of variables that are hypothetically assumed to have an influence on profitability of a corporate firm and are summarized by the following conceptual model:

$$\text{Profitability (ROAs)} = f(\text{TCA, SAL, DER, SHA, NBK, FCF, ROE}) \qquad (8.2)$$

The explanation of the variables, expected and revealed relationship sign are presented in Table 8.6. Accordingly, the findings of the study can be summed up as follows:

(1) Percent of shareholding by banks showed positive relationship with ROA indicating that, relationship banking does count in improving the profitability performance of the firms.

Table 8.6.   Descriptive statistics ($n = 174$).

Variable name	Description	Expected sign	Revealed sign
POS	The dependent variable is the profitability of firms (POS = 1 if five yearly average is in profit and 0 otherwise).		
TAS	Total assets of the company in millions of Taka	+	NSS
TCA	Total capital of the company in millions of Taka	+	NSS
SAL	Total sales volume of the company in millions of Taka	+	NSS
EQT	Total shareholders' equity in millions of Taka	?	+
LOA	Total loans taken from financial institutions in millions of Taka	?	−
REX	Interest expense of the company in millions of Taka	?	NSS
SHA	Percentage of share held by financial institutions	?	NSS
NBK	Number of banks the company maintains lending relationship	?	NSS

Note: NSS denotes not statistically significant.

(2) Whereas, the negative relationship between debt-equity ratio (DER) with profitability (ROA), indicates that, firms having higher financial leverage (loan capital) are prone to be a losing concern in terms of profitability. Thus, firms, which are taking bank loans more, are having comparatively more financial difficulties. Conversely, firms relying more on equity capital are comparatively more profitable.

8.7. Summary

The findings of the empirical studies can summarized through Tables 8.7 and 8.8.

(1) As shown in Table 8.7, relationship banking is providing positive impact to the Japanese corporate firms in the form of *increased availability of credit, rescuing in financial distress* and thus, in turn, *reducing the risk of the client firms*. The claim that *higher rents are charged* cannot be proved from this analysis. Whereas, relationship banking in the form of *corporate shareholding* is influencing positively and *easy access to credit* is influencing negatively towards the firms growth and profitability.

Table 8.7. Variables and descriptive statistics ($n = 79$).

Name of the variable	Description	Expected sign in regression model	Revealed sign in regression mode
ROA	The dependent variable is the time series mean of return on assets		
TCA	Total capital of the company in millions yen	+	NSS
SAL	Time series mean of the total sales volume of the company in millions yen	+	—
DER	Debt-equity ratio of the company	?	—
SHA	Percentage of share held by financial institutions	?	+
NBK	Number of banks the company maintains transacting relationship	?	NSS
FCF	Time series mean of financing cash flows in 100 millions yen	?	NSS
ROE	Time series mean of return on equity	+	+

Note: NSS denotes not statistically significant.

Table 8.8. Empirical findings on impact of relationship banking in Japan and Bangladesh.

Impacts	Japan		Bangladesh	
	Direction of impact	Evaluation mark	Direction of impact	Evaluation mark
Increased availability of credit	□	O	□	O
Rescuing in financial distress	□		?	?
Reduction of risk for client firms	□		□	
Higher rates charged on client firms	?	?	□	O
Corporate growth and profits:	□	O	?	?
Corporate shareholding Easy access to credit	□	O	□	□

Note: O = Yes, Δ = Moderate, X = No and ? = Not confirmed.

(2) In the case of Bangladesh, relationship banking is providing positive impact to the corporate firms in the form of *increased availability of credit* and thus, in turn, *reducing the risk of the client firms*. Whereas, regarding negative impact, the claim that *higher rents are charged* is proved to be true. But the contribution of relationship banking *in rescuing from financial distress* and impact of *corporate shareholding* on profitability cannot be verified from this analysis. *Easy access to credit* is influencing negatively towards the firms growth and profitability (see Table 8.7).

Based on the theoretical and empirical analysis results and the on-going discussion, the comparative status of relationship banking in Japan and Bangladesh can be summarized as in Table 8.9. The negative relationship between credit availability and corporate profitability can be explained by the fact that, relatively weak firms rely more on relationship banking as it is hard for them to raise funds through capital markets. Thus, relationship banking ensures easy access to credit — both to Japanese and Bangladeshi corporate firms which are relatively weak and in financial difficulties.

Table 8.9. Comparative status of relationship banking in Japan and Bangladesh.

	Japan	Bangladesh
1. Nature of financial system	Bank-based	Bank-based
2. Shape of relationship banking	Principal lender, Corporate shareholding, and Management advisory services	Principal lender
3. Positive impact of relationship banking	Easy access to credit, Rescuer in financial distress, and Corporate growth and profit	Easy access to credit
4. Negative impact of relationship banking	Weak firms rely more on relationship banking	Higher rents charged
5. Future trend	Relationship banking is flourishing by changing shape from main bank system	Under-developed capital market paving the way for the growth of relationship banking

8.8. Lessons for Bangladeshi Banking System

Based on the preceding discussions on the comparative study of the impact of relationship banking between Japan and Bangladesh, the following suggestions are put forward for the restructuring of the banking system in Bangladesh based on the Japanese experience of relationship banking.

1. Purchasing shares of the customer's firm, if adapted, might also be effective for the banking system of Bangladesh. This will enable a bank to obtain information and review firms operations and reduce mangers' ability to avoid debt payments. Even a smaller percentage of equity contribution in the form of cross shareholding would provide the base of support at the initial stage of industrialization. Bangladesh, in the primitive leg of industrialization, can utilize stockholding by banks as a means to ease the loan default problem by following the Japanese banking experience.
2. Transfer of management resources can be extremely beneficial for the banking system of Bangladesh where the client firms are seriously lacking the sufficiency of management competence and also as the board of directors are taking

seriously unjust decisions regarding the use of bank loans. Dispatched bank officials can keep a close look on the firm's activities and can prevent the managers of the firm from avoiding debt payments.

3. The loan syndication procedure can work as an important lesson for the banking system of Bangladesh where asymmetry of information is very high. Banks should try to formulate loan syndicates to share the monitoring responsibility among them. It is very time consuming and also expensive to monitor each and every borrowing firms with equal importance. This will be beneficial for both the parties, i.e., bank and the firm. As in times of financial distress, through the above-mentioned process, it would also become difficult for the banks to avoid their responsibility to rescue the troubled firms for which they were serving as main monitor. As we have seen that, in the case of Bangladesh, banks often expedite the liquidation of the distressed firm to uphold its own interest.

If the Bangladeshi banks, by adopting the above lessons, can extend the extent of relationship between the bank and the firm to monitoring and governance aspect from merely a lender–borrower relationship, then it would most likely solve the unique banking problems discussed in the earlier part of this chapter. Because, banks need not to go for retail transactions only, charge higher interest margin, ration credit, and unnecessarily delay loan decisions anymore. Due to close and long-term relationship with the client firms, banks would be able to evaluate each and every loan proposal with enough information bases and with greater control and speed. Thus, it is strongly believed that the Japanese nature of bank–firm relationship is advisable for solving the unique problems prevailing in the banking sector of Bangladesh and for crating the environment where banks get the confidence to lend to the industrial sector on the basis of more informative judgment and control.

References

Ahmed, MF (1999). Stock market, macroeconomic variables, and causality: the Bangladesh case, savings and development. *Quarterly Review*, 23(2), 109–130.

Ahmed, SU and S Uchida (2003). Multiple banking practices and its impact on the corporate borrowers. *Journal of Business and Economics*, 83(3), 245–257.

Ahmed, SU and S Uchida (2005a). Contemporary strategic aspects of relationship banking in Japan. *Annual Review of Economics*, 21, 49–59.

Ahmed, SU and S Uchida (2005b). Impact of relationship banking on the performance of corporate firms: a comparison between Japan and Bangladesh. *Journal of Business and Economics*, 85(1–2), 237–246.

Alam, K (1994). Reforms in finance and banking in Bangladesh. *Bank Parikrama*, 19(3, 4) 1–6.

Aoki, M, H Patrick and P Sheard (1995). The Japanese main bank system: survey. In *The Japanese Main Bank System: Its Relevance for Developing and Transforming Economies*, M Aoki and H Patrick (eds.), Oxford University Press.

Bangladesh Bank (2001a). *Balance Sheet Analysis of Joint Stock Companies*, Department of Public Relations and Publications, Dhaka.

Bangladesh Bank (2001b). *Bangladesh Bank Bulletin*, Various Issues, Dhaka.

Bangladesh Bank (2001c), *Scheduled Bank Statistics*, Various Issues, Dhaka.

Bangladesh Bank (2000). *Report* No. 00/25, Bangladesh: Recent Economic Developments, March 2000.

Berger, A (1999). The 'Big Picture' of relationship finance. In *Business Access to Capital and Credit*, JL Blanton, A Williams and SL Rhine (eds.), A Federal Reserve System Research Conference, pp. 390–400.

Berlin, M and L Mester (1992). Debt covenants and renegotiation. *Journal of Financial Intermediation*, 2, 95–133.

Bhattacharaya, S and G Chiesa (1995). Proprietary information, financial intermediation and research incentives. *Journal of Financial Intermediation*, 4, 328–357.

Bolton, P and DS Scharfstein (1996). Optimal debt structure and the number of creditors. *Journal of Political Economy*, 104, 1–25.

Boot, AWA, SI Greenbum and AV Thakor (1993). Reputation and discretion in financial contracting. *American Economic Review*, 83, 1165–1183.

Boot, AWA (2000). Relationship banking: what do we know? *Journal of Financial Intermediation*, 9, 9–25.

Chan, Y and AV Thakor (1987). Collateral and competitive equlibria with moral hazard and private information. *Journal of Finance*, 42, 345–363.

Choudhury, TA and MLH Moral (1999). Commercial bank restructuring in Bangladesh: from FSRP to BRC/CBRP. *Bank Parikrama*, 24(1), 92–125.

Fukuda, A and S Hirota (1996). Main bank relationships and capital structure in Japan. *Journal of Japanese and International Economics*, 10, 250–261.

Hayashi, F (2000). The main bank system and corporate investment: an empirical assessment. In *Finance, Governance and Competitiveness in Japan*, M Aoki and GR Saxonhouse (eds.), Oxford: Oxford University Press, pp. 81–97.

Hirota, S and T Horiuchi (2001). Realities and change of recent main bank relationship. *Review of Monetary and Financial Studies*, 17 (in Japanese).

Hoshi, T, A Kashyap and D Scharfstein (1990). The role of bank in reducing the costs of financial distress in Japan. *Journal of Financial Economics*, 27, 67–88.

Hosono, K (1997). R&D expenditure and the choice between private and public debt- do the Japanese main banks extract the frim's rents? *Institute of Economic Research*, Hitotsubashi University, Discussion Paper No. 353.

Kawai, M, J Hashimoto and S Izumida (1996). Japanese firm in financial distress and main banks: analysis of interest-rate premia. *Japan and the World Economy*, 8, 175–194.

Mori, A (1994). Investment of corporations and the role of main banks: empirical studies based on the information theories, *Financial Review*, 33 (Policy research Institute, Ministry of Finance), 1–40.

Nam, S (2004). Relationship banking and its role in corporate governance. *Research Paper Series*, 56, ADB Institute, pp. 1–25.

Okazaki, T and A Horiuchi (1992). Investment and the main bank. In *Structural Analysis of the Japanese Financial System* (in Japanese), A Horiuchi and N Yoshino (eds.), University of Tokyo Press, Tokyo, pp. 37–59.

Uchida, S and SU Ahmed (2004). The role of relationship banking on the performance of Japanese firms: an empirical study on small and medium enterprises. *Annual Review of South Asian Studies*, 46, 13–22.

URL: Japanese bankers association, Japanese banks: principal financial institution. Available at: http://www.zenginkyo.or.jp/en/jbank/index.html.

URL: Bank of Japan, Bank of Japan and other key statistics. Available at: http://www.boj.or.jp/en/stat/sk/ske.html.

Wahba, J and M Mohieldin (1998). Liberalising trade in financial services: the Uruguay round and the Arab countries. *World Development*, 26(7), 1331–1348.

Weinstein, DE and Y Yafeh (1998). On the cost of a bank centered financial system: evidence from the changing main bank relations in Japan. *Journal of Finance*, 53(2), 635–672.

PART 4

POLICY MODELING

CHAPTER 9

STRUCTURAL ADJUSTMENT PROGRAM AND PUBLIC FISCAL POLICY IN INDIA, 1990–1995

Dipak R. Basu

Nagasaki University, Japan

Indian economy has gone through a transitional phase during 1990–1995 where the old planning mechanisms were being replaced to make way for a complete liberalized economy. The policy planners had accepted the IMF induced "structural adjustment program". However, a large section of the public opinion is still in favor of bringing back major features of the planning system given the increasing difficulties for the poorer section of the population, although they want to maintain certain flexibilities regarding the private sector. In this paper, a mixed economic planning model is formulated to examine how the economy could have behaved during 1990–1995 if the planning authority had replaced quantitative restrictions on the private sector by various financial controls rather than privatization and liberalization of the public sector.

In a mixed economy, planning should normally take into account how the private sector formulates and revises its expectations regarding various government policies and their possible impacts on the achievability of the targets of the plan. In India, the government used to regulate the private sector by various means, such as licenses, investment quotas, tax-subsidy rates, interest rate, and by various monetary controls. The private sector, knowing the targets of the government, used to formulate its own expectations regarding the fulfillments of the targets and possible movements of various policies. It used to behave according to its expectations and realization of past expectations to allocate its resources. So, the optimum design of public policy in that framework was to direct the private sector toward the desired goals as defined by the planners taking into account the established reactions of the private sector.

In order to analyze the situation, an adaptive control model for the Indian economy was estimated. In this framework, the model and its probability structure will change continuously as the optimization progresses, thereby adapting the parameters of the model to the planned solutions. This, in a way, reflects the mixed economic plan, where the private sector reacts to the goals of the government, which in turn will modify the parameters of the model and will change the policies. A comparison is made in this paper between the simulated history and the actual history to examine the relative efficiency of the liberalized economy against the planned mixed economy that India used to have. As the character of the economy has changed too much recently, it is not possible to extend the comparison to the more recent years.

9.1. Fiscal Policy in India

In India, monetary and fiscal policies were interlinked and still are to many extents. Given the planned and non-planned expenditure the government used to raise the money either by taxation, or by borrowing from the Reserve Bank of India (RBI) and from other financial institution in return for government securities; it could also raise money from the profits of the public sector.

The deficits, which could not be financed in this way, had to be financed either by foreign borrowing or by direct money creation by the RBI. Thus, the deficit in the annual budget could be reflected in the increase in the money supply quite easily. At the same time, government bond sales to the RBI could add to the volume of high-powered money. By the standard of moat developing countries, India has followed responsible macro-economic policies. There was no hyperinflation or debt crisis. The volatility of growth rates during the planned economy has reflected the natural instability of the agricultural output.

The budget of 1985 initiated a new direction in Indian foreign trade policies. Import controls were relaxed and simplified. Exporters have received massive concessions for imports of intermediate goods. The new trade policy was designed to liberalize the economy in general to initiate a more outward-oriented economic regimes. However, in 1991 the demise of the Soviet Union, which used to account for about 20% of India's exports, along with the Gulf war and the trade embargo against Iraq, another major export market for India, had created serious balance of payments' problem.

As a result, India had decided to borrow from the IMF and as a result "structural adjustment program" to dismantle the planning system was imposed. Subsequently, most industries were delicensed, import policies were further liberalized; the rupee was made partly convertible bringing in about 42% devaluation in 1993 from its 1990 level. Most restrictions on foreign investments were removed too [Tables 9.1 to 9.4].

Table 9.1. Money supply, GNP, and price levels:
1985–1997, (Annual % changes in Rupees).

Year level	Money supply	GNP	Price
1985–1986	16.07	2.3	8.7
1986–1987	13.47	4.5	8.8
1987–1988	16.49	8.7	9.4
1988–1989	18.03	5.6	6.2
1989–1990	11.34	4.9	8.7
1990–1991	11.20	0.5	13.9
1991–1992	18.20	4.6	11.8
1992–1993	15.00	3.5	6.4
1993–1994	18.40	6.0	10.2
1994–1995	22.30	6.9	10.2
1995–1996	13.20	7.0	8.9
1996–1997	10.60	6.7	8.7

Source: Central Statistical Organization (CSO), India.

Table 9.2. Some important ratios: 1985–1995.

Year	Budget deficit/ expenditure GNP	Domestic debt/GNP	Domestic borrowing/ Public expenditure	Tax revenue/ GNP	Public GNP
1985	0.085	0.416	−48	−137	−165
1986	0.093	0.453	−49	−143	−178
1987	0.084	0.464	−41	−144	−180
1988	0.084	0.459	−43	−140	−178
1989	0.066	0.474	−34	−153	−174
1990	0.080	0.494	0.44	−137	−175
1991	0.050	0.485	0.28	−147	−147
1992	0.050	0.484	0.28	−145	−145
1993	0.070	0.516	0.41	−128	0.128
1994	0.060	0.495	0.35	−133	0.134
1995	0.060	0.479	0.31	−134	−134

Source: CSO India.

Table 9.3. Financial policy, 1985–1995 (In Rs. billions.)

Year	Public foreign expenditure borrowing	Tax revenue	Budget deficit	Domestic borrowing	Foreign borrowing
1985	430.7	361.2	−222.5	208.9	13.7
1986	518.1	420.7	−272.0	258.5	19.4
1987	597.1	480.8	−278.8	244.4	32.7
1988	700.6	554.6	−330.9	300.9	25.1
1989	769.8	675.8	−292.3	262.5	29.9
1990	924.6	723.6	−434.6	404.0	31.8
1991	1050.5	892.1	−358.2	304.4	54.2
1992	1189.3	1004.6	−399.0	340.5	53.2
1993	1363.7	1011.7	−605.3	564.7	50.7
1994	1561.3	1257.4	−616.7	553.8	39.5
1995	1743.2	1444.1	−583.9	539.3	44.6

Source: CSO.

Table 9.4. Response multiplier and endogenous variable.

Exogenous variable	Y	GBS	P	BD	CD	MS	$1R$
EXR	−0.02283	−0.00027	0.05593	0.00121	−0.00018	−0.00576	−0.00004
G	0.03178	0.00095	0.13965	0.04073	0.00041	0.01699	0.00108
TY	−0.03116	−0.00426	−0.15022	0.04091	0.00310	−0.03637	−0.01231
CI	−0.00265	0.04953	−0.00884	0.00550	−0.00210	−0.00625	0.06599

Note: [$\lambda^2 = 563.09$; the estimated Chi-Square satisfies the overall goodness of fit of estimation by the FIML method].

The IMF conditionalities, imposed upon a number of developing countries undergoing "reforms" have concentrated on two major macro-economic policies: an adequate exchange rate management and demand discipline. The latter is to be achieved through fiscal restraint and limited expansion of domestic credit. The theory is that wage-price flexibility lead to full employment equilibrium and private savings and investments are not affected by budgetary cuts. As private-sector deficits may imply deficits in the current account of the balance of payments, practical effects of any reductions in the public-sector deficit will be reflected on the improvements in the current account of the balance of payments. Inflation is to be controlled through monetary policy so that political temptations of exchange rate overvaluations do not arise. However, some required adjustment policies, including exchange rate devaluations, indirect tax increases, and reductions in subsidies imply a temporary acceleration of inflation.

This policy could be pursued within a planned mixed economy as well. Thus, the question is whether it was necessary to liberalize the economy by taking away the planning unless we can demonstrate that some extra-ordinary improvements can take place if we liberalize the economy. This paper has tried to examine this issue by solving an adaptive control model for the Indian economy for the period of structural adjustment since 1990–1991 and compare that results with the actual performances of the economy during this period.

9.2. The Method of Adaptive Optimization

It is assumed that the dynamic econometric model can be converted to an equivalent first-order dynamic system of the form

$$\tilde{x}_i = \tilde{A}\tilde{x}_{i-1} + \tilde{C}\tilde{u}_i + \tilde{D}\tilde{z}_i + \tilde{e}_i \tag{9.1}$$

where $\tilde{x}_i$ is the vector of endogenous variables, $\tilde{u}_i$ is the vector of control variables, $\tilde{z}_i$ is a vector of exogenous variables, $\tilde{e}_i$ is the vector of noises which are assumed to be white Gaussian and $\tilde{A}$, $\tilde{C}$, and $\tilde{D}$ are coefficient matrices of proper dimensions. It should be noted that a certain element of $\tilde{z}_i$ is 1 and corresponds to the constant terms. The parameters of the above system are assumed to be random.

Shifting to period $i + 1$, we can write

$$\tilde{x}_{i+1} = \tilde{A}\tilde{x}_i + \tilde{C}\tilde{u}_{i+1} + \tilde{D}\tilde{z}_{i+1} + \tilde{e}_{i+1} \tag{9.2}$$

Now we define the following augmented vectors and matrices.

$$x_i = \begin{bmatrix} \tilde{x}_i \\ \tilde{u}_i \end{bmatrix}, \quad x_{i+1} = \begin{bmatrix} \tilde{x}_{i+1} \\ \tilde{u}_{i+1} \end{bmatrix}, \quad e_{i+1} = \begin{bmatrix} \tilde{e}_{i+1} \\ 0 \end{bmatrix},$$

$$A = \begin{bmatrix} \tilde{A} & 0 \\ 0 & 0 \end{bmatrix}, \quad C = \begin{bmatrix} \tilde{C} \\ I \end{bmatrix}, \quad D = \begin{bmatrix} \tilde{D} \\ 0 \end{bmatrix}$$

Hence Eq. (9.2) can be written as

$$x_{i+1} = Ax_i + C\tilde{u}_{i+1} + D\tilde{z}_{i+1} + e_{i+1} \tag{9.3}$$

Using the linear advance operator L, such that $L^k y_i = y_{i+k}$ and defining the vectors u, z, and ε from

$$u_i = L\tilde{u}_i$$
$$z_i = L\tilde{z}_i$$
$$\varepsilon_i = Le_i$$

then Eq. (9.3) can take the form

$$x_{i+1} = Ax_i + Cu_i + Dz_i + \varepsilon_i \tag{9.4}$$

which is a typical linear control system.

We can formulate an optimal control problem of the general form

$$\min J = \frac{1}{2}\|x_T - \widehat{x}_T\|^2_{Q_T} + \frac{1}{2}\sum_{i=1}^{T-1}\|x_i - \widehat{x}_i\|^2_{Q_i} \tag{9.5}$$

subject to the system transition equation as observed in Eq. (9.4).

It is noted that T indicates the terminal time of the control period, $\{Q\}$ is the sequence of weighting matrices, and $\widehat{x}_i$ $(i = 1, 2, \ldots, T)$ is the desired state and control trajectory according to our formulation.

The solution to this problem can be obtained according to the minimization principle by solving the Ricatti-type equations (Astrom and Wittenmark, 1995).

$$K_T = Q_T \tag{9.6}$$

$$\Lambda_i = -(E_i C' K_{i+1} C)^{-1}(E_i C' K_{i+1} A) \tag{9.7}$$

$$K_i = E_i A' K_{i+1} A + \Lambda'_i(E_i C' K_{i+1} A) + Q_i \tag{9.8}$$

$$h_T = -Q_T \widehat{x}_T \tag{9.9}$$

$$h_i = \Lambda_i(E_i C' K_{i+1} D)z_i + \Lambda_i(E_i C')h_{i+1}$$
$$\quad + (E_i A' K_{i+1} D)z_i + (E_i A')h_{i+1} - Q_i \widehat{x}_i \tag{9.10}$$

$$g_i = -(E_i C' K_{i+1} C)^{-1}[(E_i C' K_{i+1} D)z_i + (E_i C')h_{i+1}] \tag{9.11}$$

$$x^*_i = [E_i A + (E_i C)\Lambda_i]x^*_i + (E_i C)g_i + (E_i D)z_i \tag{9.12}$$

$$u^*_i = \Lambda_i x^*_i + g_i \tag{9.13}$$

where u^*_i $(i = 0, 1, \ldots, T - 1)$, the optimal control sequence and x^*_{i+1}, the corresponding state trajectory, constitutes the solution to the stated optimal control problem.

It is noted that in the above equations, Λ_i is the matrix of feedback coefficients and g_i is the vector of intercepts. The notation E_i denotes the conditional expectations, given all information up to the period i.

Expressions like $E_i C' K_{i+1} C$, $E_i C' K_{i+1} A$, $E_i C' K_{i+1} D$ are evaluated taking into account the reduced form coefficients of the econometric model and their covariance matrix which are to be updated continuously along with the implementation of the control rules. These rules should be readjusted according to "passive learning" methods. It is noted, however, that the joint densities of matrices A, C, and D assumed to remain constant over the control period. The reduced form coefficients and their covariances matrix have to be updated, since the control is adaptive and the agents are adjusting their expectations.

9.2.1. *Updating Method of Reduced-Form Coefficients and Their Covariance Matrices*

The updating technique of the reduced form coefficient matrix and their covariance matrix is as follows.

Suppose we have a simultaneous-equation system of the form

$$XB' + U\Gamma' = R \tag{9.14}$$

where X is the matrix of endogenous variable defined on $E^N \times E^n$ and B is the matrix of structural coefficients which refer to the endogenous variables and is defined on $E^n \times E^n$. U is the matrix of explanatory variables defined on $E^N \times E^g$ and Γ is the matrix of the structural coefficients, which refer to the explanatory variables, defined on $E^N \times E^g$. R is the matrix of noises defined on $E^N \times E^n$. The reduced form coefficients matrix Π is then defined from:

$$\Pi = -B^{-1}\Gamma \tag{9.15}$$

Goldberger *et al.* (1961) have shown that the asymptotic covariance matrix, say Ω of the vector $\hat{\pi}$ which consists of the g columns of matrix $\hat{\Pi}$ can be approximated by

$$\tilde{\Omega} = \left[\begin{bmatrix} \hat{\Pi} \\ I_g \end{bmatrix} \otimes (\hat{B}')^{-1} \right]' F \left[\begin{bmatrix} \hat{\Pi} \\ I_g \end{bmatrix} \otimes (\hat{B}')^{-1} \right] \tag{9.16}$$

where $\otimes$ denotes the Kroneker product $\hat{\Pi}$ and $\hat{B}$ are the estimated coefficients by standard econometric techniques and F denotes the asymptotic covariance matrix of the $n+g$ columns of $(\hat{B}\ \hat{\Gamma})$, which is assumed to be consistent and asymptotically unbiased estimate of $(B\Gamma)$.

Combining Eqs. (9.14) and (9.15), we can write

$$BX' = -\Gamma U' + R' \Rightarrow X' = -B^{-1}\Gamma U' + B^{-1}R'$$

$$\Rightarrow X' = \Pi U' + W' \tag{9.17}$$

where $W' = B^{-1}R'$.

Denoting the ith column of matrix X' by x_i and the ith column of matrix W' by w_i, we can write

$$x_i = \begin{bmatrix} u_{1i} & 0 & \cdots & 0 & u_{2i} & 0 & \cdots & 0 & u_{gi} & 0 & \cdots & 0 \\ 0 & u_{1i} & \cdots & 0 & 0 & u_{2i} & \cdots & 0 & 0 & u_{gi} & \cdots & 0 \\ \cdot & \cdot & & \cdot & & \cdot & & \cdot & \cdot & \cdot & & \cdot \\ \cdot & \cdot & & \cdot & & \cdot & & \cdot & \cdot & \cdot & & \cdot \\ \cdot & \cdot & & \cdot & & \cdot & & \cdot & \cdot & \cdot & & \cdot \\ 0 & 0 & \cdots & u_{1i} & 0 & 0 & \cdots & u_{2i} & \cdots & 0 & \cdots & u_{gi} \end{bmatrix} \pi + w_i$$

$$\tag{9.18}$$

where u_{ij} is the element of the jth column and ith row of matrix U. The vector πE^{ng}, as mentioned earlier, consists of the g column of matrix Π.

Equation (9.18) can be written in a compact form, as

$$x_i := H_i \pi + w_i, \quad i = 1, 2, \ldots, N \tag{9.19}$$

where $x_i \in E^n$, $w_i \in E^n$ and the observation matrix H_i is defined on $E^n \times E^{ng}$.

In a time-invariant econometric model, the coefficients vector π is assumed random with constant expectation overtime, so that

$$\pi_{i+1} = \pi_i, \quad \text{for all } i \tag{9.20}$$

In a time-varying and stochastic model we can have

$$\pi_{i+1} = \pi_i + \varepsilon_i \tag{9.21}$$

where $\varepsilon_i \in E^{ng}$ is the noise.

Based on the above, we can rewrite Eq. (9.19) as

$$x_{i+1} = H_{i+1}\pi_{i+1} + w_{i+1} \quad i = 0, 1, \ldots, N - 1 \tag{9.22}$$

Now we need to make the following assumptions.

(a) The vector x_{i+1} and matrix H_{i+1} can be measured exactly for all i.
(b) The noises ε_i and w_{i+1} are independent discrete white noises with known statistics, i.e.,

$$E(\varepsilon_i) = 0; \quad E(w_{i+1}) = 0$$

$$E(\varepsilon_i w'_{i+1}) = 0$$

$$E(c_i \varepsilon'_i) = Q_1 \delta_{ij} \quad \text{where } \delta_{ij} \text{ is the Kronecker delta, and}$$

$$E(w_i w'_i) = Q_2 \delta_{ij}$$

The above covariance matrices are assumed to be positive definite.
(c) The state vector is normally distributed with a finite covariance matrix.
(d) Regarding Eqs. (9.21) and (9.22), the Jacobians of the transformation of ε_i into π_{i+1} and of w_{i+1} into x_{i+1} are unities. Hence, the corresponding conditional probability densities are:

$$p(\pi_{i+1} \mid \pi_i) = p(\varepsilon_i)$$

$$p(x_{i+1} \mid \pi_{i+1}) = p(w_{i+1})$$

Under the above assumptions and given Eqs. (9.21) and (9.22), the problem set is to evaluate

$$E(\pi_{i+1} \mid x^{i+1}) = \pi^*_{i+1}$$

and

$$\text{cov}(\pi_{i+1} \mid x^{i+1}) = S_{i+1} \quad \text{(the error covariance matrix)}$$

where $x^{i+1} = x_1, x_2, x_3, \ldots, x_{i+1}$

The solution to this problem (Basu and Lazaridis, 1986; Lazaridis, 1980) is given by the following set of recursive equations, as it is briefly shown in the Appendix.

$$\pi_{i+1}^* = \pi_i^* + K_{i+1}(x_{i+1} - H_{i+1}\pi_i^*) \tag{9.23}$$

$$K_{i+1} = S_{i+1}H_{i+1}'Q_2^{-1} \tag{9.24}$$

$$S_{i+1}^{-1} = P_{i+1}^{-1} + H_{i+1}'Q_2^{-1}H_{i+1} \tag{9.25}$$

$$P_{i+1}^{-1} = (Q_1 + S_i)^{-1} \tag{9.26}$$

The recursive process is initiated by regarding K_0 and H_0 as null matrices and computing π_0^* and S_0 from

$$\pi_0^* = \hat{\pi} \quad \text{i.e., the reduced form coefficients (columns of matrix } \hat{\Pi})$$

$$S_0 = P_0 = \tilde{\Omega}$$

The reduced form coefficients, along with their covariance matrices, can be updated using this recursive process and at each stage a set of "Riccati" equations should be updated accordingly so that adaptive control rules can be derived.

Once we estimate the model (described in the next section) using the FIML (full information maximum likelihood) method, we can obtain both the structural model and probability density functions along with all associated matrices mentioned above, when describing the method. We first convert the structural econometric model to a *State-Variable* form according to Eq. (9.1). Once we specify the targets for the state and control variables, the objective function to be minimized, the weights attached to each state and control variables, then it is a matter of calculations to obtain the optimization results for the entire period using Eqs. (9.6)–(9.13). Thereafter, we can update all probability density functions and all other associated matrices using Eqs. (9.23)–(9.26) which will effectively update the coefficients of the model in its *State-Variable* form. We can repeat the optimization process over and over as we update the model, its associated matrices, probability density functions and use these as new information.

9.3. Dynamic Analysis of the Model and Comparative Performances of the Economy

The policy model used in this analysis is a variation of the so-called adjustment policy model of the World Bank as elaborated by Khan and Montiel (1989, 1990) to explore the mechanism and impacts of various controls pursued by the monetary authority in order to implement objectives of the physical plan and maintain fiscal balance. Here, it is important to evaluate impacts of these policies on the private sector and to foresee the future course of action of the private sector in anticipation of these policies. Although the model defines balance of payments and money stock according to the "monetary approach" (Berdell, 1995; Humphrey, 1981; Khan, 1976), there is no explicit investment or consumption function.

The reason is that private investment was until recently controlled by various means employing licenses and quotas. It was the Planning Commission, which ultimately used to decide the nature and composition of private investment. Consumptions of essential commodities of the poorer section of the population, which means most part of the population, were controlled through the rationing system, which still exist. Non-essential consumptions were influenced by various taxes and quota restrictions, Therefore, a standard private investment or consumption based on the market behavior cannot be estimated for the economy. Instead, it is convenient for us to accept that domestic absorption can reflect the combined response of both private and public investments and consumptions to the planned target for national income, set by the Planning Commission, and to various market forces, represented by money-market interest rates, and exchange rates. The new Cambridge model of the UK economy (Cripps and Godley, 1976; Godley and Lavoie, 2002; Godley and Lavoie, 2007) has postulated a similar combined consumption-investment function of the UK but their explanation was of different nature. The money-market interest rates (money-market interest rates are different from the lending rates of the commercial banks which until recently were controlled by the RBI) can be controlled by discount rates of the monetary authority and by direct interventions of the RBI. Exchange rates under managed floating system fluctuate according to the influences of the balance of payments. This model is described in the Appendix.

9.3.1. *Dynamics of Response Multipliers*

In the adaptive control model, the response multiplier will move from one period to another. A part of the response multiplier for the initial period of planning is as follows.

As it is obvious from the response multiplier devaluation would have a negative effect on national income, it would also have negative effects on government bond sales, currency to deposit ratio, interest rate, and on the money demand. It is due to the fact that Indian exports are not normally elastic in response to devaluation whereas devaluation will reduce import abilities significantly. As a result, national income and domestic activity would have negative effects, which will depress the private sector and *CD* will go down. Due to the down-turn of the economic activity, there would be less demand for loans, so market interest rate would go down and there will be less demand for government bonds. Devaluations also can have an inflationary effect due to increased import costs.

Government expenditure, on the other hand, would have positive effects on every variable, which implies increased public expenditure would stimulate the national income and the private sector as well, despite increased interest rates. However, it would have an inflationary impact at the same time.

Increased tax revenues would depress the national income, as it would reduce government bond sales. The lower level of national income would reduce money supply, and the private sector's activity, which would be reflected on the reduced currency to deposit ratio, and the reduced level of money demand (and money supply). The reduced level of national income in this case would have lowered price levels and, at the same time, private sector activity would be less (as reflected in the currency to deposit ratio and money demand) due to an increased market rate of interest. Although government bond sales would go up, the budget deficit would be increased due to a lower level of economic activity.

The response multipliers of the system would move over time within an adaptive control framework. The movement of the response multiplier should be slow (Tsakalis and Ioannou, 1990). Movements, over the previous observations, are given in Table 9.5.

9.3.2. *Fiscal Dynamics*

We can analyze the impact of the public expenditure and tax revenues on the two most important variables, GNP (Y) and price level (P). The government expenditure (G) would certainly increase price level and the impact would be intensified. The impact of the government expenditure on the GNP would be reduced gradually, and it is consistent with the reduced impacts of the tax revenues on the GNP over the planning period. Tax revenue would have a gradually declining negative impact on the GNP and the impact will decline over time. Tax revenue would also have a negative impact on the price level. The negative impact of the tax revenue on the GNP is partly explained by the negative impact of tax revenue on the currency to deposit ratios of the commercial banks, the main indicator for private sector activities. This will have a negative effect on the growth prospects.

Government expenditure would have a gradually increasing positive impact on government bond sales due to increasing difficulties of raising taxes. However, it is not possible to analyze the full effect of monetary and fiscal policies without analyzing their optimum paths over the planning horizon. Recent experiences show, although the GDP is growing, according to the estimates of the government at about 8%, the growth is restricted to the financial and service sectors with recessions in the agricultural sector, the most important part of the economy. Private sectors' demand for loans has declined. The monetary authority has reduced the rates of interests and reserve ratios in order to stimulate credit to deposit ratios.

Table 9.5.   Response Multiplier-Period 1.

Exogenous	Y	GBS	P	BD	CD	MS	IR
EXR	−0.2254	−0.00092	−0.05458	−0.00111	−0.00020	−0.00543	−0.00092
G	0.03572	0.00403	0.14849	0.03987	0.00500	0.01466	0.00330
TY	−0.03590	−0.01017	−0.15549	0.02791	0.00399	−0.02682	−0.01996
CI	−0.00226	0.04592	−0.00606	0.00458	−0.00169	−0.00516	0.06120

Response Multiplier-Period 2

EXR	−0.02209	−0.00092	0.05336	0.00125	−0.00013	−0.00570	−0.00097
G	0.03293	0.00568	0.15603	0.03500	0.00091	0.02882	0.00599
TY	−0.02961	−0.01240	−0.15688	0.02792	0.00246	−0.04758	−0.02324
CI	−0.00273	0.94546	−0.00387	0.00488	−0.00181	−0.00668	0.06057

Response Multiplier-Period 3

EXR	−0.02199	−0.00069	0.05269	0.00133	−0.00042	−0.00573	−0.00062
G	0.03001	0.00499	0.16536	0.02924	0.05923	0.04217	0.00570
TY	−0.02470	−0.01149	−0.16281	0.02472	0.07031	−0.06325	−0.02220
CI	−0.00215	0.04676	−0.00252	0.00399	−0.00465	−0.00671	0.06228

Response Multiplier-Period 5

EXR	−0.02133	−0.00088	0.05190	0.00152	−0.00201	−0.00595	−0.00089
G	0.02058	0.00558	0.18078	0.01160	0.50890	0.07248	0.00530
TY	−0.01676	−0.00410	−0.16655	0.00695	0.55026	−0.07779	−0.01013
CI	−0.00268	0.04465	−0.00267	0.00403	−0.01967	−0.00726	0.05953

Response Multiplier-Period 7

EXR	−0.02067	−0.00116	0.04987	0.00135	−0.00104	−0.00558	−0.00129
G	0.00733	0.01033	0.16455	0.00048	0.57357	0.10760	0.01206
TY	−0.00402	−0.00345	−0.14832	0.01434	0.58067	−0.10904	−0.00869
CI	−0.00200	0.04174	−0.00236	0.00293	−0.02186	−0.00551	0.05566

9.3.2.1. Comparative performances of the planned solution and the recent history

Historical data relevant for the analysis are given in Tables 9.7 and 9.8. The target paths are given in Table 9.9 and the experimental solutions are given in Table 9.10. Target paths are according to the judgments regarding the potentials of the Indian economy and the constraints it faces. Some of the assumptions used in the solution regarding the foreign debts are given in Table 9.8. In the target path, national income and domestic absorption are expected to grow at a rate of 6% a year. Foreign borrowing should be stable; as a result, its share in the national income should be reduced. Public expenditures should go up financed by increased tax revenues and government bond sales. Newly created money stock should grow at a rate of 11% and major banking instruments like CD, RR, CI, and consequently IR should be

Table 9.6.   Fiscal dynamics.

Periods	1	2	3	5	7
$\dfrac{dP}{dG}$	0.14849	0.15603	0.16536	0.18078	0.16455
$\dfrac{dY}{dG}$	0.3572	0.03203	0.03001	0.02058	0.00733
$\dfrac{dP}{dTY}$	−0.15549	−0.15688	−0.16281	−0.16655	−0.14832
$\dfrac{dY}{dTY}$	−0.03590	−0.02691	−0.02470	−0.01676	−0.00402
$\dfrac{dGBS}{dG}$	0.00403	0.00568	0.00499	0.00558	0.01033

Table 9.7.   Debt ratios and foreign borrowings: History.

Year	Total debt/ GNP	Foreign debt/ GNP	Foreign debt/ Total debt	Foreign borrowings (Rupees in billions)
1984	0.45	0.070	0.153	13.8
1985	0.48	0.069	0.143	13.7
1986	0.52	0.069	0.133	19.4
1987	0.53	0.070	0.131	32.7
1988	0.53	0.066	0.123	24.6
1989	0.55	0.063	0.114	26.0
1990	0.55	0.059	0.107	31.8
1991	0.54	0.059	0.111	54.2
1992	0.54	0.060	0.111	53.2
1993	0.57	0.060	0.104	50.7
1994	0.58	0.054	0.098	39.5
1995	0.52	0.051	0.095	44.6

Source: Central Statistical Organization (Govt. of India) and IMF.

stable over time. Budget deficits should be more or less stable. Thus, its share in the national income should go down.

A comparison of the historical experiences during the reforms since 1991 and the experimental solution demonstrates that until 1993, growth of the GNP in the experimental solution is superior to the actual performance obtained during reform. Although, for the later years since 1996, the estimates of the government suggests

Table 9.8. Historical data (Rupees in billions, 1990 prices).

Year	Y	BP	G	TY	LR
1990	5279.9	−0123.147	924.0	723.6	239.5
1991	5298.9	−085.240	917.5	779.1	182.8
1992	5552.7	−093.076	952.2	804.3	178.9
1993	5825.4	−042.368	1010.1	749.4	194.9
1994	6295.3	−051.494	1047.1	843.3	217.7
1995	6766.1	−0182.164	1091.5	904.2	185.5

Year	FB-FP ratio	GBS	NDA	IR (in %)	CI (in %)	CD ratio	RR ratio
1990	31.8	407.0	1.006.3	15.57	10	0.75	0.15
1991	47.3	265.5	1.011.3	19.35	12	0.69	0.15
1992	42.6	272.6	931.7	15.23	12	0.69	0.14
1993	37.5	418.3	942.7	8.64	12	0.66	0.15
1994	26.5	371.4	791.9	7.14	12	0.62	0.15
1995	27.9	337.7	822.3	15.57	12	0.66	0.16
1996	17.2	365.2	1285.7	11.04	12	0.62	0.12

Year	P (CPI) index	P Rate of growth (in %)	EXR Rs/US$	GDP deflator index	BD (Rupees in billion)
1990	100	—	17.50	100	−434.61
1991	113.9	13.9	22.74	114.5	−312.82
1992	127.3	11.7	25.92	124.9	−319.45
1993	135.4	6.4	30.49	135.0	−448.37
1994	149.5	10.4	31.37	149.1	−413.61
1995	164.5	10.1	32.43	159.7	−365.62
1996	179.2	8.9	35.43	173.7	−385.03

Note: CPI = Consumer's price index.
Source: Central Statistical Organization (Govt. of India).

higher rates of growth for the GNP, it was not clear what was the source of this additional growth. Industrial sector since 1996 and until 2000 in particular, has stagnated. Agricultural growth is not at all significant. Perhaps, the service sector is the only growth factor during the recent years, at least until 2000.

Table 9.9. Target (Rupees in billions, 1990 prices).

Year	Y	BP	G	TY	LR
1990	5000	−70	1301	650	198
1991	5325	−63	1321	692	228
1992	5671	−56	1288	737	243
1993	6039	−54	1337	785	259
1994	6431	−51	1389	830	273
1995	6849	−47	1485	890	293
1996	7294	−43	1487	948	312
1997	7768	−43	1500	1009	332

Year	FB-FP ratio	GBS	NDA	IR (in %)	CI (in %)	CD ratio	RR
1990	29	350	850	9.5	9	0.75	0.12
1991	30	372	798	9.5	9	0.80	0.10
1992	33	396	850	9.5	9	0.82	0.10
1993	35	422	905	9.5	9	0.84	0.10
1994	37	450	1.025	9.5	9	0.86	0.10
1995	39	479	1.090	9.5	9	0.86	0.10
1996	42	510	1.000	9.5	9	0.86	0.09
1997	45	543	1.160	9.5	9	0.86	0.09

Year	P index	EXR Rs/US$
1990	100	17
1991	108	20
1992	116	20
1993	126	20
1994	136	22
1995	148	22
1996	160	22
1997	165	22

Source: Central Statistical Organization (Govt. of India).
(Targets are created by author's own observations on the corresponding targets of the Indian Planning Commission and the actual achievements of the economy over the historical period.)

Table 9.10. Planned solutions (Rupees in billions, 1990 prices).

Year	Y (Rate of growth (in %))	BP	G	TY	FB-FF
1990	5162.16	−98.07	877.56	672.16	27.34
1991	5345.41 (3.55)	−74.83	908.72	748.35	29.01
1992	5558.69 (3.99)	−61.14	1000.56	750.38	26.15
1993	5883.32 (5.84)	−58.83	941.33	764.83	24.29
1994	62.3.37 (5.44)	−45.82	1054.57	818.84	22.08
1995	6535.25 (5.35)	−41.74	1176.34	849.58	20.68
1996	6908.41 (5.71)	−37.54	1174.43	941.45	20.70

Year	GBS	NDA	IR (in %)	CI (in %)	CD ratio	RR ratio
1990	344.86	878.56	6	8.5	0.84	0.13
1991	370.38	908.72	5.7	8.5	0.76	0.12
1992	378.30	944.97	5.8	7.7	0.78	0.12
1993	398.72	941.33	5.8	7.3	0.78	0.10
1994	422.86	992.54	5.2	6.8	0.81	0.08
1995	434.93	1045.64	5.3	6.6	0.83	0.08
1996	450.94	1105.34	5.3	6.5	0.84	0.09

Year	P index	Rate of growth (in %)	BD	EXR Rs/ US$
1990	100	—	−361.34	16.5
1991	109.9	9.9	−374.18	17.1
1992	122.1	11.1	−377.99	18.4
1993	127.7	4.6	−405.94	19.7
1994	138.3	8.3	−434.23	20.9
1995	148.6	7.4	−444.39	22.5
1996	157.9	6.3	−455.95	23.6

The experimental solution gives much more importance to the government expenditures, bond sales, and net domestic asset creations by the central bank with reduced interest rates and reserve ratios in the commercial banks; however, budget deficits would go up slightly. In recent years, balance of payments deficits are worse than those in the experiment. This shows a basic characteristic of the Indian economy that the economy depends crucially on the public activity. The slowdown in the industrial sector during the period 1992–1996 can be directly attributable to

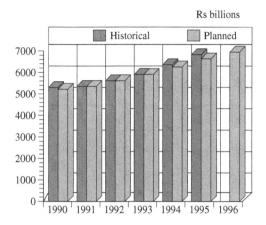

Fig. 9.1.   Comparisons: GNP.

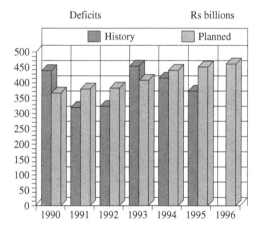

Fig. 9.2.   Comparisons: Public budget.

the reduced activities and curtailments of public investments program under the reform program.

Price level under the experiment demonstrates lower rate of inflation than the historical experience. This is due to the reduced level of interest rates and reserve ratios, which can stimulate domestic productions in the private sector and increase the level of output, which can in turn achieve lower inflation rates. Monetary policy in the experiment is expansive to support a growing economy. Net domestic asset creation by the central bank has a higher rate of growth than those in recent history. Interest rates are lower, reserve ratios are lower too, as a result credit to deposit ratios are higher, which helps growth of the real economy.

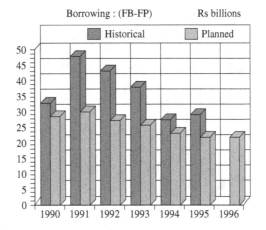

Fig. 9.3. Comparisons: Net foreign borrowing: (FB-FP).

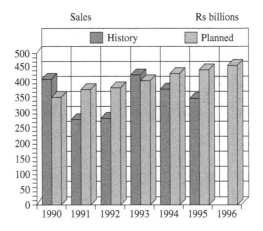

Fig. 9.4. Comparisons: Government bond sales.

The contractionary policy followed during the reform period has the result of a lower credit to deposit ratio. As a result, expansion of the private sector was not as it was expected from the reform. At the same time, in reality, public investments have suffered. The industrial recessions from 1996 to 2000 was the result of these two factors.

Even with expansionary monetary policy, the rate of inflation is lower in the experiment due to higher rate of growth of the real economy and a lower rate of devaluation. Devaluation is the cornerstone of the reform program; the objective was to expand exports. The result was a much higher cost of imports. India's imports

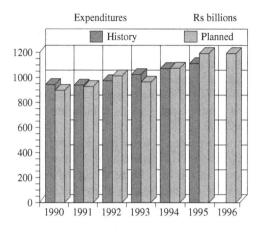

Fig. 9.5. Comparisons: Government expenditures.

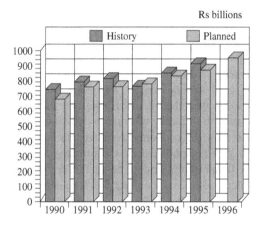

Fig. 9.6. Comparisons: Tax revenues.

are mainly essential items, so it is not possible to reduce these even if the rate of devaluation is high. The result of devaluation is increasing costs of raw material; crude petroleum is one such item, which can increase the rate of inflation.

As inflation is also the result of shortages in a developing economy, expansionary monetary and fiscal policy, by increasing real output can reduce inflation. The reform program, on the other hand, has used the logic of demand managements to reduce inflation, which is not valid for an economy like India. In the above experiment, government expenditures, bond sales, and budget deficits are higher when compared with those achieved during the reform period. These are highly desirable for a growing economy.

The idea that contractionary fiscal policy can automatically stimulate the economy by making more room for the private sector is not valid in India or in a growing economy, where growth of the private sector depends in many ways on the expansions of the public sector. Contractions in the public sector means, in this type of framework, contractions in the private sector too, which can explain the slowdown of growth in the industrial sector during the early stages of the reform program and stagnation in the small- and medium-sized industries during the reform until about 2000.

In the external sector, balance of payments' situation has not improved during the reform period; the amounts of deficits in the balance of payments, in fact, increased in some cases. In the experiment given above, rate of devaluation is much slower and the deficit in the balance of payments is lower in magnitude. India's exports increased due to devaluations only for a short period, afterwards stagnated while cost of imports went up and up. The resultant foreign debt and borrowing are higher as a result during the reform period when compared with those in the experiment given above. The expectations that reforms would bring floods of foreign direct investments has yet to be fulfilled, although in recent years there are indeed floods of short-term portfolio investments which can damage the economy in the longer run.

We have also seen that budget deficits have grown at alarming rates. If we want to reduce these, we need to reduce growth rate, which may make the debt situation worse in future. The usual solvency criteria suggest that the rate of growth of the economy should be more than the interest rate to be paid on public debt. If we assume that rates of growth of public revenues will follow rates of growth of the economy, it is possible for the economy to sustain itself with a growing public debt. However, with growing public debt, the primary deficit may outstrip the revenues and then the financial crisis may emerge. It is possible, however, for India to approach the problem from several angles, first is to increase the efficiencies of public enterprises by restructuring, redesign of managements, and more efficient supplies of raw materials. There is a need to increase the tax base of the economy by incorporating agricultural income. Public subsidies, which are not designed for the poor should be curtailed. Efforts should be made to collect the defaulted bank loans of the large private sector firms; the total amounts of the unpaid bank loans of large private sector corporations are now more than Rs.150 billion which seriously undermined the viability of the banking sector.

9.4. Conclusion

The reform process has the desired goal to create a liberalized economy in India by removing the mixed economic system that used to prevail. The results of this reform have not yet touched the majority of the people positively. Instead, there is a growing fear of loss of all benefits of the mixed economic system. The expectations of high level of inflows of foreign direct investments to substitute public investments have not materialized yet. There is no longer any political consensus either for the reforms. In view of this, it is important to examine what could have happened if India had maintained the mixed economic system and what type of monetary fiscal-exchange rate policies would be most suitable. We can see from the experiment, the mixed economic system where the private sector is regulated through monetary-fiscal policies could perform better than the so-called reform program.

Appendix A

The Policy Model

We describe below a model of the Indian economy. The model accepts the definition of balance of payments and money stock according to the "monetary" approach (Khan, 1976; Khan and Montiel, 1989) but without any explicit investment or consumption function.

Absorption function

Domestic absorption reflects the behavior of both the private and public sector.

$$\left(\frac{A}{P}\right)_t = a_0 + a_1\, E\left(\frac{Y}{P}\right)_t - a_2 E(IR)_t - a_3 XR_t + u_{1t} \tag{A.1}$$

where A_t is the value of domestic absorption, P_t is the domestic price level, Y_t is the national income, IR_t is the market interest rate, XR_t is the exchange rate between the rupee and the dollar, u_t is distributed normally with zero mean and a given variance σ^2. E signifies the expectation operator.

The relation between the national income and absorption can be defined as follows

$$Y_t = A_t + R_t \tag{A.2}$$

The government budget deficit (BD_t) is defined by Eq. (A.3)

$$BD_t = (G_t + LR_t + PF_t) - (TY_t + GBS_t + AF_t + FB_t) \tag{A.3}$$

EXR_t is the exchange rate, TY_t is the government tax revenue, G_t is the public consumption, GBS_t is the government bond sales, LR_t is the net lending by the central government to the states (which is not part of the planned public expenditure) and R_t is the changes in the foreign exchange reserve reflections of the behavior of the foreign trade sector. PF_t is the foreign payments due to existing foreign debts which may include both amortization and interest payments, AF_t is the foreign assistance which is an insignificant feature, FB_t is the total foreign borrowing assuming only the government can borrow from foreign sources.

We assume AF_t and LR_t as exogenous, whereas FB_t, G_t, and TY_t as policy instruments. PF_t depends on the level of existing foreign debt and the world interest rate WIR_t, although a sizable part of the foreign borrowing can be at a concessionnal rate.

$$PF_t = a_4 + a_5 \sum_{r=-20}^{t} FB_r + a_6 \left(\frac{WIR}{EXR} \right)_t \qquad (A.4)$$

Government bond sales (GBS_t) depends on its attractiveness reflected on the interest rate (IR_t), the ability of the domestic economy to absorb (A_t), the requirements of the governments (G_t), the alternative sources of finances reflected on the tax revenue (TY_t), and government's borrowing from the central bank, i.e., NDA_t. the net domestic asset creation by the central bank.

$$GBS_t = a_7 + a_8 A_t + a_9 IR_t + a_{10} G_t - a_{11} TY_t - a_{12} NDA_t \qquad (A.5)$$

Monetary sector

We assume flow equilibrium in the money market, i.e.,

$$\Delta MD_t = \Delta MS_t \qquad (A.6)$$

where MD_t is the money demand, MS_t is the money supply. The stock of money supply depends on the stock of high powered money and the money-multiplier, as follows

$$MS_t = \left[\frac{(1 + CD)}{(CD + RR)} \right]_t (\Delta R + NDA)_t \qquad (A.7)$$

$(\Delta R_t + NDA_t)$ reflect the stock of high powered money and the expression within the square bracket is the money multiplier which depends on credit to deposit ratio of the commercial banking sector (CD_t) and the reserve to deposit liabilities in the commercial banking sector (RR_t). Whereas NDA_t is an instrument, ΔR_t depends on the foreign trade sector. However, the government can influence CD_t and RR_t to control the money supply. RR_t, which is the actual reserve ratio depends on the demand for loans created by the private sector and commercial banks' willingness to lead. Actual reserve can be influenced by the statutory reserve limit set by the central bank. As in the case of India, the actual reserve is always at a higher level than the statutory reserve limit, so we accept, the reserve ratio for a developing country is mainly influenced by demand factors such as the market rate of interest and national income. We assume that the desired reserve ratio RR_t is a function of national income and market interest rate.

$$RR_t^* = a_{13} + a_{14} Y_t + a_{15} IR_t \qquad (A.8)$$

The commercial banks may adjust their actual reserve ratio to the desired reserve ratio with a lag.

$$RR_t^* = a(RR_t^* - RR_{t-1}^*) \tag{A.9}$$

where $0 < \alpha < 1$; we can rewrite Eq. (A.8) as follows

$$RR_t^* = \alpha a_{13} + \alpha a_{14} Y_t + a_{15} IR_t + (1 - a) RR_{t-1} \tag{A.10}$$

The ratio of currency to deposit liabilities with the commercial bank system is affected by the opportunity cost of holding currency as measured by the market interest rate and national income representing the domestic economic activity. Khan (1976) has postulated that the effect of national income should be negative because "individuals and corporations tend to become more efficient: in their management of cash balances as their income rises". However, a different logic may emerge in a developing country where the use of banks as an institution is not widespread, particularly among the labor force. If there was an expansion in economic activity, the entrepreneurs would have to maintain a huge cash balance and run down deposits simply to pay various dues, because most payments would have to be made in cash. It is possible that corporations would be more efficient, with an initial adjustment lag. We, therefore, expect the sign of the coefficient for the current national income to be positive and that for the lagged national income to be negative.

$$CD_t = a_{16} + a_{17} IR_t + a_{18} Y_t - a_{19} Y_{t-1} \tag{A.11}$$

The demand for money is assumed to be a function of the money market interest rate and the national income.

$$(MD)_t = a_{20} - a_{21}(IR_t) + a_{22}(Y_t) \tag{A.12}$$

Prices and interest rate

The money market rate of interest (IR) is determined by the supply of money, national income, and the central bank discount rate.

$$IR_t = a_{23} - a_{29}(MS_t) + a_{29}(Y_t) + a_{26}(CI_t) \tag{A.13}$$

The domestic price level depends on domestic economic activity, (particularly changes in the agricultural sector) and the import cost (IMC_t). The import cost in turn depends on the exchange rate (EXR_t) and world price of imported goods (WPM_t). We assume the desired price level (P_t) is represented by the following equation:

$$P_t^* = a_{27} - a_{28}(A_t) + a_{29}(IMC_t) \tag{A.14}$$

The desired price level reflects the private sectors' reaction to their expected domestic adsorption of the expected import cost. Suppose that the actual price will move according to the difference between the desired price in period t and the actual price level in the previous period

$$\Delta Pt = \beta(P_t^* - P_{t-1}); \quad 0 < \beta < 1 \tag{A.15}$$

Thus, we get

$$P_t = \beta a_{27} - \beta a_{28}(A_t) + \beta a_{29}(IMC_t) + (I - \beta)P_{t-1} \tag{A.16}$$

The import cost (IMC_t) is represented by the following equation

$$IMC_t = a_{30} - a_{31}(EXR_t) + a_{32}(WPM_t) \tag{A.17}$$

The exchange rate EXR_t can be an instrument variable whereas world prices of imported goods (WPM_t) is an exogenous variable.

Balance of payments

The balance of payments (R) is equal to the changes in the stock of international reserve, i.e.,

$$\Delta R_t = X_t - IM_t + K_t + PFT_t + FB_t - PF_t + AF_t \tag{A.18}$$

when X_t is the value of exports, IM_t is the value of imports, K_t is the foreign capital inflows, PFT_t is the private sectors' transactions, FB_t is the foreign borrowing, PF_t is the foreign payments by the central bank and AF_t is the foreign aid and grants; where X_t PFT_t, K_t, and AF_t are exogenous.

Import IM_t is determined by the national income, and the import cost, i.e.,

$$IM_t = a_{33} + a_{34}Y_t - a_{35}(IMC_t) \tag{A.19}$$

The above analytical structure was estimated using expected values of each variables, with expectations being adaptive. The estimated parameters were used as the initial starting point for the stochastic control model.

Estimations

The model was estimated using *FIML* (*Full Information Maximum Likelihood*) method. The *FIML* estimates are as follows (R^2 and R^2 refers to the corresponding 2 *SLS* estimates).

Estimated model

1. $A_t = 0.842Y_t + 0.024A_{t-1} - 1.319IR_t + 1.051IR_{t-t} - 284EXR_t$
        (3.48)   (1.74)   (1.34)   (1.16)   (1.29)
    $+ 55191.5$
        (4.87)
    $R^2 = 0.99, \overline{R}^2 = 0.92, DW = 1.76, \rho = 0.27$

2. $(Y_t) = A_t + R_t$

3. $(BD)_t = (G_t + LR_t + PF_t) - (TY_t + GBS_t + AF_t + FB_t)$

4. $PF_t = 1148.80 + 0.169CFB_{t-1} + 144.374WIR_t$
        (1.48)   (2.39)   (1.89)

5. $GBS_t = 0.641G_t + 0.677G_{t-1} + 1.591IR_t - 0.33AF_t$
        (1.14)   (1.41)   (1.64)   (0.23)
    $R^2 = 0.89, \overline{R}^2 = 0.84, DW = 2.36, \rho = 0.23$
                                    (1.51)

6. $\Delta MD = \Delta MS$

7. $(MS)_t = [(1 + CD_t)/(CD_t + RR_t)](\Delta R_t + NDA_t)$

8. $RR_t = 0.008Y_t - 0.002Y_{t-1} + 1.2571R_t + 2.7031R_{t-1} - 0.003T$
        (3.47)   (-1.84)   (1.87)   (1.88)   (2.87)
    $+ 0.065$
        (2.72)
    $R^2 = 0.86, \overline{R}^2 = 0.79, DW = 2.88, \rho = 0.26$
                                    (1.23)

9. $CD_t = 0.4391IR_t + 0.158CD_{t-1} + 0.0007Y_t + 0.009Y_{t-1}$
        (-1.49)   (1.16)   (1.56)   (1.73)
    $-0.0057T + 0.193$
        (-6.269)   (11.95)
    $R^2 = 0.94, \overline{R}2 = 0.92, DW = 1.22, \rho = 0.64$
                                    (4.21)

10. $MD_t = 2.733 RR_t - 2.19 IR_t + 1.713 IR_{t-1} + 1.275 Y_t - 113335.0$
        (-2.52)   (-0.24)   (2.17)   (6.67)   (-0.088)
    $R^2 = 0.86, \overline{R}2 = 0.81, DW = 1.92, \rho = 0.26$
                                    (1.31)

11. $IR_t = 0.413\ MD_{t-1} - 0.814\ IR_{t-1} + 8.656\ CI_t - 1.351\ CI_{t-1}$
       (1.93)   (1.403)   (1.68)
       $+\, 0.406\ Y_{t-1} - 7.02$
       (1.56)   (−1.84)
   $R^2 = 0.98,\ \overline{R}2 = 0.95,\ DW = 2.48,\ \rho = 0.58$
                                       (3.21)

12. $P_t = 0.0004\ A_t + 0.0002\ A_{t-1} + 0.105\ IMC_t + 0.421\ P_{t-1} + 32.895$
       (−5.71)   (1.77)   (1.48)   (3.79)   (1.87)
   $R^2 = 0.98,\ \overline{R}2 = 0.93,\ DW = 2.09,\ \rho = 0.48$

13. $IMC_t = 5.347 + 19.352\ WPM_t + 9.017\ EXR_t$
       (1.34)   (2.03)   (0.97)
   $R^2 = 0.98,\ \overline{R}2 = 0.97,\ DW = 2.07,\ \rho = 0.31$
                                       (1.37)

14. $R_t = X_t - IM_t + K_t + PFT_t + FB_t - PF_t + AF_t$

15. $IM_t = -24.04 - 0.025\ IM_{t-1} + 0.104\ Y_t - 0.089\ Y_{t-1} - 0.654\ IMC_t$
       (−0.82)   (−0.86)   (1.59)   (9.21)   (−1.26)
       $+\, 1.123\ T$
       (0.27)
   $R^2 = 0.96,\ \overline{R}2 = 0.92,\ DW = 2.52,\ \rho = -0.62$
                                    (−1.72)

16. $CFB_t = \sum_{r=-20}^{t} FB_r$
   $\lambda^2 = 563.09$

Appendix B

Stability of the Model

Characteristic roots (real) of the system transition matrix

−0.0000008

−0.0000008

−0.1213610

0.2442519

0.3087129

0.5123629

0.7824260

0.0000001

0.0000001

All the roots are real and they are less than unity, so the system is stable. (In the equivalent control system, the rank of the controllability matrix is the same as the dimension of the reduced state vector so that the system is controllable and observable, i.e., the system parameters can be identified.)

We can, however, transform our model to the following form:

$$Y_t = \rho Y_{t-1} + e_t \quad t = 1, 2, \ldots, n \tag{B.1}$$

where ρ is a real number and (e_t) is a sequence of normally distributed random variables with mean zero and variance σ_t^2. Box and Pierce (1970) suggested the following test statistic

$$Q_m = n \sum_{k=1}^{m} r_k^2 \tag{B.2}$$

where

$$r_k = \sum_{t=k+1}^{n} \hat{e}_t \hat{e}_{t-k} \bigg/ \left(\sum_{t=1}^{n} \hat{e}_t^2 \right) \tag{B.3}$$

n = the number of observations, $m = n - k$, where k = the number of parameters estimated, and $\hat{e}_t$ are the residuals from the fitted model.

If (Y_t) satisfies the system, then under the null hypothesis, Q_m is distributed as a chi-squared random variable with m degrees of freedom. The null hypothesis is that $\rho = 1$ where $\hat{e}_t = Y_t - Y_{t-1}$ and thus $k = 0$. The estimated Q_m is 3.85 where the null hypothesis is rejected at 0.05 significance level. So, we accept the alternative hypothesis that if $\rho < 1$, therefore the system is stable.

Das and Cristi (1990) have analyzed in detail the condition for the stability and robustness of the time-varying stochastic optimal control system. The condition is that the dynamic response multipliers of the model should have slow time variations. The estimated response multipliers of this model satisfy conditions of slow time-variations (Das and Cristi, 1990; Tsakalis and Ioannou, 1990).

Notations

A = Domestic absorption
AF = Foreign receipts (grants etc.)
BD = Government budget deficits
CD = Credit to deposit ratio in the commercial banking sector
CFB = Cumulative foreign borrowing, i.e., foreign debt over a period of 20 years
CT = Discount rate of the RBI

FB = Foreign borrowing
G = Government expenditure
GBS = Government bond sales
IM = Value of imports
IMC = Import price index (1990 = 100)
IR = Interest rate in the money-market
K = Foreign capital inflows
LR = Lending (minus repayments to the states)
MD = Money demand
MS = Money supply
NDA = Net domestic asset creation by the RBI
P = Consumers' price index (1990 = 100)
PFT = Private foreign transactions
PF = Foreign payments
R = Changes in foreign exchange reserve
RR = Reserve to deposit ratio in the commercial banking sector
TY = Government tax revenue
T = Time trend
WPM = World price index of India's imports (1990 = 100)
WIR = World interest rate, average of European and US money market rate
EXR = Exchange rate (Rupee/US$)
X = Value of exports
Y = GNP at constant price of 1990

References

Astrom, KJ and K Wittenmark (1995). *Adaptive Control.* Reading, Masschusetts: Addison-Wesley.

Dasu, D and A Lazaridis (1986). A method of stochastic optimal control by Baycsian filtering techniques. *International Journal of System Sciences,* 17(1), 261–280.

Berdell, JF (1995). The present relevance of Hume's open-economy monetary dynamics. *Economic Journal,* 105(432), September, 1205–1217.

Box GEP and DA Pierce (1970). Distribution of residual autocorrelation in autoregressive-integrated moving average time series models. *Journal of the American Statistical Association,* 65(3), 1509–1526.

Cripps, F and WAH Godley (1976). A formal analysis of the Cambridge economic policy group model. *Economics,* August, 43(172), 335–348.

Das, M and R Cristi (1990). Robustness of an adaptive pole placement algorithm in the presence of bounded disturbances and slow time variation of parameters, *IEEE Transaction on Automatic Control*, 35(6), June, 752–756.

Godley, W and M Lavoie (2007). Fiscal policy in a stock-flow consistent (SFC) model. *Journal of Post Keynesian Economics*, 30(1), 79–100.

Godley, W and M Lavoie (2002). Kaleckian models of growth in a coherent stock-flow monetary framework: a Kaldorian view. *Journal of Post Keynesian Economics*, 24(2), 277–311.

Goldberger, AC, AL Nagar and HS Odeh (1961). The covariance matrices of reduced form coefficients and forecasts for a structural econometric model, *Econometrica*, 29, 556–573.

Humphrey, TM (1981). Adam Smith and the monetary approach to the balance of payments. *Economic Review* (Federal Reserve Bank of Richmond), 67(6), 3–10.

Khan, MS (1976). A monetary model of balance of payments: the case of Venezuela. *Journal of Monetary Economics*, 2(3), 311–332.

Khan, MS and PJ Montiel (1990). A marriage between fund and bank models. *IMF Staff Papers*, 37, March, 187–191.

Khan, MS and PJ Montiel (1989). Growth oriented adjustment programs. *IMF Staff Papers*, 36(2), June, 279–306.

Lazaridis, A (1980). Application of filtering methods in econometrics. *International Journal of Systems Science*, 11(11), 1315–1325.

Tsakalis, K and P Ioannou (1990). A new direct adaptive control scheme for time varying plant. *IEEE Transaction; on Automatic Control*, 35(6), June, 697–705.

PART 5

POLICY ANALYSIS

CHAPTER 10

OPENNESS TO TRADE AND THE POVERTY OF FEMALE-HEADED HOUSEHOLDS IN TURKEY

Oner Guncavdi* and Raziye Selim[†]

*Istanbul Technical University and ESRC, Turkey
[†]Istanbul Technical University, Turkey

10.1. Introduction

Turkey has gone through various structural economic transformations towards higher integration with the world economy since the 1980s, and Structural Adjustment Programmes (SAPs) have been put in place for this purpose with the guidance of the IMF and the World Bank (see Aricanli and Rodrik, 1990; Nas and Odekon, 1992). In many developing countries, SAPs exhibit a close association with trade reforms, deregulating price systems and the privatization of state-owned enterprises so as to restructure the economy in the medium and long term. In some cases, like in Turkey, they occasionally include some austerity measures to stabilize the economy in the short run. These reforms, by and large, tend to disassociate poverty in adjusting countries. It is expected that economic reforms and moves towards greater openness, and an increasing reliance on the market mechanism would improve income distribution. This is due to increasing the labor-intensive economic activities and providing new opportunities to increase income for the poor, especially in rural areas after the economic reforms.[1]

---

[1]The well-known theoretical support for this expectation has been provided by the Hechscher–Ohlin theorem of international trade theory. This theory postulates an exchange of relatively labor-intensive exports with capital-intensive imports in foreign trade for countries possessing more labor than capital.

These structural changes in an economy can be expected to have some distributional consequences. However, the empirical results appear to have been very
mixed regarding the direction of these effects. The supporters of the SAPs generally
put forward the fact that economic reforms restore the confidence of international
lenders and encourage foreign direct investment (FDI). This, in turn, stimulate economic growth and ultimately helps everybody in adjusting countries to improve
their living standards. Improvements in income distribution in adjusting countries
could also happen through more liberal international trade, which brings about
more efficient factor allocation and therefore generates economic growth and higher
income. In addition, higher trade and openness are expected to bring about associated benefits such as technology and investment, stimulating economic growth
and, in turn, the opportunity of having higher income for vulnerable groups within
the countries in question. This could then be expected to generate positive distributional effects and alleviate poverty in the adjusting country.[2]

The critics of the reforms' programs, on the other hand, place emphasis mainly
on the fiscal restraints imposed by austerity measures, and point out that external
balance and reductions in aggregate demand worsen poverty in absolute terms.
Besides, the mobilizing of the labor force towards the production of exportable
goods and new incentive structures of new-trade regime may sometimes encourage
formal and/or informal employment of vulnerable groups such as women and the
unskilled labor force with extremely low wages,[3] and may even result in their
unemployment, especially in import-competing sectors. This may contribute to
an increase in poverty because vulnerable groups are often less able to insure
themselves against the effects of such transformations.

In this respect, Turkey is a promising case to launch an empirical investigation.
This is mainly because it has been widely regarded as a successful example of
countries implementing these economic reforms (Saraçoğlu, 1987). However, the
openness of the Turkish economy has never been evaluated on the basis of the
consequences regarding poverty. There has also been little empirical attention to
the income distribution issue in Turkey (see Gürsel et al., 2000; Harrison et al.,
2003; Yemtsov, 2001). Using the cross-sectional survey data, Gürsel et al. (2000),
for example, finds that overall inequality in the Turkish economy from 1987 to
1994 slightly increased. They also find that almost 16% of the total population was
below the poverty line in 1987 while it was only 15% in 1994. Despite this slight

---

[2]These positive effects would be subject to the share of wage earnings in total income. If this
share is very small, then closing the wage gap as described above would have very limited
positive distributional effects on inequality.

[3]Despite the general expectation that increased demand for unskilled labor would increase
wages in exportable sectors, institutional or legal restrictions on the wage adjustment and
high inflation could suppress the real wage for unskilled (or even skilled) labor (see Boratav,
1990).

improvement overall, there is no empirical evidence regarding the effects of trade reforms and openness on the poverty of vulnerable groups such as women.

The purpose of this paper, is therefore, to examine the level of well-being of women in Turkey, and also to assess how the poverty of women has changed over time. There could, in general, be various limitations for this kind of research. Most importantly, the published household survey data do not include any information according to the classification between men-and-women, but rather contains a classification with respect to male- and female-headed household division. Within this limitation, this paper aims to investigate the following questions: (i) is there any difference between incidences of poverty of households in different sectors? (ii) is there any significant difference in the incidences of poverty between male- and female-headed households? (iii) to what extent have these benefits or losses created by trade reforms and openness been in favor of or against the female-headed households (FHHs) within the sectors? (iv) what happened to this difference over time? (v) has the process of economic reforms in Turkey contributed positively to close the gap in poverty between male- and female-headed households?

The remainder of this paper is organized as follows. Section 10.2 summarizes the interaction between trade reforms and the well-being of women in adjusting countries. In Section 10.3, we briefly discuss the data and the methodology of measuring poverty. The empirical findings of this paper are presented in Section 10.4. Finally, Section 10.5 sets out our conclusions.

10.2. Adjustment, Poverty, and Women

The distributional effects of structural adjustment have been discussed in great detail in the context of trade reforms (e.g., Çağatay, 2001; Harrison *et al.*, 2003; Winters *et al.*, 2002). As an integral part of large-scale reform packages, trade reforms in developing countries are expected to expend the trade of these countries, and it is expected to become beneficial to not only reforming countries and their citizens but also to all participating countries. This expected result derives from mainstream trade theory, which is built upon the presumption that specialization in production according to the comparative advantages of a country leads to a more efficient allocation of economic resources and results in higher level of output and growth in reforming countries. Growth will, in turn, promote development and improve income distribution and reduce poverty. This belief is intellectually based on the fact that labor is the most abundant factor of production in many reforming developing countries, and that trade reforms and greater openness should raise the earnings of those living in poverty earlier. Proponents of this view have grown more insistent, arguing that globalization is good for the poor on account of its presumed impact on growth (see Dollar and Kraay, 2000; Edwards, 1993; Sarch and Warner, 1995). In an empirical study based on the panel data of a group of developing countries, Dollar and Kraay (2000), for example, find a favorable impact on the inequality of trade liberalization. They then come to a conclusion that a more open-trade regime positively contributes to economic growth and reduce inequality, *ceteris paribus*. Easterly (2001), which is another well-known empirical study in the literature, on the other hand, shows that the poor benefit from output growth generated by SAPs less in countries with many conditional loans than in countries with few loans. He, hence, implicitly reaches the conclusion that poor still remain poor after implementing the IMF–World Bank-based SAPs. Additionally, Garuda (2000) examines the distributional impacts of the IMF-supported programs, and finds further evidence of a significant deterioration in income distribution in countries which implements the IMF programs compared to those which do not.

Similarly, there have been a great deal of empirical studies both against and in favor of the openness-and-growth relationship, but any positive link seems to have not yet been proven. However, there is no concrete evidence that they are harmful to growth either. More recently, Rodrigues and Rodrik (2000) investigate the reason behind this divergence among the results of empirical studies in the literature, and then criticize them for their misuse of econometrics. They ultimately argue that trade plays a secondary role compared to more influential factors, such as institutions and geography. They also demonstrate that there is no satisfactory evidence to support the assumption that trade liberalization has a positive impact on economic growth. This inconclusive result of cross-section studies in literature has prompted some economists to take into account of country-specific factors and encouraged case studies which include the different features of each society and of population (see Harrison *et al.,* 2003).

Economic growth, certainly, is not the only channel, through which trade liberalization affects poverty and income distribution. Trade reforms, and increased reliance on the market mechanism create other opportunities for the poor to increase their income levels more directly than through economic growth. In this respect, Winters *et al.* (2002) report two additional channels, through which openness would influence income distribution and poverty of households. These channels relate to certain features of the poor households in a typical developing country. First, a majority of poor households are occupied in self-employed economic activities and produce goods and services for the market. An increase (decrease) in the price of something that the household is net seller in response to trade reforms may increase (decrease) its income level, and may alleviate (exacerbate) poverty. Second, these countries are labor abundant, and wage earning constitutes another major source of income for households. Structural adjustment associated with trade reforms gives particular importance to external balance and aims to move available economic resources towards the production of exportable goods, which boosts demand for labor, and in turn may increase wages. However, this adjustment does not necessarily alleviate poverty. If the poor are mostly unskilled, while the production of exportable requires skilled or semi-skilled labor, then poverty will be unaffected or possible worsened. Similarly if unskilled labor is employed primarily in the non-tradable goods sector, while exports need the use of skilled or semi-skilled labor, then the adjustment accompanied by real depreciations of domestic currency could even have a negative effect on poverty.

This is particularly true for women. Being a woman in a developing country is generally seen to be the key determinant of vulnerability. In the period of such an adjustment, women are likely to be even more vulnerable to increased unemployment and other types of insecurity. In comparison with men, women mostly suffer the burdens of economic crises and adjustment disproportionately not only in developing countries, but even in developed market economies. While men and women, for example, may lose their jobs in the case of an economic crisis and/or economic adjustment, women may find harder to regain new jobs than men due to the lack of education and skills, the life-cycle issue (younger, and even single women may be favored in job applications) and the lack of access to capital to set up their own business (e.g., Anker, 1997). Additionally, the lives of women in many developing countries are centered around child-rearing at home and have their mobility in public restricted by some social and religious norms.[4] They then become unable to benefit from new opportunities brought about by reforms. This nature of the female labor force naturally generates sex segregation in labor markets in LDCs with a male labor force in high-paid manufacturing sector activities and a female labor force in relatively low-paid manufacturing sector activities (for example, in the textile industry and service sectors) (Selim and İlkkaracan, 2002). Additionally, in the periods of economic reforms and stabilization after economic crises, women become extremely vulnerable to the removal of subsidies, increasing charges for public services, and rising prices. This issue requires particular attention in the case of a developing country like Turkey where primary sectors such as agriculture occupy a great extent of the total labor force in the economy despite their low share of the GDP. After changing the incentive structure against the agricultural sector, agricultural households, particularly FHHs, are exposed to world competition and become unable to take advantage of new opportunities created by SAPs in other sectors. This is mainly because of lack of adequate education and skill, and above all, due to the limited mobility of the female labor force.

In addition to these elements of vulnerability of women in developing countries, economic reforms and trade liberalization would also help establish positive contributions to alleviating poverty of women and FHHs. Apart from new income opportunities, reforms towards more liberal trade regimes may change the pattern and condition of paid and unpaid work for women. Help closing the wage gap between men and women and in turn alleviating women's poverty, allow them to

---

[4]Since the data we use in this paper utilize income data of households and do not contain any information that may show the social burden of the other responsibilities such as caring for children, or providing labor service to the recreation of the male labor force.

establish their own control over their assets, and even in some cases result in some changes in public provisioning of services (see Çağatay, 2001). Recent empirical studies have mostly put particular emphasis on women's participation rate into paid employment and have shown that female employment has globally increased during the particular period corresponding to trade liberalization in developing countries. Çağatay (2001) implies that this is a clear support for the thesis that greater openness and export-orientation in developing countries are associated with the feminization of paid employment. This is mainly because manufacturing exports in these countries appear to be female-labor-intensive economic activities such as textiles, apparel, and food processing, the production of which requires labor intensive technology and mostly the use of a cheap and unskilled labor force. Increases in the demand for exportable goods in the period of adjustment towards the production of tradable goods boost demand for female labor, and in some cases, substitute female for male labor. This helps to close the wage gap between men and women. Hence trade liberalization and structural adjustment in this kind can, to some extent, be seen as beneficial for women in reforming countries.

Although women and men are affected by trade reforms and openness dispro-portionately, gender has largely been ignored in the discussions concerning the interaction between poverty and trade reforms at both theoretical and empirical levels. This is primarily because of the difficulty to find gender-differentiated data in practice. Nevertheless, women are the key determinant of vulnerability and would constitute the major source of poverty in some reforming countries like Turkey. It is, therefore, important to examine how reforms and adjustment affect the poverty level of this vulnerable group even with the limitations of the available data.

10.3. Issues in Measuring Poverty

Poverty is defined as a status of a person whose social welfare level is below the minimum level of a certain living standard of a society determined by some absolute or relative measures. These measures can be constructed by a choice of a proper variable such as wealth, permanent income, annual income or consumption as an indicator of living standards. Since the wealth of households is difficult to determine, any measure based on it can be seen as unreliable. The choice of permanent income, on the other hand, requires a formation of expectation on the flow of future income, and hence a poverty measure based on it is to be subject to uncertainty and expectational errors arising from the forecast of this future income. Nominal income, however, is readily available in all household surveys and shows the potential purchasing power of households, and it is used very often in the literature, as in this research, to construct a monetary measure of poverty (see Atkinson, 1975 for further discussion).

In empirical research, there are three crucial issues that should be taken into account in measuring poverty. The first issue is the choice of an appropriate unit of analysis. The conventional analysis of poverty, which is based on the concept of income poverty or private consumption patterns, takes the *households* as the unit of analysis, implicitly assuming that all available resources are shared equally within the households. The second issue relates to the identification of the poor, and requires the construction of a monetary poverty line, so that all those below this line are considered as poor. Finally, the third issue involves the choice of proper aggregate measurement of poverty, which could capture all available information about being poor. In the following analysis, these three issues are discussed in detail.

10.3.1. *Choice of Equivalent Scale*

The first issue that should be taken into account is to answer the question of among whom income distribution should be considered. Of course, the answer for this question is individuals. However, the data in practice is collected for households but not for individuals. The standard units of assessment in statistical surveys are taken as the household, in which the incomes of all household members are aggregated. In order to have individual equivalent income measure in this respect, household income is divided by an appropriately calculated *equivalent scale*. In this regard, there are two different ways to calculate an equivalent scale (N). In the first one,

$$N = 1 + \alpha (s_a - 1) + \beta s_k \qquad (10.1)$$

where s_a and s_k are the number of adults and children in the household, respectively and α and β are their own constant parameters. Unlike in Eq. 10.1, the equivalent scale can also be calculated as follows:

$$N = S^e, \quad 0 \le e \le 1 \qquad (10.2)$$

where S is the household size, e is the elasticity of the rate of scale with respect to household size. Equation (10.2) is the most commonly used way of calculating an equivalent scale measure in the established literature. In the one extreme case where e equals unity, no economies of scale exist and a family of two requires twice as much disposable income as a family of one to reach the same level of welfare. At the other extreme situation where e equals zero, economies of scale are perfect, so that a household of two, or for that matter a household of any number, can live exactly as well as a household of one with no increase in their disposable income (see Burkhauser *et al.*, 1996 for further discussion).

Recent studies on income equality and poverty have used the equivalence scale, which is calculated as in Eq. (10.2), and the value of e varies slightly between 0.50 and 0.55. OECD (1998) and Atkinson (1995), for example, used 0.5 as a scale value of e in the studies for *OECD* and *EU* countries, respectively. In the present research, the same equivalence scale measure as in OECD (1998) is employed to convert the disposable income of households to disposable income per equivalent adult. Then, the disposable income per equivalent adult is accordingly calculated as follows:

$$Y_{ij} = \frac{R_i}{S^e} \tag{10.3}$$

where R_i and Y_{ij} stand for household income and disposable income per equivalent adult. Having discussed equivalent scale, there are two further issues left in measuring poverty.

10.3.2. Construction of a Poverty Line

The second issue that we encountered in such a study on poverty is to identify the poor among the whole population. This problem is simply resolved by selecting a properly defined *poverty line*. However, the identification of this poverty line is an arbitrary process, and any poverty measure constructed with respect to different poverty lines may give rise to different poverty rates. In the literature, a poverty line can be constructed in either absolute or relative sense. In absolute sense it is, for example, determined by the cost of minimum food requirement which is necessary for subsisting life. However, if someone wishes to compare the poverty lines of different countries, then it is appropriate to use the relative poverty line approach. This is also an arbitrary process, and generally one portion of median income (40%, 50% or 60%) is accepted as the poverty line.

There have been various independent individual attempts to construct a poverty line in Turkey. Celasun (1986) is the first of such attempts. He defines three poverty lines for three years (namely 1973, 1978, and 1980) and calculates the proportion of poor in total households. He estimates 32% of the total households being poor in 1973, 25% in 1978, and 30% in 1980. He accordingly comes to the conclusion that both the rural–urban immigration and the relative smaller share of the poor within non-agricultural households accounted for this downwards trend over time. Dumanli (1996) is another study, which determines poverty lines for Turkey for two years, namely 1987 and 1994, by using the minimum-food-energy-intake criterion. Using the poverty lines estimated by Dumanli (1996), Dansuk (1997) calculates an absolute poverty rate for Turkey, which indicates 15.2% of the total population being poor in 1987. Erdoğan (2000), on the other hand, calculates an alternative poverty line based on the 1994 *Household Consumption and Expenditure Survey* and *Income Distribution Survey* data. In order to identify poverty, she uses two criteria, namely the cost of minimum food expenditure and the cost of basic needs (including housing, clothing, and transportation and furniture expenditure). Using the first criterion, she estimates the absolute poverty line being 8.4% of the total population, whereas 23% of the total population are below the poverty line with the second criterion.

Unlike these country-specific measures, the 2.5% proportion of the total population is more commonly taken as the critical rate for absolute poverty in comparison with the internationally comparable one-dollar per day poverty line (World Bank, 2000). There is, nevertheless, no absolute poverty problem in Turkey with the low poverty rate of 7.2% (Yemtsov, 2001). This study put particular emphasis on the importance of economic vulnerability and its likely distributional consequences in Turkey. The study further brings about the fact that 36% of the total population have consumption expenditure below the economic vulnerability line, which compromises the costs of both minimum food basket and basic non-food spending. A recent study by Gürsel *et al.* (2000) also uses the same methodology as the World Bank and shows that relative income poverty improved slightly from 1987 to 1994. The present research also employs the relative poverty approach, and the poverty line was determined by the income threshold, which is the equivalent of 50% of the median disposable income per equivalent adult.

10.3.3. *Choice of Poverty Measures*

Another issue to be resolved is the choice of appropriate aggregate measures of poverty. For our empirical investigation, we employed three widely used measures (Atkinson, 1987; Foster *et al.*, 1984; Kakwani, 1980; Ravallion, 1994). They are namely *head-count ratio* (P_0), *poverty gap* ratio (P_1) and the *Foster–Greer–Thorbecke* (P_2) poverty index. The head-count ratio of poverty simply indicates the proportion of the population for whom income is less than the pre-determined poverty line; then $P_0 = q/n$ where q is the number of persons whose income lies below the poverty line, and n is the total population.

The P_1 is defined as a percentage difference between the poverty line and income of the poor, and is given as follows:

$$P_1 = \frac{1}{n} \sum_{i=1}^{q} \left(\frac{z - x_i}{z} \right) = H \times I = \frac{q}{n} \left(\frac{z - \mu*}{z} \right) \qquad (10.4)$$

where $\mu*$ is the mean income of the poor and I measures the average proportionate shortfall of income below the poverty line. P_1 also indicates the fraction of the poverty line income that would have to be generated in the economy in order to eradicate poverty under the assumption of perfect targeting. Both measures have been criticized because they may not capture differences in the severity of poverty among the poor (Ravallion, 1994). In response to this criticism, Sen (1976) develops a new measure, which takes this shortfall into account and allows the examination of income distribution within the poor population. However, this measure is not additively decomposable in the sense that the total poverty is a weighted average of the subgroup poverty levels. Foster *et al.* (1984), on the other hand, suggest a decomposable measure of poverty, which is formulated as follows:

$$P_\gamma = \frac{1}{n} \sum_{i=1}^{q} \left(\frac{z - x_i}{z} \right)^\gamma, \quad \gamma > 1 \tag{10.5}$$

where γ is a constant parameter. The larger the value of γ, the greater the weight given to the severity of poverty. For $\gamma = 0$, P_γ reduces to P_0, and for $\gamma = 1$, to P_1 and $\gamma = 2$, to P_2. Unlike others, P_2 measures the severity of poverty. P_0 and P_1 are not sensitive to income transfers among the poor, whereas P_2 is. It may further be noted that all the three measures are additively decomposable. This enables us to examine the relative contributions of different subgroups to overall poverty. In the following analysis, we use these three indices to measure the level of poverty in Turkey.

10.4. Data and Empirical Results

The cross-sectional data on which this study is based is obtained from *Household Income and Consumption-Expenditure Surveys* conducted by the *State Institute of Statistics* (SIS) in 1987 and 1994. Each survey includes rural and urban sectors, and is sufficient to enable the estimation of income and expenditure of Turkish households, which serves as the basis for constructing a money metric measure of the standard of living. One difficulty with this data set is that both surveys classify households with respect to household heads and economic activities where household heads are occupied with earning the household income. However, they do not allow us to see the other sources of income which may be obtained by other members of households through economic activities and occupations other than that of household head. Despite its importance, we are therefore unable to examine the poverty level of females within the male-headed households (MHHs) because of the lack of disaggregated income and expenditure data at each household level.

In this study, households are divided into two groups according to the gender of their household heads: namely MHHs and FHHs. Total household income was preferred for the construction of the standard of living. The measures of standard of living from both the surveys were thus the total household income, which was adjusted by household size, and was then deflated by 1987 prices using consumer price indices.

Within the main technical limitations of the data sets, there are also various conceptual issues that should be discussed before starting analyzing the results of this paper. The *first one* is the lack of data for the period before trade reforms, so that we are unable to present a comparison of the poverty levels before-and-after the trade reforms. Even though the data is available only for the post-liberalization period, it is still very difficult to distinguish the poverty effects of trade reforms from those arisen from non-trade factors.[5] With the present data set, we are unable to have a direct observation on the link between openness and poverty. However, we can establish a way of indirect observation on this link by comparing the poverty levels of households in relatively open and export-oriented sectors with those in less tradable sectors. In this type of comparison, we theoretically expect that greater openness would present opportunities to alleviate poverty levels of households by creating new job and income opportunities and closing wage differential between skilled and unskilled labor. If this theoretical expectation is proven to be true in the Turkish case, then it could be concluded that an involvement in an economic activity in a relatively open sector decreases the likelihood of a household being under the poverty line.

The *second issue* requires classifying and aggregating the sectors where the household heads are occupied, in accordance with the degree of those sectors' openness to international trade. The original data in Turkey is collected at the three-digit industry classification level, and some of these industries are relatively more internationally open industries (such as agriculture, food manufacturing, and textiles) than others (such as services and construction). In aggregating sectors, we also pay particular attention to the presence of a significant number of FHHs. Having classified all the existing industries according to their openness levels and the sufficient number of FHHs in each aggregated sector, three main sectors can be identified as being relatively open. These sectors are namely agriculture, food manufacturing, and textiles and clothing.[6] The other manufacturing industry group appears to be another sectoral group after aggregation, and it is also open to international trade, but possesses an insignificant number of FHHs in the survey to

---

[5]The Turkish economy has occasionally encountered deep economic crisis and had to undertake economic austerity programs in order to stabilize the economy. Important components of such programs, such as cuts in public expenditure and rises in the price of major public utilities, certainly have deteriorating effects on poverty. Our sample year, 1994, is one of these years in the Turkish economy. In addition, the time period spanning from 1987 to 1994 exhibits a highly volatile and insecure economic environment. In particular, the reform efforts were interrupted by a number of successive economic crises in 1988, 1991, and 1994, each of which was followed by austerity programs that might have had deteriorating effects on poverty in general and on the well-being of women in particular. Thus, they make it even more difficult to distinguish the real effects of trade reforms on poverty directly.

[6]Erlat and Şahin (1998), Erlat (1999) and Çakmaklı and Günçavdı (2005) note that these sectors are the traditional exporting sectors in the Turkish economy. In particular, Çakmaklı and Günçavdı (2005) indicate that although Turkey is traditionally an exporter of primary products, there has been a significant structural shift in the traditionality of exports towards more labor intensive manufactured goods after the 1980s such as food processing, textiles, and clothing.

allow us to draw a statistically reliable conclusion. With this classification, it is most likely to establish a link between greater openness and poverty; greater openness as a consequence of reforms would have generated more income opportunities in export-oriented sectors than others. The feminization of the labor force in these open sectors might have also acted in favor of (or against) FHHs and alleviated (or exacerbated) inequality between MHHs and FHHs by closing (or widening) the wage gap between these two groups.

In what follows, this research seeks answers for a number of questions regarding the link between openness and poverty of FHHs. We first present a brief general descriptive summary of the general pattern of poverty in Turkey based on the survey data, and then examine the presence of any statistically significant difference between the poverty levels of FHHs and MHHs. Later, we investigate the importance of the sectoral difference in the FHHs and MHHs' poverty levels. In this regard, we examine whether or not FHHs engaged in economic activities in relatively more open sectors were poorer than MHHs in the same sector and, to what extent openness helped to close (or widen) the income gaps between these two groups of households from 1987 to 1994. With a theoretical expectation that openness provides more income opportunities for vulnerable groups and alleviates their poverty levels, we examine the differences in the poverty levels of FHHs and MHHs which are engaged in different income-earning activities. With this investigation, it is also possible to see whether or not the sources of households' income can be accounted for the difference in the poverty levels of FHHs and MHHs. If there is a poverty difference between two groups of households, then we examine to what extent this difference exists in relatively more open sectors.

10.4.1. *General Summary Measures of Samples*

Table 10.1 reports the sample size and some summary statistics such as mean per household annual income (at 1987 prices) and the Gini-coefficients of the per household income distribution among individuals. Both surveys possess slightly more than 26,000 households, most of which are headed by males. As seen in Table 10.1, FHHs constitute a very small proportion of total households in the samples: almost 5% in both years. Over the period of 7 years from 1987 to 1994, the real mean annual income of household in the Turkish economy seems to have declined from 3.77 YTL in 1987 to 3.57 YTL in 1994. Whereas this decline has been very limited among MHHs, it has been very much for FHHs. Consequently, the MHHs/FHHs ratio of mean real annual income per household has widened almost by 25% from 1.24 in 1987 to 1.55 in 1994. However, the estimates of Gini-coefficients for both MHHs and FHHs appear to have improved slightly.

Table 10.2 presents the estimates of head-count ratio, poverty gap ratio, and Foster–Greer–Thorbecke poverty index separately for the whole economy, MHHs and FHHs. For the whole economy, the level of poverty in 1994 seems to have become less severe than in 1987; about 16% of the total population lived under the

Table 10.1. Basic statistics of sample.

	1987	1994
Total		
Sample size	26400	26236
Median household size	5	4
Mean household size	5.02	4.50
Mean annual income per household (YTL)	377	357
Gini-coefficient	0.46	0.45
Male-headed households		
Sample size	24295	24418
Mean annual income per household (YTL)	383	367
Gini-coefficient	0.46	0.45
Female-headed households		
Sample size	2105	2018
Mean annual income per household (YTL)	301	237
Gini-coefficient	0.46	0.43

*YTL = New Turkish Lira

poverty line in 1987 with the corresponding figure being 15.5% in 1994. While the same trend in poverty level prevailed for MHHs, the number of households under the poverty line has declined only by 5.6% from 1987 to 1994. This is an improvement in the poverty level of MHHs, and is also statistically significant as it implies that there have been poverty-reducing economic policy changes for MHHs in this period. The most striking feature of Table 10.2 is that the level of FHHs' poverty has drastically increased over seven years; as about 19% of the total FHHs were below the poverty line, this ratio raised to almost 22% in 1994. This approximate 13% increase in the head-count ratio for FHHs is statistically significant, referring not to a random increase, but to something systematically happening that negatively affects the well-being of FHHs in the Turkish economy during the period of analysis. Table 10.2 also indicates that the poverty gap has narrowed for MHHs as well as for FHHs during this period.

When we look at the values of P_2 in Table 10.2, the severity of poverty seems to have reduced both in total and at the household level. Interestingly, the result shows that while the extent of poverty increases among FHHs, the distribution of income among these poor households appears to have become better between 1987 and 1994. However, poverty still remains more severe among the poor FHHs than MHHs. The ratio Foster–Greer–Thorbecke poverty indices of MHHs and FHHs increased from 0.55 in 1987 to 0.64 in 1994, indicating a 16% increase in the gap between these two household groups.

Table 10.2.   Poverty measures.

	1987	1994	% change
Poverty line (YTL)	0.59*	0.58**	—
Total			
$P_0(\%)$	16.3	15.5	−4.9
P_1	4.9	4.1	−16.3
P_2	2.3	1.7	−26.1
Male-headed households			
$P_0(\%)$	16.1	15.2	−5.6
P_1	4.8	4.0	−16.7
P_2	2.2	1.6	−27.3
Female-headed households			
$P_0(\%)$	19.2	21.6	12.5
P_1	7.5	6.1	−18.7
P_2	4.0	2.5	−37.5

Notes: *Poverty line is 50% of median income of per equivalent adult.
**It is at 1987 prices.

So far, our initial examination shows that poverty appears to have slightly decreased from 1987 to 1994 mostly in favor of MHHs, and inequality between FHHs and MHHs has deteriorated. Following this general observation from the data available, we next investigate whether or not openness alleviates (exacerbates) poverty and creates increasing inequality (equality) between MHHs and FHHs.

10.4.2. *Openness and Poverty*

As we discussed earlier, there are some highly export-oriented sectors in Turkey which are more exposed to international market conditions. These sectors are chosen by relying on the past records of the composition of Turkish exports. These relatively more open sectors are namely; *agriculture, food processing*, and *textiles and clothing*. In addition to these sectors, our samples compose of households in other sectors such as *other manufacturing* and *services*. Although economic activities in the other manufacturing sectors compromise the production of tradable goods, this sector contains only few FHHs.[7] The service sector in our sample, on

---

[7]This sector may have the working conditions which are most likely not to be suitable for the employment of women. Economic activities in this sector require a certain level of education and established experience which most Turkish women lack.

the other hand, is mostly inward-oriented sector with less exposure to international competition.

From Table 10.3, it is evident that the great extent of FHHs are classified as non-working, which was almost 44% in 1987 and 55% in 1994. These numbers are smaller for MHHs than FHHs in both years. The data also shows that poverty

Table 10.3. Poverty measures of FHHs and MHHs (%).

Sectors	FHHs				MHHs			
	1987		1994		1987		1994	
	Population share	P_0	Population share	P_0	Population share	P_0	Population share	P_0
Non-working	43.7	11.2	55.0	19.3	6.4	10.1	10.1	15.2
Agriculture	39.6	30.8	28.7	30.0	32.4	23.4	31.2	22.7
Food manufacturing	1.0	2.6	1.2	17.8	2.8	12.0	2.4	9.5
Textile and clothing	3.6	13.6	4.1	26.5	2.8	10.4	2.9	9.2
Other manufacturing	0.4	3.4	0.6	3.4	7.5	10.6	17.3	16.6
Service	11.7	13.7	10.3	9.7	48.2	13.4	36.0	8.8
Total	100.0	19.2	100.0	21.6	—	16.1	100.0	15.2

	Poverty gap ratio P_1 (%)				Foster–Greer–Thorbecke measure $P_2^* 100$			
	FHHs		MHHs		FHHs		MHHs	
	1987	1994	1987	1994	1987	1994	1987	1994
Non-working	3.5	5.9	2.9	4.1	1.6	2.5	1.4	1.8
Agriculture	13.3	8.0	8.5	6.9	7.6	3.0	4.6	3.0
Food manufacturing	0.5	7.6	2.2	1.9	0.1	3.6	0.7	0.5
Textile and clothing	5.4	6.2	2.1	1.9	2.8	2.8	0.6	0.5
Other manufacturing	0.6	0.1	2.2	4.0	0.1	0.0	0.8	1.4
Service	4.0	1.9	3.3	1.9	1.8	0.6	1.2	0.6
Total	7.5	6.1	4.8	4.0	4.0	2.5	2.2	1.6

for both household groups seems to have deteriorated in general, but become even worse for FHHs than MHHs.

The second largest group of FHHs are occupied in agricultural economic activities in both years.[8] Whereas almost 40% of all the FHHs earn income in the agriculture sector in 1987, this share declined to almost 29% in 1994. This can be taken as an evidence for immigration from rural to urban areas from 1987 to 1994. It seems that this is mainly because of the widespread poverty among FHHs in agriculture; almost 31% of all the FHHs were under the poverty line in the agriculture sector in 1987. Despite a decline in the number of FHHs, there was almost no change in this proportion of poor FHHs in the agriculture sector in 1994.

The textiles and clothing sector is another highly export-oriented sector in the Turkish economy, and compromises 3.6% of the total FHHs in 1987 and 4.1% in 1994. However, the same figures for MHHs are 2.8% in 1987 and 2.9% in 1994, increasing the feminization of the labor force in this sector. Despite this relatively large number of FHHs in the sector, the proportion of poor is clearly higher for FHHs than MHHs. Our results show that the poverty level for FHHs seems to have deteriorated drastically from 13.6% in 1987 to 26.5% in 1994. MHHs, on the other hand, appear to have become better off from the 10.4% poor households in 1987 to 9.2% in 1994. The most striking deterioration in the poverty of FHHs appears to have taken place in the food-manufacturing sector. Despite its lower share of FHHs among other sectors (around 1% in both years), the proportion of poor FHHs appears to have jumped from 2.6% in 1987 to 17.8% in 1994. However, Table 10.3 also shows that there is a slight improvement in the proportion of poor MHHs in the same sector from 1987 to 1994.

So far, it has been evident from the results of Table 10.3 that FHHs in open and highly export-oriented sectors were poorer than the MHHs in the same sectors. Despite a general improvement in the well-being of MHHs in these sectors, it is obvious that the poverty level of FHHs seems to have deteriorated from 1987 to 1994. A particular contribution to the poverty of FHHs in both years was made largely by non-working households and those in traditional Turkish export sectors such as agriculture, and textiles and clothing, and to some extent by households in the food-manufacturing sector. FHHs in the service sector, on the other hand,

---

[8]The Turkish economy in the 2000s still shows highly agricultural features. In 2004, the agriculture sector produced only 12.5% of the total GDP while employing almost 35% of the total labor force (SPO, 2005). Despite this low productivity, the same sector requires large public funds for subsidization. Recent studies show that the total monetary value of subsidies given to the agriculture sector reached US$ 11.3 billion in 1998 (Çakmak *et al.*, 1999). Budgetary transfers to the sector, on the other hand, amount to an average of US$ 3.5 billion per annum over the last five years (Doğruel *et al.*, 2003). Despite all these costs, the sector still possesses its importance in current political debates, and any economic measure taken for reforming this sector draws considerable amount of public attention mainly because of the income distribution effects of such reforms.

comprise around 10% of the total FHHs with less than 10% of them being below the poverty line in 1994 in comparison with 14% in 1987. It, therefore, seems that households in the relatively non-tradable sector were able to have improved their well-being from 1987 to 1994. More interestingly, when we examine the poverty gap ratio (P_1), income inequality among the poor FHHs seems to have alleviated only in the agriculture sector. This is most probably due to the households which migrated from rural to urban areas from 1987 to 1994, and engaged in economic activities in other sectors (mainly in the textiles and clothing, food-manufacturing sectors, and service sectors). By examining P_2 here, on the other hand, appears to have become more difficult to eradicate poverty in the food-manufacturing sectors and textiles and clothing sectors.

10.4.3. *Occupational Difference Between Households and Poverty*

We now make a distinction between households in accordance with economic activities which the heads of households engage to earn their household income, and then examine whether or not there is a difference in poverty levels between FHHs and MHHs with respect to their occupations and the sources of income. This classification, unfortunately, is available only for the 1994 household income and expenditure survey. There are 2018 FHHs, and six different economic activities in which each household engaged in the survey in 1994. These activities are namely: wage-earning economic activities, casual working, being an employer, self-employment, being an unpaid family worker and finally being a non-working household head. As seen in Table 10.4, only 9% of the total FHHs are wage earners whereas the corresponding figure is about 37% for MHHs. The table shows that the proportion of households living under the poverty line among these wage

Table 10.4.   Income groups of households in 1994.

Employment status of household head	FHHs		MHHs	
	Population share	P_0	Population share	P_0
Wage/Salary	9.0	12.0	36.5	9.2
Casual	4.5	44.5	11.6	34.6
Employer	0.5	0.0	7.2	1.8
Self-employment	23.1	25.5	33.7	14.8
Unpaid family worker	0.1	0.0	0.1	4.7
Not employed	62.8	18.6	10.9	15.2

earner FHHs is higher than those of MHHs, indicating that female wage earners are poorer than male. Furthermore, even if openness and reform had worked to close the poverty gap between men and female, and had promoted FHHs to engage into wage-earning activities as indicated in the literature, then the share of wage-earning FHHs would have been higher, and the closing income gap between wage-earning male and female would have improved the levels of poverty between FHHs and MHHs. In fact, poverty gaps between female and male labor force could account for this larger share of the poor among wage earner FHHs than their male counterparts.

In Table 10.4, the largest proportion of FHHs is the non-working group, being 63% of total FHHs in the 1994 sample. This share is noticeably far lower for MHHs than FHHs. The great majority of FHHs — which is about 23% — engaged in self-employed economic activities like MHHs, but the proportion of the poor is higher than that of the MHHs. Poverty seems to have been widespread among the casual worker FHHs and MHHs. While 4.5% of the FHHs and 11.6% of the MHHs were occupied in casual earning economic activities in 1994, almost 45% of the FHHs had a standard of living below the poverty line. This was the largest contribution made by one occupational group in the survey. For MHHs, the same figure is 34.6%. Other occupational groups (employers and unpaid family workers), however, are relatively small. The results from Table 10.4 consequently shows that high poverty can be observed among non-working and self-employed FHHs, which compromises 85% of the total FHHs. Among all the occupational groups in Table 10.4, the proportions of households in poverty are much lower for MHHs than for FHHs. Wage-earner and self-employed MHHs predominantly compromise 70% of the MHHs, which seems to have had relatively lower poverty ratios. It can, therefore, be taken as an indication of occupational difference in the levels of poverty between MHHs and FHHs. Additionally, MHHs had more attention and have the standard of living above the poverty line than FHHs, particularly when they were engaged in self-employment economic activities. Based on these results obtained from the survey sample in 1994, it was also more likely for FHHs to be employed in relatively low-wage jobs than MHHs.

In order to examine whether or not sectoral allocation, particularly being in a relatively more open sector, accounted for the differences in the poverty levels among FHHs, we have prepared Table 10.5. The important difference between Table 10.5 and the previous tables is the sectoral aggregation level. Earlier, three sectors, namely agriculture, food manufacturing, and textiles and clothing, have been considered as open and exporting sectors basing on their large shares in the total exports in the Turkish economy. In Table 10.5, however, we aggregate them all and name the more aggregated sector as a primary export sector. The reason for this aggregation is that earlier disaggregation of the sectors together with occupational distribution leaves us with very few numbers of FHHs in each sector, and becomes very difficult to draw statistically significant inferences about the poverty level of

Table 10.5. Sectoral and occupational distribution and poverty levels in 1994.

Family Type	Non-working	Wage/Salary	Casual	Employer	Self-employment	Unpaid-family worker	Total
Female-headed households							
Non-working	1331	0	0	0	0	0	1331
Primary export sectors	0	34	46	2	400	1	483
Other manufacturing	0	9	3	0	1	0	13
Service	0	125	30	9	26	1	191
Total	1331	168	79	11	427	2	2018
Head-count ratio							
Non-working	19.3	—	—	—	—	—	19.3
Primary export sectors	—	12.4	55.4	0.0	28.1	0.0	29.2
Other manufacturing	—	0.0	15.9	—	0.0	—	3.4
Services	—	7.6	22.5	0.0	8.7	0.0	9.4
Total	19.3	8.3	42.6	0.0	26.9	0.0	21.6
Male-headed households							
Non-working	3169	—	—	—	—	—	3169
Primary export sectors	—	1451	361	226	4239	5	6282
Other manufacturing	—	1952	1579	604	403	1	4539
Services	—	5701	633	954	2928	12	10,228
Total	3169	9104	2573	1784	7570	18	24,218
Head-count ratio							
Non-working	15.2	—	—	—	—	—	15.2
Primary export sectors	—	13.0	44.0	3.1	21.5	9.7	20.8
Other manufacturing	—	11.4	30.8	2.3	8.8	0.0	16.6
Services	—	7.7	27.6	1.6	9.3	0.0	8.8
Total	15.2	9.4	32.3	2.0	17.6	2.0	15.2

such a small number of households. With this aggregation level of the economic activities in which households engage in the 1994 survey, four sectoral groups are identified, namely non-working, primary exports, other manufacturing, and services. Despite this aggregation, the small cell sizes which arise in some cases when two criteria are taken into account should be noted in interpreting the values by sectors and occupational groups of the poverty indices.

As we did earlier, the sector, which is defined as the primary export sector in Table 10.5, is considered as the relatively more exposed to international markets than the others. With this aggregation level, the distribution of FHHs and MHHs with respect to occupation and sectors can be seen in the first panel of Table 10.5. The largest number of households are the non-working groups and those in the primary export sectors and services. The majority of those in the primary export sectors appear to have been self-employed. FHHs in the service sectors, on the other hand, are employed mostly in wage-earning economic activities.

The second panel giving the values for P_0 (the head-count ratio) indicates that 21.6% of the FHHs were under the poverty line in 1994. This ratio is remarkably higher than the 15% of the poor among MHHs. The 29% of those in the primary export sectors were poor FHHs. Considering the occupational distribution, 28% of all the FHHs in the primary export sectors, which were occupied with self-employed economic activities, can be defined as poor. This ratio becomes smaller with a 12.4% value of P_0 for those which were engaged in wage-earning economic activities in the same sector, implying that wage-earner FHHs were relatively better off than the self-employed households. Looking at the wage-earner FHHs in the service sector, the proportion of the poor was smaller and 7.6% in 1994. Table 10.5 also indicates that being a casual working FHH in the primary export sector increases the likelihood of being below the poverty line in the same year. The high proportion of households engaged in agricultural activities among casual working FHHs in the primary export sector seems to account for this high proportion of the poor.

10.5. Conclusion

Since the 1980s, economic reforms and liberalization of international trade regime have been widespread practices among developing countries. As one of them, Turkey began to liberalize her trade regime in 1983. Apart from the potential benefits of more liberal and open-trade regime, it is also inevitable that this would have distributional effects on individuals. The literature has, so far, paid considerable attention to the reform-and-growth relationships and could not reach any concrete agreement on the direction of this interaction. The distributional consequences of the reforms have, on the other hand, recently gained importance in the literature. The gender issue has, however, been largely ignored. The present research is an attempt, *to some extent*, to fill this gap with empirical evidence from a well-known reforming country in the literature, namely Turkey.

The present research shows that there is a significant difference between the well-being of FHHs and MHHs, and this inequality increased against FHHs from 1987 to 1994. It is also noted that the number of FHHs involved in economic activities in relatively open sectors are lower than MHHs, and they appear to be poorer. FHHs in Turkey appear to concentrate largely in the non-working household group, so that the interaction between trade reform and the well-being of FHHs would be very limited. The poverty level of FHHs in traditionally more open sectors in Turkey, namely textiles and clothing, is higher than that of MHHs, and moreover deteriorated from 1987 to 1994. It has, therefore, been evident from the empirical result of this research that FHHs in open and highly export-oriented sectors are poorer that MHHs in the same sector. Whereas trade reform is expected to close the wage gap between FHHs and MHHs, our findings show that female wage earners are still poorer than male wage earners. In addition, self-employed FHHs, which constitute the largest fraction of the total FHHs in our survey data, still remained poorer, as the Turkish trade reforms failed to create income opportunity for the self-employed FHHs through the prices of products that the self-employed households were net sellers. The results presented in this paper should, however, not to be considered as conclusive. The limitations of the existing data and the need of more observations that would be drawn from the future surveys would allow for understanding better the distributional consequences of openness in Turkey.

Appendix

Aggregation of Economic Activities by Commodity by Commodity

Commodity group	ISIC
1- Agriculture	011–012–013–014–015–020–050–101–102–103–111–112–120–131–132–141–142–231
2- Food manufacturing	151–152–153–154–155–160
3- Textile-clothing	171–172–173–181–182–191–192

Commodity group	ISIC
4- Other manufacturing	201–202–210–221–222–223–232–233–241–242–243–251–252–261–269–271–272–273–281–289–291–292–293–300–319–311–312–313–314–315–321–322–323–331–332–333–341–342–343–351–352–353–3591–3591–3592–3599–361–3691–3692–3693–3694–3699–371–372–401–402–403–410–451–452–453–454–455
5- Service	501–502–503–504–505–511–512–513–514–515–519–521–522–523–524–525–526–551–552–601–602–603–611–612–621–622–630–641–642–651–659–660–671–672–701–702–711–712–713–721–722–723–724–725–729–731–732–741–742–743–749–751–752–753–801–802–803–809–851–852–853–900–911–912–919–921–922–923–924–930–950–990

References

Anker, R (1997). Theories of occupational segregation by sex: an overview. *International Labor Review*, 136(3), 1–5.

Aricanli, T and D Rodrik (1990). *The Political Economy of Turkey: Debt, Adjustment and Sustainability*, London: MacMillan Press.

Atkinson, AB (1975). *The Economics of Inequality*. Oxford: Clarendon Press.

Atkinson, AB (1987). On the measurement of poverty. *Econometrica*, 55(4), 749–764.

Atkinson, AB (1995). *Incomes and the Welfare State*, Cambridge: Cambridge University Press.

Boratav, K (1990). Inter-class and intra-class relations of distribution under 'structural adjustment': Turkey during the 1980s. In *The Political Economy of Turkey: Debt, Adjustment and Sustainability*, T Aricanli and D Rodrik (eds.), London: MacMillan Press, p. 278.

Burkhauser, RV, TM Smeeding and J Merz (1996). Relative inequality and poverty in Germany and the United States using alternative equivalence scales. *Review of Income and Wealth*, 42(4), 381–400.

Çağatay, N (2001). *Trade, Gender and Poverty. Background Paper. Trade and Sustainable Human Development Project*, New York: UNDP.

Çakmak, E, H Kasnakoğlu and H Akder (1999). *Tarım Politikalarında Yeni Denge Arayışlarıve Turkiye*, Istanbul: TÜSIAD.

Çakmakli, C and Ö Günçavdı (2005). The link between economic liberalisation and economic growth, the case of Turkey. In *Middle East and North African Economies: Past Perspectives and Future Challenges, Proc. of the International Conference jointly organised by ECOMOD and MEEA*, June 2–3, 2005, Brussels, pp. 135–146.

Celasun, M (1986). Income distribution and domestic terms of trade in Turkey, 1978–1983: estimated measures of inequality and poverty. *METU Studies in Development*, 13(1,2), 193–216.

Dansuk, E (1997). *Measuring Poverty in Turkey and Its Relation with Socio-Economic Structure*. Published thesis, Ankara: State Planning Organisation (in Turkish).

Doğruel, F, S Doğruel and E Yeldan (2003). Macroeconomics of Turkey's agricultural reforms. An intertemporal computable general equilibrium analysis. *Journal of Policy Modelling*, 25, 617–637.

Dollar, D and A Kraay (2000). *Growth is Good for the Poor*, Washington, DC: Development Research Group, World Bank.

Dumanli, R (1996). *Poverty and Its Dimensions in Turkey*. Published thesis, Ankara: State Planning Organisation (in Turkish).

Easterly, W (2001). *The Effects of International Monetary Fund and World Bank Programmes on Poverty*. Mimeo, Washington: World Bank.

Edwards, S (1993). Openness, trade liberalisation and growth in developing countries. *Journal of Economic Literature*, 31(3), 1358–1393.

Erdoğan, (2000). *Poverty and Its Dimensions in Turkey*. Published thesis, Ankara: State Institute of Statistics (in Turkish).

Erlat, G (1999). Diversification in Turkish foreign trade. *METU Studies in Development*, 26(3,4), 281–298.

Erlat, G and B Şahin (1998). Export diversification over time in Turkey. *METU Studies in Development*, 25, 47–60.

Foster, J, J Greer and E Thorbecke (1984). A class of decomposable poverty measures. *Econometrica*, 52(3), 761–766.

Garuda, G (2000). The distributional effects of IMF programmes: a cross-country analysis. *World Development*, 28(6), 1031–1051.

Gürsel, S *et al.* (2000). *Individual Income Distribution and Poverty in Turkey: A Comparison with EU Countries*, Istanbul: TUSIAD (in Turkish).

Harrison, GW, TF Rutherford and DG Tarr (2003). Trade liberalization, poverty and efficient equity. *Journal of Development Economics*, 71, 97–128.

Kakwani, NC (1980). *Income Inequality and Poverty Methods of Estimation and Policy Applications*, Oxford: Oxford University Press.

Nas, T and Ve M Odekon (1992). *Economics and Politics of Turkish Liberalisation*, Bethlehem: Lehigh University Press.

OECD (1998). Income distribution and poverty in selected OECD countries. Economics Department Working Papers No. 189, ECO/WKP (98) 2.

Ravallion, M (1994). Poverty comparisons: a guide to concepts and methods. http://www1.World Bank.org/wbiep/decentralization.

Rodrigues, F and D Rodrik (2000). Trade policy and economic growth: a skeptic's guide to the cross-national evidence. Unpublished Paper, Harvard University, May.

Saracoğlu, R (1987). Economic stabilisation and structural adjustment: the case of Turkey. In *Growth-Oriented Adjustment Programs*, V Corbo, M Goldstein and M Khan (eds.), World Bank, Washington D.C., 1987, pp. 251–274.

Sachs, J and A Warner (1995). Economic reform and the process of global integration. *Brookings Papers on Economic Activity*, 1, 1–117.

Selim, R and İ İlkkaracan (2002). Gender inequalities in the labour market in Turkey: some empirical evidence. *Proc. of the 6th METU International Conference in Economics*, 11–14 September 2002, Ankara, pp. 217 235.

Sen, A (1976). Poverty: an ordinal approach to measurement. *Econometrica*, 44(2), 219–231.

SPO (2005). *Economic and Social Indicators*. Ankara: State Planning Organisation.

Winters, L A, N McCulloch and A McKay (2002). Trade liberalisation and poverty: the empirical evidence. CREDIT Research Paper No. 02/22, Nottingham: University of Nottingham.

World Bank (2000). *Attaching Poverty 2000 / 2001*, Oxford: Oxford University Press.

Yemtsov, R (2001). *Living Standards and Economic Vulnerability between 1987 and 1994*, IZA Discussion Paper, No. 253, Bonn.

CHAPTER 11

CHINA'S ECONOMIC PERFORMANCE AND TRANSITION IN RELATION TO GLOBALIZATION: FROM ISOLATION TO CENTER-STAGE

Clem Tisdell

University of Queensland, Australia

11.1. Introduction

The process of economic globalization has accelerated since the early 1970s. China has played a major and increasing role in maintaining the momentum of economic globalization as a result of its open-door policies and its continuing economic reforms instigated by Deng Xiaoping. Consequently, China has become an engine for global economic growth, and a key player in the world economy. As its economy continues to grow, it can be expected to strengthen its position as a global economic powerhouse and to consolidate its status as a world political power. While these trends in China's growth can be expected to continue for much time to come, it seems unrealistic to expect them to continue forever. Eventually, the Chinese economy might be expected to catch up with the higher-income economies and experience relatively slower economic growth. Whether or not another nation will eventually replace China's leadership in international economic growth, and when, is uncertain.

It is useful to consider China's global economic situation in relation to the general process of globalization. This paper provides a background on the process of economic globalization and considers its potential social and environmental consequences, both positive and negative, as well as China's position in this process.

11.2. What is Economic Globalization? What Factors Have Favored it in Recent Decades?

Economic globalization involves the geographical extension of economic exchange and economic interdependence beyond national borders in a way that involves all countries (for more discussion, see Tisdell and Sen, 2004). In the present economic climate, this is mostly achieved by the geographical extension of markets to encompass all parts of the globe. At the same time, as markets have been extended internationally, the type of international transactions that can be made have widened. For example, not only has international trade in physical commodities risen greatly but so has global exchange in services, in intellectual knowledge, in capital, and in finance.

Many factors have helped to foster this process. They include:

(1) Reduced man-made barriers to international trade resulting from the efforts of bodies such as the WTO, e.g., reduced tariff barriers, elimination of import quotes.
(2) Reduced natural or physical barriers to international trade due to technological progress in the transport industry.
(3) Improved communication and reduced communication costs as a result of technical progress in the telecommunication industry, e.g., electronic mail and teleconferencing.
(4) Improved institutional arrangements within nations to facilitate business, such as harmonization of property rights via legal reforms and greater acceptance of international legal conventions, such as those governing intellectual property rights.

All these factors have reduced the transaction costs involved in doing international business. They have also made it easier to arrange exchanges at a distance; they have reduced the need for buyers and sellers to meet physically to arrange economic exchanges. To a large extent, technological progress in the service industries has helped to propel the expansion of globalization in recent decades.

11.3. Is Economic Globalization a New Phenomenon?

The process of extending the geographical distances over which commodities are exchanged and of increasing the range of commodities involved in such an exchange has an ancient history. However, in the modern era, it has reached unprecedented levels, and involves all inhabited areas of the world.

For thousands of years, international trade has taken place in the Mediterranean Sea. Furthermore, the Vikings engaged in considerable international trade. Florence and Venice in Italy achieved their splendor and major cultural achievements as a result of trade involving China via the Silk Route. It seems likely that the wealth of the Tang Dynasty was enhanced by international trade and commercial exchange over considerable distances. Similarly, almost 2400 years ago, the Mauryan Empire in India was well aware of the economic importance of commerce and international trade and Kautilya (1961), in his treatise on politics, statescraft, and the science of wealth, *Arthashastra* (one of the earliest known books on political economy, written about 2300 years ago), gave considerable attention to international trade. In northern Europe, during the Middle Ages, the Hanseatic towns belonging to the Hanseatic League, which depended on international trade for their prosperity, became rich and became centers of cultural creativity. Similar examples can be found in Africa and in the early Americas, e.g., Inca and Maya civilizations. Although the Australian Aborigines never achieved the wealth of these civilizations, it is known that they traded in some valuable commodities involving exchange over many thousands of kilometers. However, none of this early trade was truly global.

Global trade was eventually made possible by the European voyages of discovery beginning around the 1500s with Christopher Columbus and Vasco da Gama. The former opened the way to the Americas and the latter, after exploring the Cape of Good Hope, opened the sea route to Asia from Europe. Their discoveries ushered in a period of expanding economic globalization based on imperialism. This was a pattern that persisted into the 20th century but began to unravel after World War II, although the system persisted in the Soviet Union until the end of the 1980s.

After World War II, it is claimed that the United States was keen not to allow imperial international trading and trade preference schemes of the European powers to be re-established and favored multilateral free trade to foster its own economic interests (Svizzero & Tisdell, 2002). But soon new trading blocs began to emerge in Europe which eventually culminated in the European Union. The United States, to some extent, countered this development by setting up the North American Free Trade Association (NAFTA). While progress in globalization has been made via greater free trade (multilateralism), significant expansion in international trade has also occurred in recent years via the formation of larger international trade blocs. Whether such blocs will eventually facilitate greater free trade globally or become political obstacles to it remains to be seen (Svizzero & Tisdell, 2002).

11.4. Political Change and Transition of Former Communist Planned Systems, Especially China's, and Their Impact on Globalization

As discussed above, both increased multilateralism and the creation of new and enlarged trading blocs have contributed to growing international economic transactions. A further influence has been political changes in countries previously pursuing communist economic systems, which were based on economic planning along the lines of the former Soviet Union. These countries have become market-oriented, much more decentralized, and many have altered their political and international trading affiliations. In some cases, their borders have changed. It is only possible to sketch briefly some of the changes here and some of their consequences for international economic transactions.

For example, the Council for Mutual Economic Assistance (Comecon) was a Communist association for international exchange started in 1949 and disbanded in 1991 (Brine, 1992, pp. 11–14). The headquarters of this organization was in Moscow and it consisted principally of Eastern European Communist states and the Soviet Union. Full members at the end of the 1980s were the Soviet Union, Bulgaria, Czechoslovakia, the German Democratic Republic (East Germany), Hungary, Romania, Poland, Cuba, the Mongolian People's Republic, and Vietnam (Brine, 1992, p. 11). It might be noted that China was not a member but that Vietnam, which had hostile relationship with China, was.

It has been argued that Comecon was not very effective in fostering multilateral trade between its members. The following quotation from Wikipedia (2006, p. 2) underlines this point:

"Asymmetries of size and differences in levels of development among Comecon members deeply affected the institutional character and evo- lution of the organization. The overwhelming dominance of the Soviet economy necessarily meant that the bulk of intra-Comecon relations took the form of bilateral relations between the Soviet Union and the smaller members of Comecon.

The planned nature of the members' economies and the lack of effective market-price mechanisms to facilitate integration further hin- dered progress toward Comecon goals. Without the automatic workings of market forces, progress had to depend upon conscious acts of policy. This tended to politicize the processes of integration to a greater degree than was the case in market economies."

The existence of Comecon also impeded economic exchange by its member states with non-communist countries. Furthermore, the technological gap that became quite large between Comecon member states and the West was an addi- tional barrier to expanding East-West trade. With the collapse of the Communist governments in eastern Europe in 1989 and eventually of Comecon in 1991, the scene was set for an expansion of multilateral trade between the former Comecon members and the West. The expansion of the international exchange of the former Comecon states would, however, depend on the speed and nature of their transition to market economies. Transition was far from instantaneous, and in some respects is still incomplete. Initially, the former Comecon states were unable to make a substantial contribution to expanding world trade.

Not only did Comecon's administrative and political arrangements for exchange between member states impede their actual gains from international exchange, but the eventual souring of political relationships between the USSR and China became a significant impediment to international exchange within the communist bloc. This had adverse economic consequences for the whole communist bloc.

In the 1950s, the People's Republic of China enjoyed cordial political relationships with the USSR and Sino–USSR trade and international exchange between the USSR and China flourished. Suddenly, in 1960, Sino–USSR trade plummeted and economic cooperation between the USSR and China ceased. "In 1960, [the] USSR tore up 12 agreements [with China], recalled all the experts in China, stopped 257 technological cooperation items, refused to supply mineral resources like cobalt and nickel that China needed urgently and greatly decreased the export of machinery and important accessories. All these brought great destruction to the economy of China" (Anon, 2006, p. 2). There was virtually no economic cooperation and little trade between China and the USSR in the 1960s and 1970s. After the early 1980s, some increase in China's trade with the USSR occurred but it accounted for a very small proportion of China's international trade (less than 5%) whereas in the 1960s it accounted for around 50% of China's international trade.

Eventually, China's political disagreement with the Soviet Union and its economic isolation from the USSR would prove to be an economic blessing in disguise for China. Given the dire economic consequences of such economic isolation, China made a determined effort to establish friendly relationships with the West. In February 1972, Richard Nixon, the US President, visited China, and the Shanghai Communique was issued as the basis for the development of China–US friendship. This was an important first step in the opening up of China to the outside world. However, it was not until after Deng Xiaoping became the paramount leader in 1977 that major progress could be made in reforming China's economic system and in pursuing an open-door policy. The stage for these new policies was set when the Third Plenum of the Chinese Government Party in 1978 declared that in order to achieve economic development, [economic] reforms and an open-door policy should be followed by China (see Shawki, 1997).

By 1979, China had started on its gradual (but not so slow) process of economic reforms. It, therefore, had a headstart of over a decade in its economic transformation compared to Comecon member states. It was able to move away early from centralized planning models inherited from the Soviet Union with their excessive emphasis on heavy industries and so on (Tisdell, 1993, Ch. 8). As a result, China has become a major participant in the world economy in recent times. The next section outlines trends in economic globalization in recent times and compares these with measures of China's increasing openness and participation in the world economy.

11.5. Measuring the Recent Pace of Economic Globalization and China's Involvement

There are many different possible indicators of expansion in globalization. Because the process is multidimensional, no single measure adequately captures its extent. It must be considered from many different points of view.

One indicator of the extent of economic globalization is the proportion of global GDP traded internationally. This is graphed in Fig. 11.1. This has been trending upwards since the 1950s, but after the 1970s showed dramatic acceleration. After World War II, many nations developed inward-looking economic policies but more and more nations began to depart from these policies beginning in the 1970s.

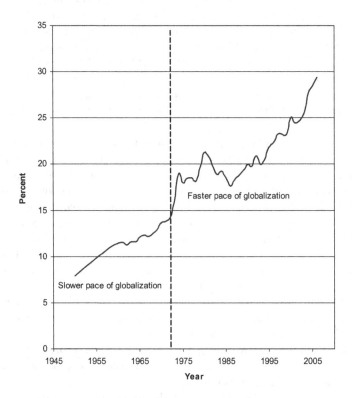

Fig. 11.1. World exports as a percentage of global GDP, 1950–2006.

Sources: World Bank, 2006, World Development Indicators, available online at: http://devdata.worldbank.org/dataonline/ (for 1960–2004); IMF World Economic Outlook Database, April 2006, available online at: http://www.imf.org/external/pubs/ft/weo/2006/01/data/index.htm (projections for 2005 and 2006); United Nations Statistical Yearbook 1970 (for 1958); Doha WTO Ministerial 2001 Briefing Notes (for 1950). Data are based on current US$.

However, it is interesting to note that even when inward-looking policies were in vogue, the trend in international trade as a percentage of global GDP was upwards.

Although inward-looking economic policies were the rule, the extent of economic globalization still rose considerably in the 1950s, and continued to rise in the 1960s but more slowly. However, as Fig. 11.1 illustrates, the pace and extent of globalization increased decisively and significantly after the early 1970s, even though global exports fluctuated as a percentage of global GDP. The major upward trend in world exports, beginning in the early 1970s, is shown in Fig. 11.2.

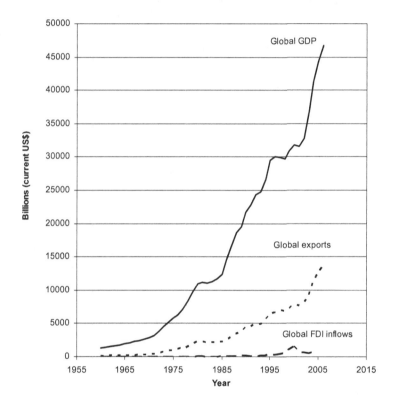

Fig. 11.2.   World economic indicators, 1960–2006*.

Sources: For global GDP and global export — World Bank, 2006, World Development Indicators, available online at: http://devdata.worldbank.org/dataonline/ (for 1960–2004); IMF World Economic Outlook Database, April 2006, available online at: http://www.imf.org/external/pubs/ft/weo/2006/01/data/index.htm (projections for 2005 and 2006).

Note: *For global FDI inflows, the data presented are from 1970 to 2004 — World Bank, 2006, World Development Indicators, available online at: http://devdata.worldbank.org/dataonline/.

Policies on foreign direct investment (FDI) began to be relaxed by many nations, including China, in the latter part of the 20th century. However, the process did not progress as quickly as international trade liberalization. Nevertheless, from 1970 onwards there was a general tendency for global FDI inflow as a percentage of gross GDP to rise, with a spike occurring in 2000 (Fig. 11.3). Despite the fall after 2000 in global FDI as a proportion of global GDP, there appears to have been a permanent rise in FDI inflows globally.

Figure 11.4 shows China's exports as a percentage of her GDP. These display a massive increase following the commencement of China's economic reforms. Prior to China's economic reforms beginning in 1979, China's exports as a percentage of its GDP were of the order of 5% or less but by 2003 had reached almost 35% (Fig. 11.4). Furthermore, from the late 1970s onwards, the value of China's exports in current US$ accelerated as is illustrated in Fig. 11.5.

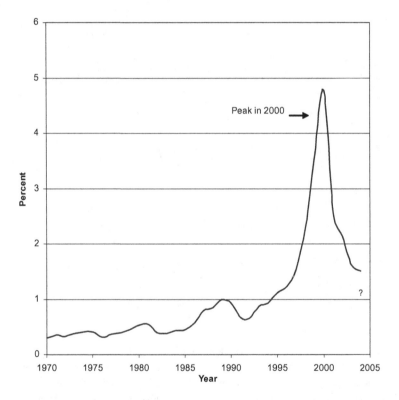

Fig. 11.3.   Global FDI inflow as a percentage of global GDP, 1970–2004.
Source: World Bank, 2006, World Development Indicators, online at: http://devdata. worldbank.org/dataonline/. Data are based on current US$.

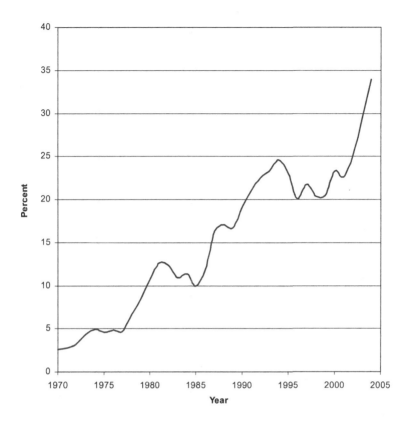

Fig. 11.4.   China's exports as a percentage of its GDP, 1970–2004.

Source: As for Fig. 11.3. Data are based on current US$.

Figure 11.6 compares China's export to GDP ratio with that for the world as a whole. It shows how this ratio has progressed from being below that for the world as a whole to exceeding it. It indicates that China has increasingly become an export-led economy. The year 1990 marks an important cross-over point for China.

Inflows of FDI to China, after beginning from negligible levels prior to 1979, began to grow. They have followed the pattern as shown in Fig. 11.7 as a proportion of China's GDP, and in US current dollars, the pattern illustrated in Fig. 11.4. Note that the trend in FDI in China was almost stationary in the period 1989–1990. This was a result of social disturbances and pro-democracy demonstrations in China in April and May 1989 culminating in early June in the Tiananmen Square tragedy. These led to international uncertainty about the future political and economic directions of China. However, FDI in China increased markedly after 1990 (see Fig. 11.8). Possibly, this was a result of the assurance given by Deng Xiaoping

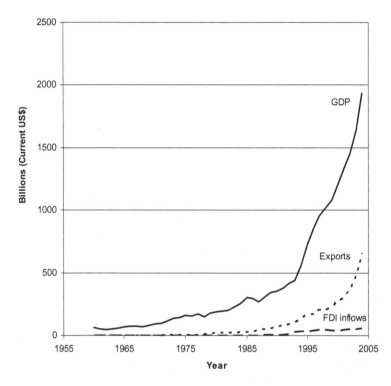

Fig. 11.5. China's aggregate economic indicators (GDP, exports and FDI inflows), 1960–2004.

Source: As for Fig. 11.3.

that China's economic reforms would continue and because of the concrete steps taken in 1991 in this regard (Tisdell, 1993, p. 12).

Figure 11.9 compares China's inflow of FDI as a percentage of its GDP with global FDI inflows as a percentage of global GDP. This percentage grew rapidly for China during the 1980s, and since 1984, has exceeded the global percentage in most years, the year 2000 being the exception. This is a further indication of China's increased economic openness and its incorporation into the global economy. It can also be deduced from Fig. 11.9 that FDI inflows to China have also been much more sustained than in the rest of the world.

There has also been a massive increase in the amount of short-term international financial flows in recent times. These exceed by many times the amounts needed to finance international commerce. These movements are activated by large banks and financial institutions, and to some extent, are speculative. Other indicators of the pace of globalization include the extent of growth in global telecommunications

Fig. 11.6. China's exports as a percentage of its GDP compared to global exports as a percentage of global GDP, 1970–2004.

Source: As for Fig. 11.3. Data are based on current US$.

traffic (Tisdell, 2005a, p. 9), the growth in international tourist arrivals as a proportion of the world's population (Tisdell, 2005b, p. 427), and increased global media exposure (Tisdell, 2005a). All have accelerated in recent decades, even though terrorist activities have dampened international growth in tourism.

It should be observed that the extent to which different types of economic resources have been able to participate in the globalization process is uneven. International population and labor movements continue to be restricted but nevertheless considerable international movements of labor and population are occurring in response to economic disparities. While barriers to international movement of skilled labor are less substantial than for unskilled labor, large short-term movements of relatively unskilled labor can also be observed.

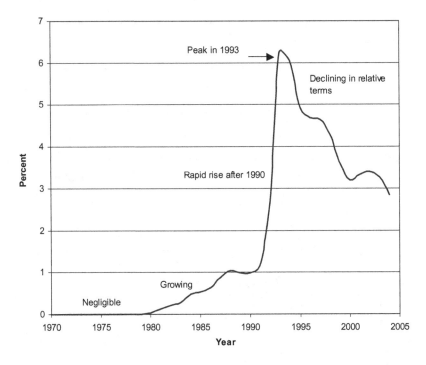

Fig. 11.7.   China's FDI inflow as a percentage of its GDP, 1970–2004.
Source: As for Fig. 11.3. Data are based on current US$.

11.6. Positive and Negative Socioeconomic Impacts of Economic Globalization

Both Western classical economic theory (Adam Smith, 1910, Ricardo, 1817) and neoclassical economic theory have extolled the economic benefits of international free trade. Adam Smith supported it on the grounds that it would result in reduced production costs by promoting the increased division of labor. The increased division of labor could provide economies of scale in industrial production. David Ricardo argued that international trade would allow countries to specialize in production in accordance with their comparative advantage, thereby adding to their economic abundance. Neoclassical economists refined this theory. For example, the Hecksher–Ohlin theorem supported the proposition that nations are likely to have a comparative economic advantage in producing commodities that use most intensely their relatively most abundant factor of production. It was also shown that countries may gain from international trade even when none has a comparative

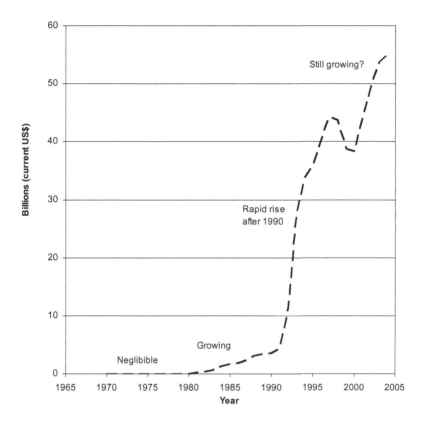

Fig. 11.8.   China's FDI inflow, 1970–2004.

Source: As for Fig. 11.3.

advantage in production provided that the tastes of their citizens differ. However, the theory was based on static considerations rather than on dynamic analysis.

Schumpeter (1942) pointed out that static analysis does not capture the essence of contemporary corporate capitalism, which is better modeled by taking into account dynamic forces motivating innovation in the economy. The dynamics of globalization require account to be taken of FDI, technology transfer, R & D and innovation, and the economic motives of multinational enterprises. In the latter respect, neotechnology theories of international trade and investment are particularly relevant (Posner, 1961; Tisdell, 1981; pp. 42–46). Companies which develop superior intellectual knowledge compared to others stand to gain considerably from the process of globalization provided their knowledge can be legally (or otherwise, such as via secrecy) protected. Both they and countries which purchase their products, or host their subsidiaries, may gain economically from their activities.

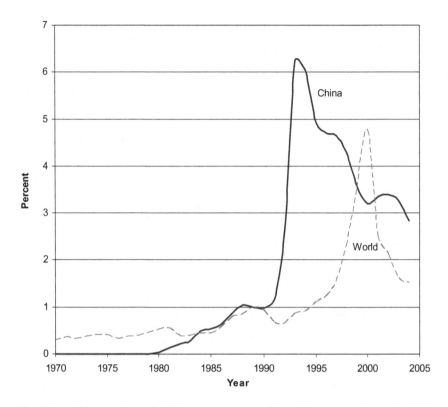

Fig. 11.9. China's inflow of FDI as a percentage of its GDP compared to global FDI inflows as a percentage of global GDP, 1970–2004.

Source: As for Fig. 11.3. Data are based on current US$.

To take a simple case, suppose a company develops a unique product for which it is able to obtain a patent and, as a result, secure a monopoly. Assume that there is sufficient demand in the home market (market I) to make production of the commodity profitable. Its production for the home market will benefit buyers and add to consumers' surplus at home, and yield a monopoly profit for the company. If this product can be profitably sold abroad, and possibly produced abroad, this will further add to the company's profit, assuming that its intellectual property rights can be protected. Consumers abroad will also benefit from the sale of the product. So, a win-win situation may occur. On the other hand, such processes in the absence of adequate institutional arrangements in peripheral countries can result in their increasing economic dependence on corporations in certain countries. To avoid this, a degree of economic and scientific self-reliance needs to be maintained by host countries.

The process of growing economic globalization appears to stimulate economic growth in the short-to-medium term. If the Kuznets' hypothesis about the relationship between economic development and the distribution of incomes being a reversed U-shape applies (Kuznets, 1963), then one might expect that growing globalization would be associated with reduced inequality of income, at least in more-developed countries (Kuznets, 1963). However, in more-developed countries growing globalization has been associated with rising income inequality because the income of the skilled or better educated has risen relative to that of the less skilled or educated. In the United States, for example, income inequality after having fallen from the 1930s through to the 1960s has risen and its income inequality is reported to be as great in the 1930s. The pattern that has emerged is like the reclining S-pattern as shown in Fig. 11.10 (Tisdell and Svizzero, 2004).

It has also been observed (Costa, 1998) that while the income of skilled persons has risen relative to the less skilled in higher-income countries such as the US, so have the hours of work of the skilled. Their higher income has been purchased to some extent by a reduction in their leisure time.

Several explanations have been advanced as to why income inequality has increased in recent decades, particularly between skilled and unskilled laborers. This increase in inequality came to be noticed in the late 1970s and has coincided with accelerating economic globalization. One school of economic thought attributes it to the Stolper–Samuelson effect (Stolper and Samuelson, 1941). According to this point of view, freer world trade has made it easier for unskilled or low-skilled workers in less-developed countries (LDCs) to compete through imports of labor-intensive products with their counterparts in more-developed countries (Wood, 1998). Another school of thought argues that the root cause is rapid technological progress which has increased demand for skilled labor relative

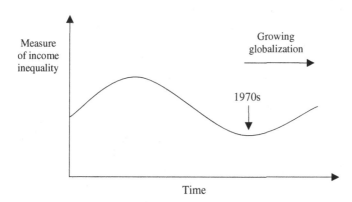

Fig. 11.10. A Kuznets' income distribution curve modified to reflect the recent experiences of more-developed countries.

to unskilled labor or labor with little skill (Aghion and Williamson, 1998). To a considerable extent, new technologies have resulted in substituting capital for labor with little or no skill.

It is interesting to note that as early as 1977, Joan Robinson pointed out that technological progress could be a powerful force making for income inequality; it increases the demand for skilled workers relative to the unskilled. She states: "It is characteristic of modern industry to require highly trained personnel, while it has no use for the labor power of a great mass of unskilled workers" (Robinson, 1977, p. 1333). Svizzero and Tisdell (2002) have suggested that growing globalization has stimulated non-neutral technological change which has increased demand for skilled labor relative to unskilled labor, and that growing income inequality has also been partly due to the operation of the Stolper–Samuelson effect as well as other factors associated with growing globalization (Tisdell and Svizzero, 2004, pp. 235–238).

With growing globalization, income inequality has risen in LDCs (Ghosh, 2004) as well as higher-income countries. It is, however, difficult to disentangle how much of this rising inequality is due to their being in the early phases of economic growth and how much should be attributed to the globalization effect. Both effects may be present and may reinforce one another.

11.7. The Catching-up Phenomena and the Evolutionary Dynamics of Economic Growth

It has been suggested that the normal pattern of development of economies may follow a pattern like that of a logistic growth curve (Fig. 11.11). Less-developed countries that are experiencing economic take-off, such as China, are in the strong growth phase of it, developed or mature economies are in its slow growth phase, whereas stagnant LDCs show little or no economic growth. Lim (2005) has described the latter as turtle economies, the fast-growing economies, such as China, as horse economies, and the mature economies, such as Japan and the US, as elephant economies.

Not all LDCs are able to escape from economic stagnation but those that do enter a catching-up phase (phase II in Fig. 11.11) in relation to more-developed economies, largely adopt and imitate technologies developed in the mature economies, as, for example, Japan did, then Korea did, and as China is doing now. Their technology gap in the beginning is usually large but progressively narrows, and as such countries approach the global technology frontier, their rate of economic growth slows. Eventually, they also become mature economies and their economic growth is then determined, to a large extent, by the global rate of technological progress.

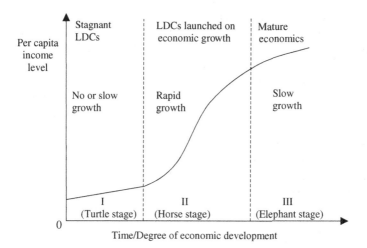

Fig. 11.11. Possible stages in the economic growth of nations.

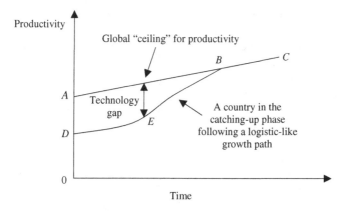

Fig. 11.12. Possible growth path of a nation catching up with mature economies as a result of transfer of technologies in its opening up process. The difference between line *AB* and curve *DEB*, the productivity gap, reflects a technology gap.

This technology-driven view of LDCs launched on successful economic growth is illustrated in Fig. 11.11. In Fig. 11.12, *ABC* represents the global frontier of productivity determined by intellectual knowledge. A nation may follow the logistic type of curve shown by *DEB* in its catching-up phase. At first, the economic growth of the nation is not so fast but it accelerates as the country assimilates foreign technologies, before decelerating as the nation approaches the global productivity frontier determined by global technological progress.

It is possible that China may catch up more quickly with the mature economies than did countries that began their catching-up phase earlier, such as Japan. This may be due to globalization technology transfer occurring at a faster rate than in previous times (Gao and Tisdell, 2005).

Economies in their catching-up phase, especially if large or potentially so (such as the economies of China, of India, and Russia), can add substantially to global economic growth and provide economic benefits to mature economies that otherwise might not be available. However, as the above theory suggests, the rapid economic growth of nations in a catching-up phase is unlikely to last forever. After nations currently catching up complete their catching up, will other LDCs also go through a similar phase? And if so, when? Will the whole global economy approach a mature phase? If so, will corporate capitalism in its mature phase then fall into the type of economic stagnation and social deterioration envisaged by Schumpeter (1942)?

A major challenge for the former planned economies has been the reform of their science and technology systems. Although it was common in the West to attribute deficiencies in economic performances in the planned economies mostly to misallocation of resources as a result of centralized bureaucratic regulation of production, possibly a more serious problem was the failure of the system to stimulate technological progress and innovation adequately, particularly in relation to consumer goods. For example, it has been said that "in the 1970s, Comecon member states became aware of the technological gap between their economies and [those of] the West. They realized that there was a need for intensive rather than extensive growth" (Beata, 2004). Yet, because to address the matter would require major institutional change, these economies were unable to address the matter effectively until their Communist Planned system was dismantled.

China too had a centralized state-controlled R & D system when it embarked on its economic reforms in 1979. A feature of such a system was the separation of research bodies from production units. Research was driven by the desires of bureaucrats rather than those of users, buyers or consumers of commodities. It was not at all market-driven, and economic incentives for creating economically valuable inventions and for innovating were weak.

The above discussed points signify that when China embarked on its market reforms in 1979, its science and technology system was not designed to complement the use of the market system in guiding the availability of commodities. It was not until 1985 that China took the first step to reform its science and technology system to make it more market-oriented (Gao and Tisdell, 2004). As discussed by Gao and Tisdell (2004), China confirmed in 1985 its support for market-oriented reforms in science and technology systems as recommended by the State Science and Technology Commission. There were moves to treat research results as marketable commodities and the view became common that revenue received could be used to provide incentives for further research. The practical steps for this commercial transition in technology started in the mid-1980s and are still ongoing. The establishment of a unified, open technology market has been seen as a significant shift in China's science and technology system (World Bank, 1995), helping to break vertical and horizontal institutional barriers and accelerate technology transfer and diffusion (Gao and Tisdell, 2004, p. 321).

In accordance with the philosophy of Deng Xiaoping, reforms to China's science and technology system have been carefully planned and paced. These reforms were intended to tailor China's science and technology system to its market system for commodities. Furthermore, the reforms would have undoubtedly facilitated China's transfer of technology from abroad by increasing its capacity to select the required technology and absorb it. In the future, as China draws nearer to the international technology frontier, its reformed science and technology system will become more important for generating inventions and new technologies in China and therefore, for its future pace of economic growth.

11.8. Could Globalization Result in Economic Growth that is Unsustainable Because of Adverse Environmental Impacts Generated by it?

Economic growth is heavily dependent on the use of the environment and natural resources both as a source of raw materials, e.g., for producing energy, and as a sink for wastes from economic production and consumption. While technological progress is often resource-saving and frequently reduces wastes, total resource use has continued to rise with global economic growth (Tisdell, 1997). Natural resources are being converted into economic commodities at a growing rate and greenhouse gas emissions continue to rise. There is considerable scientific evidence that the latter is triggering climate change and may generate sea-level rises. There is speculation that changes in the natural environment caused by human economic activity will eventually undermine global economic prosperity.

This is the opposite scenario to that suggested by the environmental Kuznets' curve. This type of Kuznets' curve is hypothesized to be of a reverse U-shape; the intensity of environmental pollution/degradation is portrayed as first rising with the economic growth of a nation and then declining. The optimistic conclusion that may be drawn here is that economic growth will eventually solve all environmental problems. However, the environmental Kuznets' curve scenario is too simplistic and of doubtful validity when the natural environment is assessed from a global point of view, as is pointed out by Tisdell (2001).

Although greater economic globalization may stimulate global economic growth in the short- to medium-term, such a growth could be unsustainable in the long run for environmental reasons. Robinson (1977, p. 1336) in pointing out that economic growth may not be the solution to major economic problems also mentions that "the consumption of resources, including air to breathe, has evidently impoverished the world".

China has become a major world user of the globe's natural resources and a large contributor to global pollution and environmental change. As China's economy continues to grow, these effects will magnify. The self-interest of the West has helped foster China's economic growth by FDI and trade. As time goes on, it will become more evident that China is a strong international competitor for the use of environmental and natural resources, and this may lead to conflict with other countries. Political pressure may, for example, mount on China to curb its emissions of greenhouse gases (which it is not presently required to do so under the Kyoto Protocol) and China may come into conflict with other countries in securing its oil imports and international economic interests. China's economic growth has not only enhanced its international political power but may increasingly require, or result in, the exercise of this power.

11.9. Concluding Comments

Naturally, the further into the future we try to predict economic conditions, the more uncertain we must be about our outlook. This is particularly so when predictions are made about economic globalization, its economic and social consequences, and the pattern of future global economic development. This is made even more difficult because the operation of natural biophysical systems and levels of economic activity are becoming increasingly interdependent. This means that the future development of the global economy cannot be predicted without taking into account the biophysical consequences of economic growth. It is unlikely that the global economy can continue growing as it has done in modern times without experiencing major biophysical crises. While China might have justifiably ignored such issues in the past, in its new and emerging global economic position it can no longer do so. It must be part of the solution to global problems.

China's economic growth in recent decades as a result of its economic reforms and opening up to the outside world has been remarkable. A strong incentive for China's opening up was to overcome its adversity caused by the Soviet Union's decision in 1960 to abandon its economic cooperation with China, although this was not the only reason. The economic havoc caused by the Cultural Revolution also played a part. As a result of its early adversity, China started earlier than other planned Communist economies on its economic reforms. As a result, it has already secured itself a strong economic and political place globally.

References

Aghion, P and JG Williamson (1998). *Growth, Inequality and Globalization*, Cambridge: Cambridge University Press.

Anon (2006). Sino-Russian Forum. http://www.essays.cc/free_essays/b2/iev205.shtml.

Beata, O (2004). COMECON: Council of mutual economic assistance — Comecon's trade relations with Poland and GDR. www.wsgn.euv-frankfurt-o.de/vc/Ws2004/Sch_SeminarDDR/Hausarbeit__Wirtschaft_und_Gesellschft_DDR_Bea.PDF.

Brine, J (1992). *Comecon: The Rise and Fall of an International Socialist Organization*, Oxford, England: Clio Press.

Costa, DL (1998). The unequal work day: a long-term view. *The American Economic Review*, 88, 330–334.

Gao, Z and C Tisdell (2005). Foreign investment and Asia's, particularly China's rise in the television industry: the international product cycle reconsidered. *Journal of Asia-Pacific Business*, 6, 37–61.

Gao, Z and C Tisdell (2004). China's reformed science and technology system: an overview and assessment. *Prometheus*, 22, 311–331.

Ghosh, BN (2004). Globalised capitalist development and income inequalities: what does the data from East Asian economies tell us? In *Economic Globalisation: Social Conflicts, Labour and Environmental Issues*, C Tisdell and RK Sen (eds.), pp. 210–226, Aldershot, UK: Edward Elgar.

Kautilya (1961). *Arthashastra*, 7th Ed. (Translated by R Shamasastry) Mysore: Mysore Publishing House. (Original work completed in about 300 B.C.)

Kuznets, S (1963). Quantitative aspects of economic growth of nations, distribution of income by size. *Economic Development and Cultural Change*, 1, 1–80.

Lim, CY (2005). Economic theory and the East Asian region. *Proc. of the Singapore Economic Review*, 50 (Special), 495–512.

Posner, NV (1961). International trade and technical change. *Oxford Economic Papers*, 13, 323–341.

Ricardo, D (1817). *The Principles of Political Economy and Taxation*. London: Dent. (Reprint 1955).

Robinson, J (1977). What are the questions? *Journal of Economic Literature*, 15, 1318–1339.

Schumpeter, J (1942). *Capitalism, Socialism and Democracy*, 2nd Ed, New York: Harper.

Shawki, A (1997). China: Deng's legacy. *International Socialist Review*, Issue 2, Fall (online edition). http://www.isreview.org/issues/02/China_Part2.shtml.

Smith, A (1910). *The Wealth of Nations*. 1st Ed. (1776). London: JM Dent and Sons.

Stolper, WF and PA Samuelson (1941). Protection and real wages. *Review of Economic Studies*, 9, 58–74.

Svizzero, S and C Tisdell (2002). Reconciling globalization and technological change: growing income inequalities and remedial policies. *Intereconomics*, 37, 162–171.

Tisdell, CA (2005a). An overview of globalisation and world economic policy responses. In *Globalisation and World Economic Policies*, CA Tisdell (ed.), pp. 3–16. New Delhi: Serials Publications.

Tisdell, CA (2005b). Tourism development and globalisation: experiences and policies of China and Australia. In *Globalisation and World Economic Policies*, CA Tisdell (ed.), pp. 421–436, New Delhi: Serials Publications.

Tisdell, CA (2001). Globalisation and sustainability: environmental Kuznets curve and the WTO. *Ecological Economics*, 39, 185–196.

Tisdell, CA (1997). Capital/natural resource substitution: the debate of Georgescu-Roegen (through Daly) with Solow/Stiglitz. *Ecological Economics*, 22, 289–291.

Tisdell, CA (1993). *Economic Development in the Context of China: Policy Issues and Analysis*, London: Macmillan and New York: St. Martin's Press.

Tisdell, CA (1981). *Science and Technology Policy: Priority of Governments*, London: Chapman and Hall.

Tisdell, CA and RK Sen (2004). An overview of economic globalisation: its momentum and its consequences examined. In *Economic Globalisation*, C Tisdell and RK Sen (eds.), pp. 3–23, UK: Edward Elgar and USA: Northampton.

Tisdell, C and S Svizzero (2004). Globalization, social welfare, public policies and labour inequalities. *Singapore Economic Review*, 49, 233–253.

Wikipedia (2006). Comecon. Available from: http://en.wikipedia.org/wiki/Comecon.

Wood, A (1998). Globalisation and the rise in labour market inequalities. *The Economic Journal*, 108, 1463–1482.

World Bank (1995). *Staff Appraisal Report: China — Technology Development Project*. World Bank, Washington DC: Report No. 2814-CHA.

PART 6

GLOBALIZATION AND
INTERNATIONAL BUSINESS

CHAPTER 12

GLOBALIZATION AND CREATION OF ORGANIZATIONAL CITIZENSHIP IN THE DEVELOPING COUNTRIES: A CASE STUDY OF TOYOTA IN INDIA

Victoria Miroshnik

University of Glasgow, U.K.

12.1. Introduction

A successful multinational company can create its unique organizational culture and in turn create a set of values among its employees to form affective commitments on the part of its employee. We can describe this commitment as the indicator of effective corporate performance, as commitment leads to its success. We call this commitment as "organizational citizenship". This organizational citizenship can be transmitted from the head office to the subsidiaries in another part of the globe by a successful multinational company. Creation of this organizational citizenship provides a multinational company some unique competitive advantage.

"Flat World" is the term coined by Thomas Freedman (Freedman, 2006) to describe a world where people have the "Jet-Set Culture" (Triandis, 2006) of the high Anglo-American executive class, with similar language, education, tastes, and preference but with varied citizenships and nationalities. Emergence of this global culture is the result of globalization process that has started since 1990. Globalization is defined as the freedom of the multinational companies to invest anywhere they like across the world, with products and services being produced in different parts of the world where the costs would be cheapest. This has created a new breed of managerial class whose culture is global, not national. If this is the case, organizational systems that were developed using national characteristics are undergoing changes to include global characteristics.

I propose that there is a set of unique values in each successful multinational company which forms its organizational culture and create a set of values, which in turn would form commitments on the part of its employees which is the indicator of effective corporate performance, as commitment leads to its success. We can call this commitment as organizational citizenship. This organizational citizenship can be transmitted from one part of the globe to another by a multinational company. By creation of this organizational citizenship from its organizational culture, a multinational company creates unique competitive advantages as its international strategy. This is a new theoretical development because it is different from the existing theoretical explanations of the transmission of values from the social or national environment to the organizational values (O'Reiley, 1989; O'Reiley, Chatman and Caldwell, 1991).

12.2. Multinational Companies and Global Culture

Kluckhohn (1951) has defined culture as shared standards operating procedures, unstated assumptions, practices, tools, myths, art, kinship, norms, values, habits about sampling the environment, and shared meanings. We used to think that different national cultures are different and these give rise to different organizational cultures (Hofstede, 2002). Globalization has created a new cultural concept, called "Jet-Set Culture" or global culture (Triandis, 2006). The idea is that multinational companies are spreading a US corporate culture and other cultures would be submerged into it. The implications are that ultimately there would be one global corporate culture instead of separate cultures.

Triandis (1989) has divided the people of the world into two parts. People in individualistic cultures (in north and western Europe and North America) have complex culture while the people of the collectivist cultures (Asia, Africa, and South America) along with fascists, communists, and religious fundamentalists have a simple culture. The "Jet-Set Culture" is complex, sophisticated, multicultural, materialistic, and supports liberalism, humanism, and rationalism. The people with collectivist mind emphasize soul, instinct, and intuition. There are two types of collectivist cultures. Vertical collectivist culture (Indian villages) emphasizes in-group cohesions, respect for in-group norms, and directives of authorities (Triandis, 1995). Horizontal collectivists are less authoritarian. People in this kind of culture are interdependent with in-groups (Markus and Kitayama, 1991), give priority to the goals of their in-groups (Triandis, 1990), and behave in general communal way. They value patriotism, bravery, loyalty, and self-sacrifice (Triandis and Trafimow, 2001).

The individualistic culture of the "Jet-Set Culture" emphasizes self-reliance, competition, uniqueness, hedonism, and emotional distance from in-group. Vertical individualistic culture (US corporate culture) values competitiveness. Horizontal individualistic culture (Australia, Sweden) de-emphasizes hierarchical differentiations (Triandis and Gelfand, 1998). Effects of globalization is the creation of a "Jet-Set Culture" who belong to an emergent global culture, which promotes primarily the vertical individualistic US corporate culture irrespective of national boundaries (Clark and Knowles, 2003). This global culture consists of people who are attached to other members of this global culture through a process of self-selection. Core values of global managers are not derived from ethnic group, national origin but from a cultural cross-pollination (Bird and Stevens, 2003).

Historically speaking, globalization is nothing new. Karl Marx and Engels wrote 150 years ago in 1872 about globalization initiated by the industrial revolution in Britain where, "The need of a constantly expanding market for its products chases the bourgeoisie over the whole surface of the globe. The bourgeoisie has through its exploitation of the world market given a cosmopolitan character to production and consumption in every country. It compels all nations to adapt the bourgeois mode of production; it compels them to introduce what it calls civilization into their midst, i.e., to become bourgeois themselves. In one word, it creates a world after its own image"(Marx and Engels, 1872).

Baron Macauley, who went to India in 1834 to reform the education system of the British India wrote, "We must at present do our best to form a class who may be interpreters between us and the millions whom we govern; a class of persons, Indian in blood and colour, but English in taste, in opinions, in morals, and in intellect" (Macauley, 1860).

Indeed, both the British and the French empires had created a class of people in their empires very similar to the British or French but that had not changed the cultures of the countries in the British or French empires even after 150 years. Thus, the predictions of Triandis or Freedman, just like that of Marx–Engels or Macauley before, may not materialize.

12.3. Global Citizenship (Global Managerial Culture) Vs. National Managerial Culture

Husted (2003) has pointed out that the assumptions of Bird and Stevens (2003) that global culture is homogeneous is questionable. Collectivist values, which place priority of the group over individual, are in the interests of individuals who dominate the group. Thus, the US corporate values are the values of the dominant group in the USA, which may not be shared by everyone in the society. While national culture is heterogeneous, there are heterogeneous cultures in the world, which may cross the national boundaries. This creates a number of global cultures for each affiliated groups not a single global culture. The second question is adaptation of a particular practice (for example, Just-in-Time or TQM from Japan or down-sizing from the USA) does not mean cultural adaptation. These affect the culture at the superficial level but not at the level of "deep mental programming" referred by Hofstede (2002).

Globalization may be an optical illusion, because most global trends were originally local practices. The introduction of foreign cultural practices in a new culture often results in hybridization. TQM had its origin in the USA in the early 20th century; Japan has adapted it and refined it as an "organizational software of mind" and now came back to USA as a Japanese management culture. The adopted practice can never mean the same to the adopting culture as it did to the original culture. Globalization, localization, and hybridization are complex and interrelated phenomena and these are a continuation of an old process of cultural change that has taken place for millennia (Clark and Knowles, 2003; Husted, 2003; Ralston, 1999; Ricks, 2003).

Sheth (2006) has pointed out that instead of a global culture based on US corporate culture, a fusion of cultures of different countries may emerge which will combine the best from all managerial values.

Because of the rising economic power of Asia (Japan, China, and India), "Global" enterprises may organize around global centers of excellence taking into account different types of efficiency of different types of people. Increasingly, US companies are having their manufacturing units in China, R&D centers in Russia and India and main corporate centers in the USA, which will lead a confusion of different cultures but not one single dominant culture.

Sociologists have always promoted their own culture as the basis for efficient economic growth and higher business productivity. Weber (1930) has promoted protestant virtues for superior economic performances of organizations in the Western countries and has condemned the Asian, particularly Confucian culture for backwardness. Now, Hofstede (2002), Kahn (1979) and Leung (2006) are promoting Confucian values as the basis for superior economic performances of East Asia. Hofstede (2002) has moderated this extreme nationalism by defining certain values those promote organizational efficiency as "long-term orientations"; the same values are characterized by Triandis (1989) as "collectivist" values. However, Hofstede (1991) has shown that there are important differences between Japanese, who emphasizes traditional male role associated with achievement, control and power, and Chinese or Koreans who are more materialistic and much less communal. Japanese work as a group and have great faith on social institutions; Chinese work as individuals, have great mistrust of people and social institutions (Leung, 2006).

Managerial cultures are spreading in the world from East Asia mainly by Japanese multinational companies and Japanese management practices are influencing the rest of the world in a significant way (Adler, 1997). It was observed that firms that cultivate "collectivist" values or "long-term orientations" are performing more efficiently. Rise of Toyota, as the most important automobile company of the world outperforming even GM or Ford is an example. Values are shifting from materialistic to a post-materialistic set of values emphasizing long-term orientations (Hitt *et al.* 2006; Inglehart and Baker, 2000).

Marcouliades and Heck (1993) have opined that values that characterize an organization's culture significantly affect performance without specifying which values are most closely related with positive outcome. O'Reilly, Chatman and Caldwell (1991) have identified certain dimensions of organizational culture called OCP (organizational culture profile) values that promote performances. These values are innovation, stability, respect for people, outcome orientation, detail orientation, team orientation, and aggressiveness (or determination). These values resemble the values in Cameron and Freeman's (1991) model of organizational culture types. Deshpande, Farley and Webster (1993, 1997) found that higher levels of business performance were closely associated with a market culture (emphasizes result and determination) and adhocracy culture (values flexibility and innovation).

The results obtained by Dennison and Mishra (1995) and Basu (1999) also support this conclusion. These values are closely related to what Triandis (2006) has described as "collectivist" values which must give way to the "individualistic" values in a fully "globalized" value system according to the supporter of the "Jet-Set Culture". However, as we can see "collectivist" values from the East are associated with superior business performances and are affecting the psychology of the "Western" managers more and more. Thus, the direction for the "global" culture as suggested by the supporters of the globalization may not be a correct one.

12.4. National Managerial Culture Vs. Organizational Citizenship

There are important differences as mentioned by Triandis (2006) between the western (individualistic) and eastern (collectivist) organizational culture. These differences were explained in detail by Hofstede and Bond (1984), Hall and Hall (1990), Goodman (1981), Yeh (1995), and others mentioned below. The cultural value system in Japan for example, promotes hard work and attention to detail, group orientations, and consensus orientations. It emphasizes conflict avoidance, respect and concern for people, importance of long-lasting relationship with others, harmony, and uniformity. The end result is a very high level of loyalty for the company (Lazer, Murata and Kosaka, 1985). This has led to lifetime employment, slow evaluation, and a non-competitive workforce. The US corporate culture, on the other hand, promotes more communication and coordination and short-term performance evaluations (Ueno, 1992).

Hofstede (2002) has concluded that national culture moderates the organizational culture and organizational culture created by one specific national culture may not be implemented in a different nation because of the differences in national characteristics. There are some basic characteristics that shape the national culture (Hofstede, 2002):

(a) Individualism vs. collectivism, i.e., the degree of preference for acting as individuals rather than as group members;
(b) Power distance, i.e., the degree of inequality among people considered as normal;
(c) Uncertainty avoidance, i.e., the degree of preference for structured over unstructured situations;
(d) Masculinity vs. feminist, i.e., the relative prevalence of values such as assertiveness, performance, success and competition vs. values such as quality of life, warm personal relations, service, care for the weak and solidarity; and
(e) Long-term vs. short-term orientations, i.e., importance of achievements over a longer time horizon over a shorter time preference. Nations can be categorized according to these characteristics, which determine organizational cultures of the firms emerging from these cultures.

Hofstede has characterized various nations according to their national culture and organizational culture, which are closely linked together. Recently, the GLOBE project (Gupta, Hanges and Dorfman, 2002) is trying to characterize nations, following Hofstede, according to both leadership culture and organizational culture. In Hofstede's analysis, national culture is related to the national characteristics regarding the organizational culture and national performances. There can be important differences within a nation among various firms regarding their organizational culture, leadership culture and thus their performances can vary.

However, according to a number of authors, organizational culture but not national character is the most important explanation for competitive advantages of a company. A company with effective organizational culture, irrespective of national origin of the company, can demonstrate superior performance. Cameron and Quinn (1999) have mentioned that the most important competitive advantage of a company is its organizational culture. According to their theory of "Competing Value Framework", it is possible to characterize firms into four separate organizational types with different criteria for leadership, effectiveness, and basic management philosophy; these are: clan, adhocracy, hierarchy, and market. In the "clan" type of organization, leaders are facilitators, mentors, and parents. The effectiveness criterion is a combination of cohesion and proper development of human resources. The basic management philosophy is: participation fosters commitments. In the "adhocracy" type of organization, the leaders are innovators, entrepreneurs, and visionaries. The effectiveness criterion is creativity and growth of the company with the most advanced technology. The management philosophy is: innovations foster new resources. In the "hierarchy" type of organization, the leaders are coordinators, monitors, and organizers. The effectiveness criterion is efficiency, timeliness, and smooth functioning of the organization. The management philosophy is: control fosters efficiency. In the "market" type of organization, leaders are hard-drivers, competitors, and producers. The efficiency criterion is the market share, goal involvements, and defeats of the competitors. The management philosophy is: competition fosters productivity.

If an organization has a "strong culture" with "well integrated and effective" set of values, beliefs and behavior, it normally demonstrates high level of corporate performances (Cameron and Quinn, 1999; Kotter and Heskett, 1992; Mintzburg, Simon and Basu, 2002; Ouchi, 1981; Owens, 1987). Some of the characteristics of organizations mentioned above may have relationship with successful administrative practices, positive attitudes of the workers and as a result higher levels of productivity (Deal and Kennedy, 1982; Gordon, 1985; Mercoulides and Heck, 1993). If a company can influence its employee with a strong organizational culture, it can override influences of national characters and can have a superior organizational culture throughout the organization irrespective of national boundaries. Ouchi (1981) has analyzed how a Japanese clan type of organizational culture can make an organization efficient. Peters and Watermann (1982) along with Carroll (1983) and van de Ven (1983) have demonstrated how companies with progressive human resources practices can improve their performance. Similar study by Gordon (1985) has demonstrated that organizational cultures emphasizing creativity, autonomy, and participatory management can improve productivity. Mintzburg, Simon and Basu (2002) have analyzed how unselfish and socially responsible behavior of the firms can improve their performances. Calori and Sarnin (1991) in their study of the French management system have shown that this link between organizational culture and performance is not restricted to any particular culture. Kotter and Heskett (1992) and Cameron and Quinn (1999) have put forward the argument that there is no link between national culture and organizational culture. There are only strong cultures, weak cultures, and flexible cultures in organizations, which can be designed and transportable from one national culture to another.

The above analysis leads us to a concept called "organizational citizenship", a product of the organizational culture of a multinational company. Organizational citizenship does not depend on nationality but on the company irrespective of national boundaries.

12.4.1. *Organizational Citizenship*

Organizational citizenship can be defined as the reflection of the reason for the existence of the company or the organizational culture. Pascale and Athos (1981) have mentioned that the values of the organizational culture create super-ordinate goals or purpose of the company, which binds the corporation to its members in spirit (Basu, 1999). Drucker (2002) has expressed certain specific features of that super-ordinate goals or mission, productivity, responsibility, and purpose.

Leadership defines these features in practical terms in order to disseminate these
to its employees. These provide guidelines for decision-making and coordination.

Organizational culture through its beliefs and assumptions influences behavior,
which in turn affects decision and actions of the members of the organization and
creates a citizenship or membership, which is ideal for the organization to satisfy
its purpose (Lasch, 1995; Sathe, 1983). Organizational citizenship is formed for a
multinational enterprise first in its home territory but it spreads in the subsidiaries
located in various parts of the world creating a common organizational culture
throughout the organization. Company citizenship differs from one company to
another, as the organizational culture of a company is different from that of another
company.

Thus, instead of a common global citizenship or common global culture, which
has never existed, we have a common organizational citizenship throughout the
world for a specific multinational company. There can be as many company citizenship as the number of multinational companies. Instead of a single global
culture, thus, we have a multiplicity of organizational citizenship, which differs
from each other as the organizational culture of Toyota differs from that of Ford.

Organizational culture became a phenomenon in the management literature by
four seminal works by Ouchi (1981), Pascale and Athos (1982), Kotter and Heskett
(1992), and Peters and Waterman (1982). The first two authors suggested that
Japanese business success could be attributed in large part to Japanese corporate
culture. All the four authors suggested that corporate culture was the key to organizational performance and that corporate culture could be managed to improve
a company's competitive advantage. If an organization decides its objectives, it
is necessary to define the organizational culture that will help the organization to
achieve its objectives and ensure the implementation of that organizational culture
to ensure effective organizational performance. The management literature has
emphasized the importance of organizational culture in motivating and maximizing
the value of its human resources (Calori and Sarnin, 1991; Cameron and Quinn,
1999; Denison and Mishra, 1995; Mintzburg, Simon and Basu, 2002).

12.4.2. *Organizational Commitment as the Outcome of Organizational Culture*

Selznick (1957) argued that various commitments entered into by organizational
stakeholders that defines an organization's character and bestows upon it a distinctive competence in the conduct of its affairs. For Selznick, commitment is an
enforced component of social action — as such it refers to the binding of an individual to particular behavioral acts in the pursuit of organizational objectives. Such
commitments, in turn, define an organization's character for good or ill, thereby
bestowing upon it a distinctive competence. One of the chief strengths of Selznick's

perspective is its emphasis on group and organizational levels of analysis. Because organizations are social systems, goals, policies or procedures tend to achieve an established, value-impregnated status. Commitment to established or institutionalized patterns is thereby accomplished, restricting choice and enforcing specific behavioral standards. Selznick (1957) argues that, it is through commitment, enforced as it is by a complex web of factors and circumstances, and operating at all levels within an organization, that social actors influence organizational strategies and outcomes. However, these commitments do not evolve spontaneously; they are shaped by "critical decisions" that reflect or constitute organizational culture. Thus, organizational commitment is the outcome of organizational culture.

Knudsen (1994) suggested that Selznick's (1957) institutional theory as a suitable process-based perspective to augment the outcome-centric view of organizational competence prevalent in the literature on the "resource-based theories" of Barney (1986). Selznick's institutional theory captures the dynamics of the continuous exchange and interrelationships between an organization's latent competencies and its structure and processes. Knudsen argues that these are a consequence of human design and "intentionality" as expressed by the commitments.

Selznick's work, therefore, provides appropriate behavioral foundations for the resource-based view (RBV) of the firm, which has hitherto operated from the perspective of bounded rationality. Ulrich (1998) calls for a focus on the relationship between commitment and competence formation through organizational culture. Winograd and Flores (1986) highlight the role of commitment in shaping the design of such system of effective organization. In this research, I like to take it further by understanding the relationship between organizational culture and commitment as a source of competitive advantage for the multinational companies.

12.4.3. *Organizational Culture as a Source of Competitive Advantage*

If an organization has a "strong culture" with "well integrated and effective" set of values, beliefs and behavior, it normally demonstrates high level of corporate performances (Cameron and Quinn, 1999; Kotter and Heskett, 1992; Mintzburg, Simon and Basu, 2002; Ouchi, 1981). Some of the characteristics of organizations mentioned above may have relationship with successful administrative practices, positive attitudes of the workers and as a result higher levels of productivity (Deal and Kennedy, 1982; Gordon, 1985; Heck and Mercoulides, 1993). Calori and Sarnin (1991) found that there is a significant relationship between a firm's growth over a short period and cultural intensity and cultural homogeneity. Zammuto and O'Connor (1992) also have demonstrated relationship between organizational culture and technology adaptations using competing values model of organizational culture.

Kotter and Heskett (1992) have put forward an analysis to evaluate the need for organizational culture changes and their relationships with performances of the related companies. A strong culture, by creating a high level of motivation among the employees, can enhance the performance of an organization. Thus, organizations with strong cultures in terms of effective beliefs, values, and behavioral patterns, are mainly successful organizations, although there are some exceptions (Kotter and Heskett, 1992). Leaders create certain visions or philosophy and business strategy for the company, when they implement these in a firm people behave according to their guided philosophy (Kotter and Heskett, 1992). Then, a corporate culture emerges that reflects the vision and strategy of the leaders and experiences they had while implementing these. Japanese leaders are nurtured from the organization itself; they have work their way up through the ranks. As a result, there is no outsider among the leaders. Leaders are cultivated by the organizational culture and the human resources management system of the organization.

This is the reason why "human resources management system", which creates the values of the organization through continuous training of the employees, is so vital for any Japanese organization. Leaders, i.e., president, vice-presidents, members of the board of directors are normally the former directors of the "human resources management" department. Leadership is also collective with leaders acting as coordinators. Decisions are made collectively; they do not depend on any individual. As a result, the western literature on leadership is invalid in the context of Japanese corporate culture. As Japanese national culture is collectivist (Hayashi, 1989; Nakane, 1970), its corporate culture is also collectivist, demonstrating the direct link between the values of the Japanese national culture and leadership culture (Basu, 1999; Morita, 1992; Ouchi, 1981; Toyoda, 1985).

In a nationally representative sample of firms in these countries, Deshpande, Farley and Webster (1997) found unsurprising differences in organizational cultures (the Japanese businesses had more clan-oriented cultures and the French firms more hierarchical ones, for instance). Despite these differences, however, they found that successful firms transcended national culture differences to develop a common pattern of drivers of business performance. These included a primary focus on organizational innovativeness, a friendly climate, and a competitive culture. Organizational climates that encouraged trust, participativeness, and entrepreneurial behavior were effective across all the five countries. According to them, organizations with relatively flexible, externally oriented corporate cultures perform better. Even when a national culture tended to be more insular, this result held. All organizations in the sample see themselves as mixtures of four types of organizational cultures: market, adhocracy, hierarchy, and clan. Relative emphasis on one or another of these is often subtle. Various combinations may produce good results; for example, successful Japanese firms, while generally hierarchical and clan oriented, also tended to develop relatively strong market cultures. The best-performing firms in all the five countries have similar corporate cultures. There is no strong evidence of country-specific slope differences for relationships between organizational culture and performance.

12.4.4. *Organizational Commitment as Competitive Advantages: Resource-Based Views*

How organizational culture can enhance competitive advantages was studied by a number of researchers. Penrose (1959) conceives the firm as a collection of competencies that embody its knowledge. Following Hayek (1945), Penrose argues that a firm's competitive position is dependent on the manner in which the experiential knowledge of its personnel is developed and leveraged, i.e., its organizational culture. Deal and Kennedy (1982), Ouchi (1981) and Peters and Waterman (1982) indicated organizational culture that can increase productivity, improve relationships with suppliers, customers and employees and as a result increase profitability of the firm.

Barney (1986, 2001) has indicated certain qualities, which are essential for an organizational culture in order to enhance corporate performance. The culture must enhance economic values of the organization. It must be unique for a firm in order to give competitive advantage. It also must be such that other firms cannot imitate it quickly.

Organizational culture reflects the personalities of its leaders, the historical contexts of its growth and experiences it has obtained since its foundations. As a result, it may be difficult for other firms to have similar organizational culture. Uniqueness of the culture gives the firm competitive advantages, its rival companies do not have. When this uniqueness provides increased profitability, the firm can outbid its rival companies using this uniqueness (Barney, 1986).

The fundamental statement is "that valuable and rare organizational resources can be a source of competitive advantage" (Barney, 2001). Barney has mentioned resources as including "all assets, capabilities, organizational processes, firm attributes, information, knowledge, etc. controlled by a firm that enable the firm to conceive of and implement strategies that improve its efficiency and effectiveness" and as "firm attributes that may enable firms to conceive of and implement value-creating strategies" (Barney, 2001). He defines resources as valuable "when they enable a firm to conceive of or implement strategies that improve its efficiency and effectiveness" and "when they exploit opportunities or neutralize threats in a firm's environment" (Barney, 2001). Barney defines competitive advantage as a firm "implementing a value-creating strategy not simultaneously being implemented by any current or potential competitors"; further, he reasons that competitive advantage cannot exist for identical firms, because since "these firms all implement the same strategies, they will improve their efficiency and effectiveness in the same way, and to same extent". Rarity is not specifically defined but is used in its general sense.

These attributes can be written as follows (Priem and Butler, 2001):

1. "Uncommon organizational attributes that enable firms to conceive of and implement value-creating strategies can be a source of implementing a value-creating strategy not simultaneously being implemented by any current or potential competitors";
2. "Uncommon organizational attributes that enable a firm to conceive of or implement strategies that improve its efficiency and effectiveness can be a source that may enable a firm to conceive of or implement strategies that improve its efficiency and effectiveness"; and
3. "Uncommon organizational attributes that exploit opportunities and neutralize threats in a firm's environment can be a source of implementing an opportunity-exploiting and threat-neutralizing strategy not simultaneously being implemented by any current or potential competitors".

Uniqueness of the organizational culture makes the organizational culture difficult to imitate. Values, symbols, beliefs are difficult to describe and are not transferable (Barney,1986) as there are unspoken, unperceived commonsense of the organization. The reasons that make organizational culture of a firm rare are also the factors prohibit imitations of the culture. Oliver and Wilkinson (1992) described how a large number of British firms had tried to imitate the organizational culture of Japanese firms during the 1980s but could not implement. Certain outward aspects of a firm can be imitated but the intrinsic aspects of the culture are difficult to imitate. This can be a source of competitive advantage of the firm.

An organization's productive knowledge is to be found in its operational routines. Routines allow organizations to cope with complexity and uncertainty under the conditions of bounded rationality; in addition, they provide an efficient way of storing an organization's accumulated experiential knowledge. Nelson and Winter also posit that organizational routines are the basis of a firm's distinctiveness and are, therefore, the source of its competitiveness. Thus, the RBV considers the firm as a repository of knowledge (Fransman, 1998).

Teece *et al.* (1997) define dynamic capabilities as "the ability to integrate, build, and reconfigure internal and external competencies to address rapidly changing environments". The concept of dynamic capabilities arose from a key shortcoming of the RBV of the firm. The RBV has been criticized for ignoring organizational factors surrounding resources, instead assuming that they simply "exist". Considerations such as how organizational resources are developed; how they are integrated within the firm, and how they are released have been under-explored in the literature.

Dynamic capabilities attempt to bridge these gaps by adopting a process approach: by acting as a buffer between organizational resources and the changing business environment, dynamic resources help a firm adjust its resource mix and thereby maintain the sustainability of the firm's competitive advantage, which otherwise might be quickly eroded. So, while the RBV emphasizes resource choice, or the selection of appropriate resources, dynamic capabilities emphasize organizational resource development and renewal. Kaizen or continuous development in the Japanese multinational companies can be considered as a major dynamic capability of their organizational culture.

According to Wade and Hulland (2004), IS (Information System) resources may take on many of the attributes of dynamic capabilities, and thus may be particularly useful to firms operating in rapidly changing environments. Thus, even if IS resources do not directly lead the firm to a position of superior sustained competitive advantage, they may nonetheless be critical to the firm's long-term competitiveness in unstable environments if they help it to develop, add, integrate, and release other key resources over time.

The concept of dynamic capabilities incorporates two valuable observations: first, the shifting character of the economic environment renders it dynamic — for example, decreasing time to market for products, shifting barriers to entry through technological change, globalization of national economies, and environmental uncertainty caused by political strife; second, organizational capabilities lie at the source of competitive success. Commitment of the employees create this dynamic capability which is rare, non-imitable and unique for a specific multinational company, i.e., satisfies all requirements of Barney as a source of competitive advantages.

Core capabilities must be "honed to a user need", must be "unique", and "difficult to replicate". They present an analytic framework that incorporates a set of descriptive dimensions or attributes in organizational culture that create such capabilities. Organizational culture includes the patterns of current practice and learning in a firm, tangible evidence of which is to be found in its routines. For example, integration processes are concerned with the efficient and effective internal coordination of organizational activities and production. In knowledge-intensive firms, integration is also concerned with routines and mechanisms for knowledge sharing. Learning processes involve repetition and experimentation to enable tasks to be performed better and more rapidly — this occurs at the level of the individual, group, organizational, and inter-organizational levels. Re-configuration and transformation processes relate the capabilities required to evolve a firm's asset structure. Assets include a firm's endowment of technology and intellectual property (as indicated by its difficult-to-emulate knowledge assets) as well as its relational assets with partners, customers, and suppliers.

12.4.5. *Toyota's Organizational Citizenship as a Competitive Advantage*

I elaborate the argument as follows with Toyota as an example. The purpose of Toyota Corporation is to fulfill its super-ordinate objectives, which can be categorized into some subdivisions (Basu, 1999, p. 188):

1. Operational objectives are to reduce cost, improve profit to have sustained growth and
2. Dominant objectives are to provide employee's satisfaction, fulfill its obligation to Japan to enhance its honor.

The organizational culture of Toyota is designed in such a way so as to achieve these objectives by molding its employees into active agents to fulfill these objectives both in its Japanese operations and in its overseas operations.

The organizational culture of Toyota would form a company citizenship throughout its worldwide organization disregarding national boundaries. Toyota has a strong organizational culture, which is rooted in its values, beliefs, and assumptions (Basu, 1999, p. 235). To the employees of Toyota, the company is a living entity. The continuous growth of the company is needed for the preservation of these values. Continuous progress and respect that can be gained to be associated with a company with continuous growth is the end objective of the employees of Toyota. A deep religious value to perpetuate growth is also the objective of the corporate growth of Toyota. Toyota's employees think and operate with their outlook for the long-term prospect of the organization and harmony with the work-place and broad social environment. These feelings lead them to develop a family feeling within the work-place and responsibility towards the fellow employees and the community at large. They believe that they have a responsibility towards the organization and the local and global societies, as Toyota is now a global organization. Irrespective of the location, Toyota is striving to inject these values to its employees across the globe creating an organization citizenship, which would carry the essential values of the Toyota as a global organization. The fear of loss of face due to non-achievements of its objectives to the employees, Japan and the global community are the motives for Toyota's efforts to mold every employee irrespective of their nationality to a company citizen. The then president of Toyota in 1995, Shoichiro Okuda said that his task is "to encourage a change in nationality through globalization — to transform Toyota Motor Corporation into Toyota, a company with a world nationality" (Okuda, 1995).

In order to understand whether Toyota has managed to create a corporate citizenship in its India plant, I compare the corporate management system and operations management systems in Toyota plants in Bangalore in India and in Toyoda in Japan. Interviews of the most senior managers in both of these plants were conducted in order to understand their systems and to set up the survey of opinions of the 150 managers in both of these plants. The results are given below.

12.4.5.1. *Results of the survey*

The results of the survey conducted in Toyota, in Japan, and India are summarized into forms, which can be analyzed in future publications. We have identified certain key variables to characterize the corporate management system and operations management; we provide below the initial statistical analysis (Tables 12.1–12.4). We have identified the following variables for corporate management:

1. Community feelings
2. Innovations
3. Consultations
4. Stability
5. Employee welfare
6. Contributions to organization

We have identified the following variables for operations management:

1. Awareness of return to investment
2. Continuous improvement

Table 12.1. Analysis of the data from survey in Toyota India: correlation matrix: corporate management.

Variable	Mean	SD	1	2	3	4	5
1	3.9	0.36					
2	3.9	0.52	0.72*				
3	4.5	0.42	0.79*	0.55*			
4	4.3	0.35	0.78*	0.63*	0.69*		
5	3.9	0.55	0.76**	0.65*	0.81*	0.79**	
6	3.9	0.59	0.79*	0.81**	0.72*	0.68*	0.69*

Notes: *Significant at 5% level.
**Significant at 10% level.

Table 12.2. Analysis of the data from survey in Toyota Japan: correlation matrix: corporate management.

Variable	Mean	SD	1	2	3	4	5
1	4.5	0.35					
2	4.8	0.55	0.72*				
3	4.2	0.42	0.81*	0.53*			
4	4.9	0.25	0.74*	0.63*	0.74*		
5	4.1	0.25	0.82*	0.68*	0.83*	0.87*	
6	4.7	0.33	0.84*	0.78*	0.69*	0.68*	0.71*

Notes: *Significant at 5% level.

Table 12.3. Analysis of the data from survey in Toyota India: correlation matrix: operations management.

Variable	Mean	SD	1	2	3	4	5
1	3.9	0.26					
2	4.9	0.51	0.82*				
3	4.2	0.32	0.89*	0.85*			
4	4.7	0.55	0.88**	0.73*	0.89**		
5	3.9	0.35	0.79*	0.85*	0.86*	0.89**	
6	4.4	0.55	0.89*	0.85*	0.79*	0.88*	0.89**

Notes: *Significant at 5% level.
**Significant at 10% level.

Table 12.4. Analysis of the data from survey in Toyota Japan: correlation matrix: operations management.

Variable	Mean	SD	1	2	3	4	5
1	4.6	0.26					
2	4.4	0.58	0.82*				
3	4.7	0.32	0.87*	0.83*			
4	4.5	0.55	0.84*	0.83*	0.84*		
5	4.7	0.35	0.89*	0.88*	0.83*	0.87*	
6	4.5	0.53	0.81*	0.88*	0.89*	0.88*	0.81*

Notes: *Significant at 5% level.
**Significant at 10% level.

3. Total quality management
4. Customers satisfaction
5. Facilitations
6. Goal orientations

In both the cases, we can accept Toyota in Japan as the bench mark and compare the corresponding tables in India to examine whether these are similar or very different. If they are similar, then we can demonstrate that Toyota is successful in implementing its organizational culture and particularly its corporate management system and operations management system. In Tables 12.1–12.4, the basic characteristics of corporate management system and operations management systems are identified and the opinions of the managers provide the quantitative measures of the degree of correlations among these characteristics. If these matrices are similar, it will prove that the corporate management systems and operations management systems of both these plants are similar.

To examine the similarities or differences between these two sets of matrices, the Likelihood-ratio test of comparison of two covariance matrices (Manly and Rayner, 1987) was employed. The results do not reject the hypothesis that matrices are not different. Thus, there are close similarities of corporate management system and operations management system of Toyota in Japan and Toyota in India. It signifies that although Toyota in India is a new company of about 10-years old, organizational culture is very similar and the mentality of the managers is not very different from their Japanese counterparts despite of the vast differences of their culture. Thus, Toyota has managed to surpass the national differences to implement its organizational citizenship in Indian plant as it did across the globe.

What is true about Toyota is also true about major multinational companies of the world who have a strong organizational culture and who have a vision and strategy for long-term growth to maintain both technological and business success. Multinational companies with a weak organizational culture may not have any vision for the future and as a result they may allow their subsidiaries to develop their own distinct national organizational culture rather than a global organizational culture such as what can be seen in Toyota.

12.5. Conclusion

To conclude, a firm's organizational culture can be a valuable resource to enhance corporate performance and create competitive advantages. In the context of a Japanese firm, culture has certain economic dimensions or resources, which should not be ignored. Collectivism as represented by the organizational culture of Japanese firms can be a very important competitive advantage for a Japanese firm and thus, it may be responsible for a superior corporate performance. Creation of commitments is an index of corporate performance, which in turn creates a organizational citizenship. Successful multinational firms transcended national cultural differences to develop a common pattern of drivers of business performance by creating organizational citizenship. These included a primary focus on organizational innovativeness, a friendly climate, and a competitive culture. Organizational climates that encouraged trust, participativeness, and entrepreneurial behavior were effective across all countries. Organizations with relatively flexible, externally oriented corporate cultures perform better. Thus, what is important is the effective organizational culture, which promotes successful corporate performance. It is essential for us to explore the ingredients of organizational culture and how these lead us to successful corporate performance.

Every multinational company wants to create its own citizenship; however, not all of them can be successful. The example provided by Hofstede (1991, 2002) for IBM that national citizenship, i.e., national character rather than organizational culture shaping managerial characteristics is an example of a weak organizational culture, which has failed to create an organizational citizenship. For a company with strong organizational culture, we may get results, which can negate the observations made by Hofstede. Kotter and Heskett (1992) provide a number of examples of weak and strong organizational culture. A multinational company with weak organizational culture cannot provide a global company citizenship but a company with strong organizational culture can; Toyota provides the example. Thus, it is highly likely that instead of a "global culture" we are going to have organizational citizenships of various multinational companies according to their organizational cultures.

In this paper, a conceptual idea of the organizational citizenship is presented, which can be transformed into an operational tool to examine the theory of organizational citizenship. It is possible to find out the factors that constitute the organizational culture of a Japanese multinational company by taking into account the views of the employees of that organization and then examine the similarities with the factors that affect organizational culture of a subsidiary unit in a different country in an alien national culture. It is possible to relate the organizational culture of the home unit to the organizational commitment through a structural equation model and we can compare it with a similar structural equation model relating organizational culture in a subsidiary unit with the organizational commitment of the employees in that foreign country. In that case, it would be possible for us to examine decisively the validity of the theory of organizational citizenship.

References

Adler, N (1997). *International Dimensions of Organizational Behavior*, 3rd Ed, Cincinnati, OH: South-Western.

Barney, JB (1986). Organizational culture: can it be a source of sustained competitive advantage? *Academy of Management Review*, 11(3), 656–665.

Barney, JB (2001). Is the resource-based view a useful perspective for strategic management research? *Academy of Management Review*, 26(1), 41–57.

Basu, S (1999). *Corporate Purpose*, New York: Garland Publishers.

Bird, A and M Stevens (2003). Toward an emergent global culture and the effects of globalisation on obsolescing national cultures. *Journal of International Management*, 9, 395–407.

Calori, R and P Sarnin (1991). Corporate culture and economic performance: a French study. *Organization Studies*, 12(1), 49–74.

Cameron, KS and R Quinn (1999). *Diagnosing and Changing Organizational Culture*, Reading, Massachusetts: Addison-Wesley.

Cameron, K and S Freeman (1991). Cultural congruence, strength and type: relationships to effectiveness. In *Research in Organizational Change and Development*, RW Woodman and A Passmre (eds.), Vol. 5, Greenwich, CT: JAI Press, pp. 23–58.

Carroll, D (1983). A disappointing search for excellence. *Harvard Business Review*, November–December, 78–88.

Clark, T and L Knowles (2003). Global myopia: globalisation theory in international business. *Journal of International Management*, 9, 361–372.

Deal, TE and AA Kennedy (1982). *Corporate Cultures: The Rites and Rituals of Corporate Life*, Reading, MA: Addison-Wesley.

Denison, DR and A Mishra (1995). Toward a theory of organizational culture and effectiveness. *Organization Science*, 6(2), March–April, 204–223.

Deshpande, R, J Farley and F Webster (1993). Corporate culture, customer orientation and innovativeness in Japanese firms: a quadrad analysis. *Journal of Marketing*, 57, January, 23–37.

Deshpande, R, J Farley and F Webster (1997). *Factors Affecting Organizational Performance: A Five-country Comparison*, Cambridge, MA: Marketing Science Institute.

Drucker, P (2002). *The Performance Measurement*, Cambridge-Massachusetts: Harvard Business School Press.

Fransman, M (1998). Information, knowledge, vision, and theories of the firm. In *Technology, Organisation, and Competitiveness: Perspectives on Industrial and Corporate Change*, G Dosi, D Teece and J Chytry (eds.), pp. 147–192, New York, NY: Oxford University Press Inc.

Freedman, T (2006). *The World Is Flat: The Globalized World in the Twenty-first Century*, New York: Picador.

Goodman, G (1981). American samurai. *Sales and Marketing Management*, 127, October 12, 45–48.

Gordon, GG (1985). The relationship of corporate culture to industry sector and corporate performance. In *Gaining Control of the Corporate Culture*, R Kilman, MJ Saxton and R Serpa (eds.), San Francisco, CA: Jossey-Bass, pp. 65–80.

Gupta, V, PJ Hanges and PW Dorfman (2002). Cultural clustering: methodologies and findings. *Journal of World Business*, 37(1), 11–15.

Hall, ET and MR Hall (1990). *Hidden Differences: Doing Business with the Japanese*, New York: Doubleday Anchor Books.

Hayashi, S (1989). *Culture and Management in Japan*, Tokyo: University of Tokyo Press.

Hayek, FA (1945). The use of knowledge in society. *American Economic Review*, 35, 519–532.

Hofstede, G (1991). *Cultures and Organizations: Software of Mind*, Cambridge: McGraw- Hill Book Company.

Hofstede, G (2002). *Culture's Consequences: Comparing Values, Behaviors, Institutions, and Organizations Across Nations*, CA: Sage Publications.

Hofstede, G and MH Bond (1984). Hofstede's culture dimensions: an independent validation using Rokeach's value survey. *Journal of Cross-Cultural Psychology*, 15, 417–433.

Husted, BW (2003). Globalization and cultural change in international business research. *Journal of International Management*, 9, 427–433.

Iglehart, R and WE Baker (2000). Modernization, cultural change and the persistence of traditional values. *American Sociological Review*, 65, 19–51.

Kahn, H (1979). *World Development: 1979 and Beyond*. London: Croom Helm.

Kluckhohn, C (1951). Value and value orientations in the theory of action. In *Toward a General Theory of Action*, T Parsons and E Shils (eds.), Cambridge, MA: Harvard University Press, pp. 388–433.

Knudsen, C (1994). The competence view of the firm: what can modern economists learn from Philip Selznick's sociological theory of leadership? In *The Institutional Construction of Organisations: International and Longitudinal Studies*, WR Scott and S Christensen (eds.), pp. 135 163, Thousand Oaks, CA: Sage Publications Inc.

Kotter, JP and JL Heskett (1992). *Corporate Culture and Performance*, New York: Free Press.

Lasch, C (1995). *The Revolt of the Elites and the Betrayal of Democracy*, New York: W.W. Norton & Company.

Lazar, W, S Murata and H Kosaka (1985). Japanese marketing: towards a better understanding. *Journal of Marketing*, 49, Spring, 69–81.

Leung, K (2006). The rise of East Asia: implications for research on cultural variations and globalisation. *Journal of International Management*, 12, 235–241.

Macauley, TB (1860). Minute on Indian education, 1935. In *Miscellaneous Writings and Speeches*, pp. 237–251.

Manly, BFJ and JCW Rayner (1987). The comparison of sample covariance matrices using likelihood ratio tests. *Biometrika*, 74, 841–847.

Marcoulides, G and RH Heck (1993). Organizational culture and performance: proposing and testing a model. *Organization Science*, 4(2), May 1993, 209–223.

Markus, H and S Kitayama (1991). Culture and self: implications for cognition, emotion, and motivation. *Psychological Review*, 98, 224–253.

Marx, K and F Engels (1872). *The Communist Manifesto*. London: Samuel Moore.

Mintzburg, H, R Simon and K Basu (2002). Beyond selfishness. *Sloan Management Review*, Fall, 44(1), 67–74.

Morita, A (1992). A moment for Japanese management. *Japan-Echo*, 19(2), 44–52.

Nakane, G (1970). *Japanese Society*, Harmondsworth: Penguin.

Okuda, S (1995). *Second Founding*, Tokyo: Nihon Keizai Shimbun.

Oliver, N and B Wilkinson (1992). *The Japanization of British Industry*, Oxford: Blackwell.

O'Reilly, C (1989). Corporations, culture and commitment: motivation and social control in organization. *California Management Review*, 31, 19–25.

O'Reilly, C, JA Chatman and D Caldwell (1991). People and organizational culture: a Q-sort approach to assessing person-organization fit. *Academy of Management Journal*, 34, September, 487–516.

Ouchi, W (1981). *Theory Z*, Reading, MA: Addison-Wesley.

Owens, R (1987). *Organizational Behavior in Education*, Englewood Cliffs, NJ: Prentice-Hall.

Pascale, R and A Athos (1982). *The Art of Japanese Management: Applications for American Executives*, New York: Simon & Schuster.

Penrose, E (1959). The *Theory of the Growth of the Firm*. London: Basil Blackwell.

Peters, T and R Watermann (1982). *In Search of Excellence*, New York: Harper and Row.

Priem, RL and JE Butler (2001). Is the resource-based "View" a useful perspective for strategic management research? *Academy of Management Review*. January, 26(1), 22–40.

Sathe, V (1983). Implications of corporate culture: a manager's guide to action. *Organizational Dynamics*, 12, 4–23.

Selznick, P (1957). *Leadership in Administration: A Sociological Interpretation*, New York: Harper and Row.

Sheth, JN (2006). Clash of cultures or fusion of cultures: implications for international business. *Journal of International Management*, 12, 218–221.

Teece, DJ, G Pisano and A Shuen (1997). Dynamic capabilities and strategic management. *Strategic Management Journal*, 18(7), 509–533.

Toyoda, E (1985). *Toyota: Fifty Years in Motion*. Tokyo: Kodansha International.

Triandis, HC (1989). The self and social behavior in different cultural contexts. *Psychological Review*, 96, 506–520.

Triandis, HC (1990). Cross-cultural studies of individualism and collectivism. In *Nebraska Symposium on Motivation*, J Berman (ed.), pp. 41–133, Lincoln: University of Nebraska Press.

Triandis, HC (1995). *Individualism and Collectivism*. Boulder, Co: Westview Press.

Triandis, HC (2006). Cultural aspects of globalisation. *Journal of International Management*, 12, 208–217.

Triandis, HC and M Gelfand (1998). Converging measurements of horizontal and vertical individualism and collectivism. *Journal of Personality and Social Psychology*, 74, 118–128.

Triandis, HC and D Trafimow (2001). Cross national prevalence of collectivism. In *Individual Self, Relational Self, Collective Self*, C Sedikides and M Brewer (eds.), pp. 259–276, Philadelphia, PA: Psychology Press.

Ueno, S (1992). The influence of culture on budget control practices in USA and Japan: an empirical study. *Journal of International Business Studies*, 23(4), 659–674.

Ulrich, D (1998). Intellectual capital = competence × commitment. *Sloan Management Review*, 39(2), 15–26.

van de Ven, A (1983). Review in search of excellence. *Administrative Science Quarterly*, 29, 621–644.

Wade, M and J Hulland (2004). The resource-based view and information systems research: review, extension, and suggestions for future research. *MIS Quarterly*, 28(1), 107–142.

Weber, M (1930). *The Protestant Ethnic and the Spirit of Capitalism (Translated by Parsons, T)*, New York: Scribners.

Winograd T and F Flores (1986). *Understanding Computers and Cognition: A New Foundation for Design*, Norwood, NJ: Ablex Publishing Corporation.

Yeh, RS (1995). Downward influence styles in cultural diversity settings. *International Journal of Human Resources Management*, 6, September, 626–641.

Zammuto, RF and EJ O'Connor (1992). Gaining advances manufacturing technology's benefits: the roles of organization design and culture. *Academy of Management Review*, 17, 701–728.

Index